University of Plymouth
Charles Seale Hayne Library
Subject to status this item may be renewed
via your Voyager account

http://voyager.plymouth.ac.uk
Tel: (01752) 232323

Early Childhood Programs as the Doorway to Social Cohesion

Early Childhood Programs as the Doorway
to Social Cohesion:
Application of Vygotsky's Ideas
from an East–West Perspective

Edited by

Aija Tuna and Jacqueline Hayden

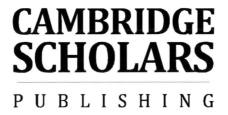

**CAMBRIDGE
SCHOLARS**

P U B L I S H I N G

THIS WORK WAS CREATED AS AN INITIATIVE
OF THE INTERNATIONAL STEP BY STEP ASSOCIATION

Early Childhood Programs as the Doorway to Social Cohesion:
Application of Vygotsky's Ideas from an East-West Perspective,
Edited by Aija Tuna and Jacqueline Hayden

This book first published 2010

Cambridge Scholars Publishing

12 Back Chapman Street, Newcastle upon Tyne, NE6 2XX, UK

British Library Cataloguing in Publication Data
A catalogue record for this book is available from the British Library

ISBN (10): 1-4438-2390-2, ISBN (13): 978-1-4438-2390-6

TABLE OF CONTENTS

LIST OF BOXES, FIGURES, AND TABLES

Boxes

Figures

Tables

ACKNOWLEDGMENT

This volume was created through the initiative of the International Step by Step Association (ISSA). It was a team effort, encompassing authors and editors across the world, and would not have been possible without the significant support and partnership of the Bernard van Leer Foundation and the Open Society Institute. This volume also builds upon ISSA's partnership with the European Early Childhood Education Research Association (EECERA); the essays collected herein are based upon presentations from the 2007 EECERA Conference, hosted by ISSA.

ISSA is a membership organization that connects professionals and organizations working in the field of early childhood development and education. ISSA promotes equal access to quality education and care for all children, especially in the early years of their lives. Established in the Netherlands in 1999, ISSA's network today stretches across the globe from Central and Eastern Europe to Central Asia, Asia, and the Americas. ISSA's core members are the 29 nongovernmental organizations located primarily in Central/Eastern Europe and Central Asia which implement the Step by Step Program initiated by the Open Society Institute in 1994. Within its network, ISSA supports a wide array of programs that collectively provide a comprehensive set of educational services and advocacy tools intended to influence policy reform for families and children, with a special focus on the years from birth through primary school.

ISSA's mission is to support professional communities and develop a strong civil society that influences and assists decision makers to:

- provide high quality care and educational services for all children from birth through primary school (age 0–10), with a focus on the poorest and most disadvantaged

- ensure greater inclusion of family and community participation in children's development and learning

- ensure social inclusion and respect for diversity.

ISSA's overarching goal is to promote inclusive, quality care and education experiences that create the conditions for all children to become active members of democratic knowledge societies. ISSA does this through: raising awareness of the importance of quality care and education, developing resources, disseminating information, advocating, strengthening alliances, and building capacity to create conditions where all children thrive. ISSA's vision is of a world where families and communities support every child in reaching his or her full potential and developing the skills necessary for being a successful and active member of a democratic knowledge society.

In 2009 ISSA launched *Competent Educators of the 21st Century: Principles of Quality Pedagogy*, a revised version of its Pedagogical Standards, a network-developed tool that defines quality in teaching practices and classroom environment. This document represents a framework of principles for quality pedagogy and can provide guidelines for teacher preparation and continuous professional development, supporting early years professionals from the classroom to the policy level. This document serves as a basis for professional discussion, building and expanding partnerships, improving practices, and bringing change into the lives of young children in the countries of the ISSA network and beyond.

www.issa.nl

INTERNATIONAL
STEP by STEP
ASSOCIATION

FOREWORD

Perhaps more than at any other stage of life, experiences in early childhood have the potential to affect an individual's life over the long term, including health and general well-being. The first years of life are marked by rapidly increasing mobility, development of communication skills and intellectual capacities, socio-emotional development, and swift shifts in interests and abilities. What supports this development and what experiences will be most conducive to positive growth and learning is a topic of endemic interest and focus for professionals from many sectors of society. During recent decades, early childhood has also become increasingly visible on agendas of international agencies and decision makers at all levels.

Recent research findings have identified a relationship between quality early childhood experiences for young children and enhanced early school performance that leads to more successful learning and achievements throughout life. Early childhood services are also associated with poverty reduction through employment opportunities and reduced welfare dependency. It is also increasingly clear that early childhood services may be a significant entry point for meeting new social goals—those associated with facilitating social cohesion and respect for diversity in changing demographics, economic, social, and political environments.

Early childhood has great potential to be the meeting point for all families and all members of a community in order to recognize and identify the need for early support and intervention when necessary, to get to know each other, and to build social cohesion using all existing diversity and potential.

During the last two decades, the countries of Central and Eastern Europe and Central Asia have been working on rebuilding and improving early childhood programs and policies, ready to learn from early childhood structures, policies, and systems of service delivery in the West, but also building upon their own traditions and knowledge. This is a unique and privileged position of developing new systems and structures, in which the good and useful features of a previous system can be preserved and enriched with new knowledge and experiences from across the world. In this situation, a timely window of opportunity is opened and can be used for the benefit of children and societies in general.

Meanwhile, the industrialized countries in the West (Western Europe, the Americas, and Australasia), amongst other changes, are dealing with tensions between an increasing emphasis on market forces versus social justice and equity issues for citizens–all this within a paradigm of increased government attention to the early years of life and increased demand for accountability for public expenditures. Recent financial turbulences across the globe have added new challenges to both placing and protecting the position of early childhood development (ECD) in a prominent place in the political and social agendas of countries from East to West.

There is growing agreement that ECD issues, including various services for young children and their families, should be approached and decided from the perspective of the interests of the child. As education stakeholders grapple more and more with issues such as children's rights and universal approaches along with the importance of cultural specificities in program development and delivery, the social and economic implications of early childhood development have become common areas for investigation by researchers and common topics of international conferences and seminars. Theories and practice from different parts of the world have been reviewed, compared, deconstructed, and, in some cases, consolidated.

Researchers, practitioners, and policy makers from any part of the world can benefit from an exploration of early childhood programs through the reciprocal sharing of perspectives and experiences. The legacy of Russian psychologist L. S. Vygotsky provides a unique example of how the belief in the importance of early childhood and attempts to provide the best support to children's development have crossed borders and developed, in spite of distances, varying and often opposing political regimes, and diverse socio-economic conditions.

The 17th Annual Conference[1] of the European Early Childhood Education Research Association (EECERA), which took place in Prague between 29 August and 1 September 2007, represented such a forum. The International Step by Step Association (ISSA),[2] with more than 10 years of experience in early childhood education in Central Eastern Europe and Central Asia, co-hosted the conference.

The focus of the conference was the legacy of L. S. Vygotsky and his astounding ability to be a driving force for early childhood practice and policy in both the East and the West–despite their significant differences in terms of culture, politics, and socio-economic conditions.

---

[1]   For more information about the conference visit: www.easyprague.cz/eecera2007.

[2]   For more information on ISSA visit: www.issa.nl.

While following on a number of similar international forums, the Prague conference, entitled *Exploring Vygotsky's Ideas: Crossing Borders*, had some unique and seminal features. It was the largest EECERA conference to date, as well as the first time that a significant cohort of early childhood professionals had gathered at the EECERA Conference from such diverse geographical and sociopolitical regions. Of the 780 early childhood specialists in attendance, about half came from Western nations and half from the former communist countries of Central and Eastern Europe and the Commonwealth of Independent States (CEE/CIS).

During the conference, representatives of major universities and other research and implementation agencies from CEE/CIS and Western nations took the opportunity to review the influence of Vygotsky in relation to how young children are viewed and how programs for children are developed in different contexts.

It was inspirational and gratifying to note that the rich history and the huge leaps in early childhood development and education in the Eastern regions and Central Asia were not only acknowledged, but embraced by colleagues from the West.

As a way to embrace and memorialize the good will, mutual respect, and collaborative approaches which took place at the conference, ISSA endeavoured to gather a group of papers representative of the wealth of knowledge shared at the conference and to develop the collection of papers into a book—this book!

Combining contributions from both East and West presented challenges in incorporating different styles of scholarly writing in one publication, but also allowed the expansion of the body of professional knowledge for both sides. Another outcome of this book is to show that some aspects of globalization are positive!

In this case, the opportunity to note our common touchstone and to discuss how one theorist has affected our diverse systems has resulted in a feeling of global comradeship. As a result of the 2007 Conference, many collaborative initiatives and consortia have been developed in the intervening years, many involving ISSA's own members. Both East and West have been enriched by sharing information about research, policy, and practice in early childhood education.

On a practical level, the chapters in this book are presented to facilitate the learning of students in teacher preparation programs for early childhood education, social psychology, social work, and other child related disciplines about how Vygotsky's work has shaped our current approaches to quality in early childhood care and education. The book will be useful as well to civil society organizations involved in piloting and implementing quality early childhood programs, and to decision makers at national and international levels who want to support good practice in education programs and systems.

As a peer reviewed, academic publication, this volume is meant to suggest ideas and build links between theory and practice, as well as to stimulate development of new ideas for successful implementation of quality early childhood education.

Moving Forward Together: Early childhood programs as the doorway to social cohesion. An East–West Perspective is a product of many forces. ISSA, as a leading network of early childhood education organizations from CEE/CIS has been in a perfect position to gather those forces together. ISSA's long-term cooperation with and support from the Open Society Institute (OSI), successful partnership with EECERA, and generous financial assistance from the Bernard van Leer Foundation helped make this book a possibility. The authors from Australia, Azerbaijan, Canada, Denmark, Italy, Singapore, Latvia, the Netherlands, Poland, Portugal, Russia, USA, and the United Kingdom, have brought our vision to life.

Those of us who had the good fortune to experience those intense days in Prague came away with a feeling that divisions can be overcome and that diversity can be an inspiration and strength. It is our hope that this book will contribute to the growing cooperative movement amongst educators, decision makers, and civil society for the benefit of children, their families, and communities.

This book aims to be a strong step towards this mutual sharing and knowledge enhancement.

We acknowledge everybody who has contributed to the development and publishing of the book, with very special thanks to Taryn Paladiy, Coordinator of the project, for her hard work, patience, and commitment.

Liana Ghent, *Executive Director, ISSA, Hungary*
Jacqueline Hayden, *Macquarie University, Australia*
Aija Tuna, *Program Specialist, ISSA, Latvia*

July 2010

Part I

Introduction

CHAPTER ONE

MAKING A DIFFERENCE—EAST AND WEST MEET VYGOTSKY

JACQUELINE HAYDEN

Making a Difference

The recent *Report Card 8 from UNICEF* identifies internationally applicable benchmarks for early childhood care and education. The benchmarks refer to macro social and fiscal policies which are seen to have indirect effects on the quality of an early childhood system. These global benchmarks include policies for poverty reduction, parental leave, access to health services, and other structural issues. The benchmarks also include regulatory items such as adult to child ratios and teacher training requirements (Box 1-1).

While there is no doubt that the global early childhood sector needs to promote and advocate for these macro policies and state regulations, the benchmarks may seem to be outside of the immediate sphere of influence of most early childhood teachers. In fact, knowing about these benchmarks for quality care can be de-motivating: Classroom teachers may well feel that their efforts towards effective service delivery are wasted if these 10 macro policies are not in place.

This book represents an important message: While we must never stop advocating for macro changes, there is a realm over which early childhood professionals do exert direct control—and that is the environment within each setting. It is at this level that our focus and energies can make an immediate difference for every child and parent with whom we come into contact.

Using Vygotsky as a common baseline, the following chapters provide some guidelines, review some issues, and present some innovative and inspirational examples for making a difference in the lives of all young children, regardless of the context; of the number of international benchmarks which have been met; or whether programs emanate from the East or the West.

Box 1-1

**Internationally Applicable Benchmarks
for Early Childhood Care and Education (UNICEF, 2008)**

1. Parental leave of 1 year at 50% of salary.
2. A national plan with priority for disadvantaged children.
3. Subsidized and regulated child care services for 25%of children under 3.
4. Subsidized and accredited early education services for 80% of 4 year-olds.
5. 80% of all child care staff trained.
6. 50% of staff in accredited early education services tertiary educated with relevant qualification.
7. Minimum staff-to-children ratio of 1:15 in preschool education.
8. 1.0% of GDP spent on early childhood services.
9. Child poverty rate less than 10%.
10. Near-universal outreach of essential child health service.

Vygotsky and Quality—A Global Approach

The very existence of internationally applicable benchmarks for early childhood care and education reflects the importance which is placed on the sector. Early childhood programs worldwide are increasingly recognized for their potential to address myriad social, educational, cultural, and economic issues. Indeed, the correlation of early childhood programs to educational, psychosocial, and bio-medical outcomes for children, and concomitant increased employment, reduced poverty, enhanced education and human capital, and other macro level social and economic outcomes is a common argument for support and commitment by a growing number of nation states and global initiatives. As a result, the call for increased access to early childhood programs is common in nearly every nation on the globe.

But access alone does not guarantee nurturing environments for young children. As Box One implies, it is not merely *more* spaces which we aim for, but assurances that children, when they obtain access, are being exposed to quality programs.

This has been emphasized throughout the literature, and especially in the findings from longitudinal studies of early childhood programs (Schweinhart 2005, Lynch 2004, Kagitcibasi, Sunar, Bekman, Baydar, and Cemalcilar 2009).

Over and above the international benchmarks, few researchers would argue with the notion that even when all benchmarks are met, what constitutes quality service delivery is dependent upon, and consistently reconstructed by, the dynamics of context and community values.

However, there is one construct which can be universally applied: Relationships within settings is a fundamental indicator of quality programming!

This truism stems from the work of Lev Vygotsky. His insistence that full cognitive development requires social interaction defines the essence of his theory and is both universal and timeless.

For Vygotsky, human development is dependent upon social relationships, and experiences in the early years of life set the foundation for healthy development. His works provide a guideline for establishing these critical relationships. Studies from East, West, North, and South have shown that within their classrooms, even if they are under resourced, overcrowded, housed in poor facilities, and/or set up in the middle of toxic environments, early childhood teachers can make a difference to the children they engage with by engaging with them in appropriate ways.

This book gives an insight into the wisdom and timeliness of Vygotsky's legacy.

The chapters herein apply Vygotsky's theories to diverse contexts: Azerbaijan, Canada, Croatia, Greece, the Netherlands, Poland, Italy, Russia, the United Kingdom, and the United States and beyond, and attest to the universality of his offerings about the way that human beings learn and develop.

But this book is not merely an explanation of applied Vygotsky-ism. Indeed, there are hundreds of publications about Vygotsky, and we were not compelled to add to that already rich literature. Rather, our purpose for this book is to serve as a reminder of the basic teaching of Vygotsky: *It is through others that we become ourselves.*

All early childhood professionals influence the children in their care, at every moment, through every interaction. It is not a role that can be taken lightly. We developed this book because more than at any other time, we early childhood professionals need to be reminded and inspired to fulfil our role: We might not have the power to create social transformations in the immediate future, but we are social provocateurs. We can change

children's lives within whatever context we find ourselves, and we can turn
to Vygotsky for support.

Despite the detailing of very different issues and approaches, each
chapter illuminates an aspect of the influence of Vygotsky in the practice of
early childhood education. The book serves as a reminder of the importance
of Vygotsky and provides examples for many of his terms which permeate
the early childhood sector around the globe: *zone of proximal development,
mature play, leading activity, mediation, socially constructed approaches,
intersubjectivity, mediations by a knowledgeable other.* In clarifying the use
and meaning of these terms, there is also a warning—misunderstanding and
misuse of Vygotsky is a common practice across divides.

The culmination of the chapters makes it very clear that within the
setting walls, much of what we associate with quality, contextually relevant
early childhood education owes its development to Vygotsky.

Beyond our original goals, to highlight the impact of Vygotsky, as the
chapters rolled in, another purpose for this book emerged. We noted a global
collegiality amongst those who care about the day to day experiences of
young children. The chapter by Mathias Urban (which we kept for last)
provides a good description of this. Early childhood teachers constitute a
community of professionals who communicate despite language, geography
and huge differences in historical and political backgrounds. This common
purpose is what we hope the book will reflect and reinforce.

In this unsettling era of global movement and rapid change, we think
the chapters in this book will remind early childhood teachers in the East,
West, North, and South to remember why they chose this profession—and
to realize the profound impact they can have in their day to day interactions
(*mediations*).

Vygotsky and National Policy

Zylicz describes a diminished sense of self-efficacy as an outcome of the
post-communist era, whereby the state promoted obedience, and state
teaching practices favoured passive reproduction of knowledge with little
or no attempt to relate this to the daily lives of children. Since the fall of
Communism in Poland and other countries, preschools and schools have
had to reconceptualise themselves from being instruments of ideological
influence, to agents of change. The notion of citizenship is no longer state
driven but based on self-efficacy. Poland and similar countries need self-
reliant, active, and engaged individuals in order for the countries to be
active and viable members of the European Union.

Zylicz reports that Vygotsky's ideas about child development, and his emphasis on the importance of embedding programs within the sociocultural environment, have guided the highly successful *Where There Are No Preschools* (WTANP) program in Poland. WTANP faced great opposition during its development and throughout its expansion era, because it challenged the traditional, highly hierarchical, and top down approaches to education.

Zylicz's article is especially important because it presents one of the few comparative studies of children who have experienced child-centred/play-based programs with those who did not have access to the WTANP program. Although these are not necessarily validated research methods, the studies undertaken show definite indications that children exposed to particular (Vygotskian influenced) preschool programs score higher than their peers on tests of locus of control, self-confidence and persistence. Longer term outcomes of enhanced social skills and curiosity were also recorded. The study is seminal. Polish authorities now have evidence that it is not merely attendance at preschool which makes a difference, but that particulars of classroom engagement (as per Vygotskian ideas) which facilitate healthy development in children.

Ang picks up the theme of creating reflective, thinking citizens as an outcome of early childhood practice. She uses the example of a Christian school that caters to a large percentage of non-Christian families to make her point. The teachers post plans and follow what seems to be a predetermined, set curriculum, yet somehow, at every moment, the classroom reflects child-centred, spontaneous (yet purposeful) activities, which to the untrained eye might seem chaotic. Ang concludes:

> An effective curriculum is not just about meeting educational outcomes, setting clear aims, or careful planning. Equally important, it is to enable children to take ownership of their learning, independently as well as collaboratively, and to create contexts in which their learning is sustained in an environment where they can create and co-construct their own experiences. In essence, the key processes of early childhood education are not derived just from a carefully planned curriculum or programme, but from the opportunities that children are given to undertake tasks, make choices, and partake in activities with the adults and peers around them (this volume).

This is the gist of Vygotsky's gift to the field of early childhood education. Ang goes on to describe a music lesson which, to her non-Singaporean eyes, seemed unsuccessful. She later discovers that there were goals to the lesson which reflect the sociocultural context *"We are brought up to listen. A good child's one who listens."* and concludes that in the Vygotskian sense, there is no one way to "do Vygotsky." Indeed, the role of the early childhood teacher involves finding the balance between promoting and facilitating the inquiring child and the need for all children to learn the skills of cultural and social negotiation.

The role of cultural historical psychology in facilitating child outcomes at the classroom level is the focus of the chapter by **Yudina**. She investigates what she calls *the teachers' position* and how this impacts child outcomes, particularly in relation to extending a child's zone of proximal development (ZPD): Teachers positions towards children exist along a continuum of *authoritarian* through to *no guidance given.* Those who fall too close to either end of this continuum cannot engage in the important joint activity which facilitates extension of the zone of proximal development.

Yudina goes on to describe research studies across three contexts and three diverse educational systems (Russia, Latvia, and USA) and shows that teachers' *declared position(s) frequently differ from their actual position.* In some cases, teachers are more authoritarian than they believe and in other cases, less authoritarian. Meanwhile, differences between Russian and American children on the 'perception of the child' scale show very different cultural expectations: in Russia a child is seen as a vessel to be filled with knowledge; in America teachers are more apt to view the child as a partner in his or her own development. In her seminal analyses, Yudina shows that beyond any curriculum it is the *teacher's position*, or teachers' sets of attitudes toward the child, which determines how effective they can be in guiding development. As she puts it, *the set of attitudes towards the child (is) the key participant of the educational process,* (because these attitudes) impact on the character of the child-adult joint activity which Vygotsky tells us leads to real learning and development. Yudina concludes by raising questions about how cultural attitudes are developed in teachers, how they might be 'moved' to ensure maximum effect for leading activities within the ZPD.

We close this section of the book with a case study of Vygotsky's influence upon early childhood education programs and practices in one nation. **Mantovani** describes the influence which Vygotsky has had on Italian approaches to early childhood education, most notably on the renowned Reggio Emilia programs. She reminds us that despite his application to guiding practice, Vygotsky's ideas are truly political in a deep sense, attributing to school and education a fundamental role for understanding and changing society.

Vygotsky and Classroom Practice

The next section of the book is dedicated to pragmatic ideas for classroom practice, based upon Vygotskian principles.

Broström provides an example of how a Vygotskian approach can develop literacy and aesthetic development. He gives the example of using specific-ended questions—a kind of scaffolding—(such as *'What surprised you about this story?)* to demonstrate how reading one simple book can provide myriad opportunities for creativity, fantasy, language, and social development.

Lee points out how Vygotskian thinking lies behind the values which we place upon diversity, participation, and respect for different ways of knowing. She uses several examples to illustrate how young children have been given voice through teaching strategies which do not depend on competence in oral or written language skills. Her examples remind us of the many languages of children and the many ways in which communication—social interaction—can take place. Lee provides poignant examples of the myriad (non-verbal) ways in which children communicate. When a young boy was asked to draw a picture of what he liked about school, but drew instead a picture representing sadness and fear, this presented a portal for understanding the boy's social reality. When a group of children were instructed to draw a picture depicting 'what is math' and drew several non-numerical designs, the teacher knew that her students had understood the concept of *math-in-context*. When children were asked to take photos of *hot spots* in their school, administrators became aware of the physical infrastructure needs and could address areas which were causing alarm to young children. Children found ways of communicating their fears in ways that were meaningful to them.

Portugal et al demonstrate the Vygotskian principles behind *The Portugal Curricular Orientations for Preschool Education* (COPSE). Rather than prescribing activities and outcomes, COPSE offers strategies which reflect learning through play, working in the zone of proximal development, promoting significant, differentiated learning, and considering social reality as a source of development. In addition, COPSE points out the importance of taking into consideration the children's cultures of origin, the type of partnership to be established with the family, and the appropriation of pertinent symbolic-cultural instruments and other concepts.

Portugal et al's chapter is especially interesting in light of its presentation of the Child Follow-up Instrument (CFI) which is used to assess the context including the socio emotional environment of the classroom as a tool for assisting teachers to construct appropriate group interventions.

Mikailova and Karimova describe how Vygotsky's theories are facilitating the radical transformation in attitudes and strategies for teaching children with disabilities in Azerbaijan.

In many ways, they report, the teaching profession has been conditioned towards a system of "defectology" promoted by the previous Soviet regime. Under that system children with disabilities were given lesser attention and resources and were kept far away from mainstream classrooms. The authors point out that new policies are working to dispel old procedures. While integration is now recognized as a human right and an effective strategy, teachers need support and training to overcome old biases.

This chapter describes a pilot project which addresses these needs. The theories of Vygotsky are shown to be highly effective in the development of the children with disabilities and the overall achievement educational goals for the whole group. The chapter describes how classroom teachers were scaffolded themselves as they learned to observe children, build relationships, assess and work within zones of proximal development, and finally to mold a learning environment which could accommodate the needs of all children.

Van Oers reminds us of the central role of teachers in applying Vygotsky's theories within the classroom—especially as they transition from traditional approaches to a play-based curriculum for the early primary school years. He describes a project from the Netherlands which shows how facilitating the integration of Vygotsky based theoretical ideas and the tools for teachers culminated in more independent and creative classroom practices; and why the interaction between teacher educator, teacher, and pupils is fundamental to sustainable learning outcomes.

Global Implications

The two final chapters, by Bodrova and Urban, serve as a summary, a reminder, and a tribute to the importance of Vygotsky on a global scale.

Bodrova identifies a (perhaps *the)* fundamental issue which is defining the concept of early childhood education worldwide: As Bodrova points out, both the east and the west—with such diverse backgrounds in terms of rationale and evolution of early childhood programs—are facing similar pressures today. The perceived co-relationship of school success for individuals to national productivity, reduced poverty, and concomitant decrease in social unrest is having profound effects in both regions.

Concerns about children not being ready for school, as well as concerns about children falling behind in their later academic learning, is creating what

Bodrova calls the *miniature schools movement,* whereby early childhood programs focus superordinately on 'school knowledge' and test preparation. Bodrova does not mention this, but we are acutely aware that there is global reinforcement for this notion. In a recent report from UNICEF, Secretary General, Ban Ki-moon states

> Pre-primary schooling differs substantially from one country to another, but the strongest programmes share three basic characteristics. First, they support parents during the children's earliest years; second, they integrate educational activities with other services, notably health care, nutrition, and social services; and third, *they provide children with educational experiences that help ease the transition to primary school* (Ban Ki-Moon cited *in* UNICEF 2007, 45). (Emphasis is the editors'.)

While we applaud the fact that the Secretary General acknowledges the importance of early childhood education, we fear that the term *educational experiences* may not be seen to encompass the broad spectrum of development beyond school related skills.

Bodrova addresses this when she describes how early childhood specialists in both the East and the West are working hard to promote a counter movement to the promotion of academic focus for young children. However, and this is a controversial but important point, according to Bodrova, in our enthusiasm to counter prevailing notions of schooling, an upswing towards the notion of child centeredness can go too far! In its extreme form, child centeredness over-privileges the notion of following the child's lead. This can diminish what Vygotsky identifies as the most important aspect of early childhood teaching—adult mediation in meaningful children's play.

In fact Vygotsky has very specific ideas about what constitutes play as a source of development. Bodrova's description of how play provides the foundations for abstract thought should be read by anyone who has ever had doubts about the relationship of play to academic (especially literacy) skill development. However, not all play, and certainly not all play materials, are meaningful. This is an important and vital chapter!

Urban provides a final chapter which focuses on the issues that most early childhood professionals are facing worldwide As indicated in the Bi Moon quote above, as early childhood education and care moves up in the international policy agenda, the push for an educational outcome and the discourse on 'curriculum' and other means of regulation is predominant—as are national policies which emphasise access and cost benefits for a myriad of goals which may have little to do with enhancing the quality of a child's day to day experiences, and much to do with developing an employable citizenry. The economic/human capital discourse creates tensions with early childhood professionals who do not see themselves as technicians, but who emphasise the importance of critical reflectiveness, professional autonomy, and habitus over the mere acquisition of skills. Meanwhile, professionals everywhere are expected to achieve predetermined outcomes in a working context that is increasingly diverse and unpredictable. Urban demonstrates how Vygotsky is critical in steering us toward s the possibility of policy-practice relationships that allow for and encourage the development of critical thinking and embrace 'untested feasibilities,' rather than predetermined outcomes.

Conclusion

Despite deep differences between the east and west, there is little doubt that early childhood professionals across these borders are united by a similar goal: We all want to contribute to healthy and stimulating environments which will facilitate optimal developmental trajectories for all children.

Undoubtedly in many regions of the world, the socio-political environment works against this goal. Children and families, who are exposed to violence and conflict, discrimination and stigma, poverty and ill health, have huge barriers to overcome. And yet there is a significant body of research which supports the notion that early childhood programs services can make a significant contribution to the health and wellbeing of young children—even within unstable, fragile, and/or conflict ridden contexts (Connolly and Hayden 2007).

We may not be able to influence immediate peace and security, nor might we have direct influence on the global indicators in Box One, but we *can* create environments for young children which are stimulating, creative, and effective, despite the macro context—and in this way we can move every child we come into contact with closer to actualizing their full cognitive (and social-emotional) development.

The following chapters provide some guidelines.

References

Connolly, P. and J. Hayden. 2007. *From conflict to peace building.* Seattle: Exchange Press.

Hayden, J. 2007. Making a difference: Promoting social inclusion and respect for diversity. Keynote presentation delivered at the Diversity in Early Childhood Education and Training (DECET) Conference, October 17, 2007, in Brussels, Belgium.

Kagitcibasi, C., D. Sunar, S. Bekman, N. Baydar, and Z. Cemalcilar. 2009. Continuing effects of early enrichment in adult life: The Turkish Early Enrichment Project 22 years later. *Journal of Applied Developmental Psychology,* 30 (6): 764–779.

Lynch, R. 2004. *Exceptional returns—Economic, fiscal, and social benefits of investment in early childhood development.* Washington: Economic Policy Institute.

Schweinhart, L.J. 2005. *Lifetime effects: The High/Scope Perry Preschool study through age 40.* Ypsilanti: High/Scope Press.

UNICEF. 2007. *Children and the millennium goals.* New York: UNICEF.

———. 2008. *The child care transition, Innocenti Report Card 8.* New York: UNICEF.

Part II

Vygotsky and National Policies

CHAPTER TWO

WHERE THERE ARE NO PRESCHOOLS: AN EDUCATIONAL PROGRAM FOSTERING SELF-EFFICACY IN POLISH RURAL AREAS

PIOTR OLAF ZYLICZ

The educational situation of children in Polish rural areas does not differ much from other post-Communist countries in the region. Large numbers of Poles live outside cities. Twenty years after the end of the Communist era in Poland and a few years after joining the European Economic Union (EU), low income households predominate in the rural areas of Poland (except for a small percentage of very rich new era farmers).

The situation is especially challenging for children living in villages which formerly operated within the state-run system of collective farms. Their inhabitants adjusted to the fact that an external power, the state, through its agencies, provided all necessary supplies and did not reward personal engagement and creativity. In these new times the Polish state no longer serves such a strong provider role. However, there remains a growing learned helplessness—the feeling that one can do very little to manage one's personal situation. In this climate, the most self-reliant, active, and often the most education-oriented people tend to move to the cities, significantly depopulating rural areas.

The attitude among adults toward education in rural areas has traditionally been unfavourable. There was a strong conviction that long years of engagement with education did not pay off. In educational institutions, including preschools and schools, the lingering effects of this heritage are still present.

Under Communist rule, schools were meant to be a critical instrument of ideological influence (Levitas and Herczynski 2002, 113–189). In rural areas, the educational approach of *"Just listen and follow instructions"* had been backed by a traditional appreciation of the authority of elders. Teaching practices favoured passive reproduction of knowledge which had little to do with the daily lives of the children (Karpov 2006; Harkness, et al. 2007, 113–135). Despite large changes as the aftermath of the fall of the former system, little has changed in this respect. Thus, the development of **self-efficacy and attitudes of agency** seems to be a critical focus for change in Polish citizens, especially for children living in rural areas of Poland.

Self-Efficacy

Maddux and Gosselin (2003, 218–238) define self-efficacy as beliefs (regardless of their accuracy) about one's competencies and one's ability to exercise these competencies in certain domains and situations. Self-efficacy beliefs (Bandura 1994, 71–81; Schwartzer 1992) determine how people feel, think, motivate themselves, and behave. A strong sense of efficacy enhances human accomplishment and helps one to perceive difficult tasks as challenges rather than as problems. Persons of high self-efficacy set themselves challenging goals and maintain strong commitment even in the face of failure. People's beliefs about their efficacy can be developed foremost by personal mastery experiences, vicarious experiences provided by social models, and social persuasion (the belief that one has the capabilities to master given activities).

Schools play a major role in developing the cognitive competencies, knowledge, and skills essential for participating effectively in society. In the school setting, knowledge and thinking skills are continually tested, evaluated, and socially compared. As children master cognitive skills, they develop a growing sense of their intellectual efficacy.

Schunk and Pajares (after Yuen, Westwood, and Wong 2008, 110–119) showed that students who feel efficacious for learning are more involved, work harder, persist longer in the face of difficulties, and demonstrate higher rates of achievement. Students of low self-efficacy, on the other hand, have a constantly deteriorating self-concept because they repeatedly compare themselves unfavourably to others.

Where There Are No Preschools Program Principles

The Comenius Foundation for Child Development is a Polish non-governmental organization that seeks to equalize life opportunities for children aged zero through ten years. Its program called "*Where There Are No Preschools*" (WTANP) was launched in 2002 to address structural educational inequities faced by young children, especially those living in rural areas where unemployment levels were high (usually well over 20%). Official Polish statistics (FRD 2009) show that in 2006 preschool attendance was 16% in rural communities and 34%in urban communities, an unsatisfactorily low proportion compared to the EU average. In 2007, WTANP was implemented in 28 communities, with more than 800 children attending 75 centres in various parts of Poland. Over 4,000 teachers have been trained by the Comenius Foundation on its approach to early education. The Foundation runs its centres where no other preschool education services are offered. The standard number of hours a child spends in the program is nine per week. The intention has been to keep program costs low so that the program can be replicated in rural areas throughout Poland.

WTANP draws on child-centred approaches to early education. These approaches have had a long tradition, from Comenius through Locke, Rousseau, Pestalozzi, Fröbel, Montessori, Dalton, Isaacs, Anna Freud, and Lilian Katz.

The assumptions of WTANP very much suit Vygotsky's (1986) approach to education. Vygotsky believed individual cognitive development is embedded in the socio-cultural environment that provides tools for thinking. Children's interactions with others in the Zone of Proximal Development (ZPD) provide children with opportunities to carry out cognitive processes that are more advanced than they would manage independently. In an adaptation of the teacher-child interaction which is usually associated with stimulation within the ZPD, Ryba and colleagues (2001) proposed a *"Collective" Zone of Proximal Development*. Here, a group of students form a collective in which there is potential for all members to advance their learning through guidance from more capable peers, fostered by the efforts of the teacher. The authors indicate that within the community, individuals gain a sense of self-efficacy through reflective practice. This sense of self-efficacy is enhanced as individuals experience successes that are recognized and rewarded by others.

This is how the WTANP program works. The WTANP program incorporates learning through exploration and play, observational behaviour modelling, creative activities, teachers' sensitive receptivity, parental involvement, and developing relationships with local authorities.

It became evident quickly that WTANP represents a clear challenge to the formal educational services which had been founded on hierarchical and rigidly governed 'top-down' educational processes. Indeed the program has been continually criticized by the traditional associations of teachers who still hold on to beliefs and practices strongly embedded in the past. The notion that children can set and realize their own goals, for example, is seen as disrespectful to elders and a threat to traditional teaching systems. Consequently, children's spontaneity, flexibility and questioning habits have been interpreted (correctly or incorrectly) as disobedience, or non-compliance with group-accepted rules. There is also concern that the self-efficacy which takes place in the WTANP program will generalize to other domains of children's lives, eventually resulting in social disobedience and even anarchy.

Evaluation of WTANP Program

In 2006 an evaluation of the effectiveness of WTANP was undertaken. It focused on the psychological functioning of the participants. While some of the data are yet to be published, (Żylicz in press), this paper reports on a number of the findings to date.

Direct information on self-efficacy, persistence, and self-confidence (the two latter categories being strongly related to self-efficacy) was gathered from interviews with children and through instruments to measure persistence, self-confidence, and locus of control. The differences and similarities between children who did and did not attend WTANP were investigated.

Research Project 1

The first research study (2006) included students in primary school reception classes in two small rural localities in the Eastern part of Poland. Twenty one six and seven year old graduates of the WTANP program and twenty same-aged peers who did not attend any systematic preschool program took the *Locus of Control in Children Questionnaire* (Szmigielska 1996). The questions focused on perceptions of responsibility behind events (i.e., did children see themselves, or external circumstances such as other people or good or bad luck, as having control). Questions included hypothetical situations such as being successful in fixing a toy or spilling soup at a family meal. Half of the questions were about success, and the other half were about failure. The questionnaire also made it possible to calculate the global locus of control index (LoCI) by adding the success and failure indices.

Figure 2-1

Average Locus of Control Levels: Control of failure, Control of success and global
Locus of Control Index in WTANP graduates vs. children without preschool education

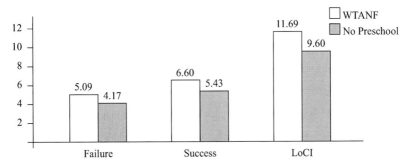

Table 2-1

Average Locus of Control Levels: Global Index (LoCI) and failure/success in
WTANP graduates vs. children without preschool education (non-WTANP)

	t	Significance
LoCI	2.23	$p < 0.05$
Subscales		
Failure	1.65	$p > 0.05$
Success	2.15	$p < 0.05$

The identified statistical differences are of particular importance as the numbers of children in the compared groups are relatively low. A partial locus of control (successes) and a general locus of control was shown to be higher in WTANP children than in those who did not attend any preschool program. This research did not take into account children who attended preschool programs other than WTANP. Therefore, it is difficult to identify the specific influence of WTANP. However, it is reasonable to presume several WTANP practices played a role in the contrast between the two groups.

Discussion

Why did WTANP Children Demonstrate a Higher Locus of Control?

First, the relatively small groups in WTANP classes enabled teachers to pay focused attention to contacts with children, to follow their patterns, and to actively provide assistance when appropriate. Teachers were trained to provide encouragement to explore and to undertake experiential learning. They expressed appreciation for the outcomes of children's efforts.

An important aspect of the program is the opportunity for care takers (mostly mothers) to participate in the classroom activities, and thus to have the chance to observe the teachers' approach to play and learning. It is believed that watching these frequent examples of positive interactions helps parents to acquire new behaviors and attitudes. They not only become more conscious and capable as parents, they also tend to become more proactive in a broader sense. In one of the localities, for example, parents threatened social disobedience if local authorities stopped supporting the Program!

Longitudinal studies will show whether a heightened sense of self-efficacy persists in children and caregivers—and whether this is addressed by traditionally educated teachers who may find the WTANP children to be too self-confident and independent.

Second Evaluation of Project

A second evaluation made use of the Children Behaviour Questionnaire (Żylicz in press). This questionnaire was developed to measure perceptions by teachers and parents about the persistence, social skills, self-confidence, and curiosity of children aged three to seven years old.

The questionnaire has two versions: one for parents and the other for teachers.[1] Previous research shows it is important to consider both perspectives—home and school—as this can reveal diverse images of children's psychological/social functioning (Herling and Wahler 2003, 119–130).

---

[1]   The above mentioned locus of control scale related mostly, as expected with positive significant correlations, with persistence and self-confidence reported by parents and teachers. The only exception was for self-confidence of children as assessed by teachers. Surprisingly, sense of locus of control in the case of failures correlated negatively, although insignificantly, with the reported self-confidence of children. The relationships have been particularly strong in parents: self-confidence and persistence of children as reported by parents accounted for by 56 percent of the variance of children's general locus of control.

Analyses of the findings showed that WTANP graduates, when compared with children without preschool education, were scored by parents significantly higher in each developmental area. Primary school teachers' scores were higher for WTANP graduates on only two of the four areas: self-confidence and curiosity. In broader, cross-sectional comparisons it was found that WTANP 5-year-olds, who were currently attending the Comenius educational centres, scored higher on social skills and curiosity than peers who had graduated from WTANP centres a year before! This phenomenon of unexpected deterioration is discussed below.

Comparisons were also made between current WTANP beneficiaries and children attending other forms of preschool education in Poland. One of the differences is the amount of time children attended preschool per week. In traditional forms of education, children attend preschool for over twenty hours, compared to the standard nine hour attendance per week in WTANP centres.

Children attending WTANP (41 children from diverse centres[2]) were compared with children attending other preschool institutions in two contexts: small towns and villages (91 children) and cities (72 children). Some surprising findings emerged:

No differences were identified in respect to levels of self-confidence. However, significant differences were shown for perseverance.

Children from preschools located in small localities as well as from WTANP centres showed higher persistence than the children who attended preschools in cities: No differences were found between children from small localities preschools and those from WTANP centres.

Evaluation Study Three

Focus groups were held with teachers and parents of children attending WTANP centres. Here, several excerpts are presented to enrich an understanding of the specificity of functioning of WTANP children in respect to self-efficacy (or related categories—self-confidence and persistence).

A total of eleven teachers from seven localities were interviewed in two group interviews. These teachers reported that WTANP graduates differed from the others in levels of self-confidence. WTANP graduates were

---

[2]   For these comparisons only data for WTANP children who attended the basic standard of 9 hours per week were used.

reported to make suggestions easily and to come up with their own ideas for art activities. They were reported to be less afraid than other children, to ask questions, and to make decisions more quickly than other children.

WTANP graduates' self-confidence was also revealed in situations that involved interaction with unrelated adults.

> *"When the head teacher comes into the classroom* [where WTANP children are a majority] *the children don't really notice her, they are natural, relaxed, they aren't afraid of her. A few years back they would have stood to attention."(Teacher)*

Sometimes WTANP children's self-initiative, and evidently sense of self-efficacy, comes as a big surprise to adults who are used to children being more dependent, which was illustrated by one class where WTANP graduates were a majority. Six months into the school year, the head teacher had a surprise visit from a delegation of WTANP children, who came to her office on their own initiative to ask her to be their substitute teacher because their regular teacher was ill. They said they did not want "just any teacher" to teach them. The children's power of persuasion was so strong that the head teacher did as she was asked, even though, to do that, she had to find a substitute teacher to teach her own class!

According to teachers, there is no common tendency with regard to persistence that is characteristic of all WTANP children. Persistence seems to be a genuinely personal trait of character, heavily dependent on the child's individual dispositions. However, many teachers point out that WTANP graduates are, in general, more mobile and initially find it hard to keep their minds on the task at hand for too long, especially if they are distracted or tempted to play. This is why many WTANP children do not apply themselves to manual activities (e.g., cutting with scissors) and are described as doing things in a "slapdash fashion," just to be able to say "I'm finished." Apparently, WTANP children are more persistent, but they can only stay on tasks of their own choosing or on tasks they find interesting. (This would comply with the overall findings of the *Children's Behaviour Questionnaire.*) The above may serve to explain the lack of difference in persistence between WTANP graduates and children without preschool education.

On the other hand, a number of reception-class teachers voiced some criticism of WTANP's educational approach, which favours learning by exploration and encourages self-reliance, making it difficult for the teacher to do obligatory—and sometimes undeniably boring—classroom work. In time, however, these children become more systematic and able to stay on those much-hated manual tasks, and the differences between them and their other classmates gradually fade away. It seems it is the children's approaches, rather than the teachers' expectations, which adapt to the situation.

On the one hand it is an inevitable process for WTANP children to adapt to the more structured and more obligatory tasks imposed by the school system (as compared to self-exploration and independent action in WTANP centres). On the other hand, this adaptation to the traditional schooling system (curricula and teachers' approach) often causes a deterioration in curiosity and social skills (as mentioned above).

Two groups of six teachers from diverse WTANP centres participated in the group interviews as well. These teachers revealed crucial information on the factors underlying the building up of the self-efficacy in social situations in the participating children. They cited many noteworthy events to illustrate children's need and determination to explain and follow group rules. This is what one teacher at a WTANP Centre had to say:

"My children react when someone misbehaves. They say, 'We don't run around with our food because the room can get messy,' or 'You chatterbox, don't talk and eat, or you'll choke.'"

Another teacher stated what many others had indicated in terms of agency and ownership of the classroom behaviour by the children themselves:

"Most importantly, we laid down these rules together. These are children's rules, not something that school staff put on the notice board, like a poster with children's rights that nobody will ever read. Our children decide for themselves who should do what. And they make sure these decisions are followed. As a matter of fact, they are stricter than me in this respect."

This approach to the formulation and acceptance of the group rules encourages the development of an internalised locus of control, i.e. the child's conviction that whatever happens to him/her depends on his/her own efforts, and the children repeatedly refer to these rules in their daily functioning in the centres.

Parents of current WTANP children were questioned about how their participating children's behaviour compared with their other children's behaviour at the same age, and with non-participating children from the neighbourhood. Parents cited examples of children becoming more sociable, independent, and open-minded communicators. They reported that their children had learned to speak in public, to be more assertive, to defend their own boundaries and opinions, and to stand up for other peoples' rights. As one mother stated, her daughter will point out when she, the mother, is not correct in her own behaviour: *"(The daughter) tells me what I shouldn't do. It's great!"* In light of powerful traditional hierarchic relationships between parents and children, this is seen as a breakthrough of self-confidence for the young daughter.

Persistence is the most difficult topic to discuss with parents. Persistence is 'invisible.' It is lack of persistence rather than too much persistence that is more likely to attract attention. The significance of persistence can only be appreciated at a later age, when educational tasks become more and more demanding, especially in the contexts of the assessment tests taken by primary and middle school leavers. Difficulty focusing attention is one of the greatest challenges for children's persistence on tasks everywhere, not only in rural areas. Passive television watching, which is an overwhelmingly common pastime, plays a critical role here (almost every family in Poland has a television). Television viewing reinforces the natural tendency for children of this age group to be distracted. One mother of a three year old proudly told the story of a face mask:

"One day, not long ago, they were painting a fun face mask. The children were about to finish... I'd come to collect Z. Her teacher said: 'Z. is really persistent.' They'd been working for four hours, and she wouldn't put that mask away because she wanted to finish it, put it on and give a scare to her Grandpa. She wouldn't put that mask away, even though she's the youngest of them all, and she asked the teacher to let her take her fun mask home."[3]

Another sign of persistence is the eagerness with which children listen to stories. The following statement of a father is typical. He said:

"They are good listeners. Sometimes they want me to read them a story. They have their stories. They keep quiet and listen, even though they already know the story by heart."

---

[3]   Żylicz (in press).

Discussion

Vygotsky pinpointed educational practices in the Soviet system (including in Poland), which were based on mechanical memorization and procedural knowledge largely non-transferable into real life (Karpov 2005). The WTANP program specifically aims to change the approach and the product of the education system.

Self-efficacy has been found to be an important agent that substantially helps children from disadvantaged rural areas to overcome the low educational expectations of their parents and the limitations of traditional education (which all of these children will inevitably continue to encounter for many years to come).

There are three classifications of self-efficacy in children (Sulda, et al. 2007): emotional, social, and academic.

Our research suggests that the WTANP program effectively enhances self-efficacy (identified through locus of control, self-confidence, and persistence measures). The high congruence of findings between teachers and parents makes the findings more robust.

The WTANP program, in its focus on an experiential approach to educating children, operates on the assumption that facilitating self-confidence and persistence in young children will help them to cope with less than favourable academic situations when they are older. The educational communities of WTANP centres function as "collective" ZPDs (Ryba, et al. 2001) with adults who are more facilitators of the educational processes than traditionally conceived instructors.

In the light of practical implications, the comparisons of psychological effectiveness of WTANP with other, more traditional preschool education programs run in rural, small towns and larger population localities shows the following: offering a nine-hour-per-week curriculum in WTANP is not less effective, in terms of developing self-confidence, than the more expensive traditional programs offering twenty hours per week. Meanwhile, rural WTANP students have been shown to outscore their counterparts from the traditional kindergartens in Polish cities on measures of persistence. This combination of relatively low costs combined with effectiveness suggests the WTANP or similar programs could serve as a serious alternative to the traditional preschool programs in the region. (Specific WTANP teacher education provided by the Comenius Foundation, plus on-going support and supervision, were identified as the causes of the program's effectiveness.)

Additionally, the research addresses the issue of cooperation between prevailing traditional and more modern, progressive approaches (including

WTANP). It was found in cross-sectional comparisons that children of the primary school reception classes who had graduated from WTANP centres scored lower on social skills and curiosity than current program beneficiaries—who were, on average, one year younger. The effect is attributable to the challenges that WTANP (as an example of the child-centred and experiential learning focused programs) children face on entering the traditional education system. It seems highly desirable, for the sake of children, that more traditional institutions actively cooperate with less traditional ones (state run schools vs. centres like WTANP) to ease the transition between the systems. Much of the mutual mistrust between the institutions of both types currently makes this goal of cooperation difficult to fulfil.

While we are aware of the limitations of the research presented here, especially the lack of longitudinal data and the small sample sizes, we are confident that our evaluations have indicated positive outcomes for children and parents who participate in the WTANP program(s)—and confident that Vygotsky would approve of our processes.

References

Bandura, A. 1994. Self-efficacy. In *Encyclopedia of human behavior*, ed. Vilanayur S. Ramachaudran, vol. 4, 71–81. New York: Academic Press.

FRD. 2009. http://www.frd.org.pl.

Harkness, S., M. Blom, O. Oliva, U. Moscardino, P.O. Zylicz, M.R. Bermudez, X. Feng, A. Carrasco-Zylicz, G. Axia, and C. 2007. Teachers' ethnotheories of the 'ideal student' in five western cultures. *Comparative Education*. 43: 1, 113–135.

Herling, M. and R. Wahler. 2003. Children's cooperation at school: The comparative influences of teacher responsiveness and the children's home-based behavior. *Journal of Behavioral Education*, 12: 2, 119–130.

Karpov, Y. 2006. *The neo-Vygotskian approach to child development*. Cambridge: Cambridge University Press.

Levitas, T. and J. Herczynski. 2002, Decentralization, local governments and education reform in post-Communist Poland. In *Balancing national and local responsibilities. Education management and finance in four Central European countries,* ed. Kenneth Davey. Budapest: Open Society Institute/Local Government and Public Service Reform Initiative.

Maddux, J.E., and J.T. Gosselin. 2003. Self-efficacy. In *Handbook of self and identity*, eds. M.R. Leary and J.P. Tangney, 218–238. New York: Guilford Press.

Ryba, K, L. Selby, and M. Mentis. 2001. Analyzing the effectiveness of on-line learning found in communities. [Electronic version]. http://www.ecu.edu.au/conferences/herdsa/main/papers/nonref/pdf/KenRyba.pdf.

Schwarzer, R., ed. 1992. *Self-efficacy: Thought control of action.* Washington, DC: Hemisphere.

Suldo, S.M. and E.J. Shaffer. 2007. Evaluation of the self-efficacy questionnaire for children in two samples of American adolescents. *Journal of Psychoeducational Assessment*, 25, 4: 341–355.

Szmigielska, B. 1996. *Skala poczucia kontroli u dzieci przedszkolnych—SPK-DK.* [A scale of self-efficacy in pre-school children—SPK-DK]. Warszawa: PTP.

Vygotsky, L.S. 1978. *Mind in society: The development of higher psychological processes.* Cambridge: Harvard University Press.

———. 1986. *Thought and language.* Cambridge: MIT Press.

Yuen, M., P. Westwood, and G. Wong. 2008. Self-efficacy perceptions of Chinese primary aged students with specific learning difficulties: A perspective from Hong Kong. *International Journal of Special Education*, 23, 2: 110–119.

Zimmerman, B.J. 2000. Self-efficacy: An essential motive to learn. *Contemporary Educational Psychology*, 25: 82–91.

Żylicz P.O. (in press). *Where there are no preschools: Programme evaluation.* Manuscript to be printed in *Practice and Reflections* series of Bernard van Leer Foundation.

CHAPTER THREE

CROSS-CULTURAL PERSPECTIVES IN EARLY CHILDHOOD EDUCATION: VYGOTSKIAN INFLUENCES AND ETHNOGRAPHIC INSIGHTS INTO ONE PRESCHOOL IN EAST ASIA, SINGAPORE

LYNN ANG

Introduction
Early Childhood Education: A Cross-Cultural Perspective

At the core of Lev Vygotsky's work is the notion that children develop in their socio-cultural context, as a result of their interaction with the environment and world around them. This chapter looks at the ways in which Vygotsky's theories have influenced our understanding of how children develop and learn. Vygotsky has contributed extensively to the field of early childhood education, through his notion that children's knowledge and experiences are influenced not only by the social contexts in which they live, but also by the role of adults in creating and facilitating appropriate environments for learning. Vygotsky's ideas inform us of the importance of adopting a holistic perspective of early childhood education. More importantly, it also emphasizes the significance of taking into account a cross-cultural perspective, not least because children develop and learn in the context of their culture and society, and one is inconceivable without the other.

The influence of Vygotsky's theories is evidenced by the extent to which the theories inform current thinking and practice. With reference to an ethnographic study of a preschool in Southeast Asia, Singapore, the following narrative offers insight into a different culture and society and the factors that influence children's learning and development. The discussion reveals how early childhood education is interpreted from a non-Western perspective and is shaped by the cultural realities and lives of the children and teachers. The vignettes are part of a larger ethnographic study of preschools in Singapore that emerged from a study funded by the British Academy. The research entailed visits across a period of 10 weeks, during which time my role as researcher allowed me unprecedented access to the kindergarten to observe the teachers and children in their daily interactions. The chapter poses essential questions such as, "whose knowledge are we using as a yardstick to support children's learning?" and "what purpose is being served when we talk about a quality early childhood curriculum?" The discussion explores these questions from a cross-cultural perspective, and offers ways of examining how we can re-think notions of early childhood education.

Early Childhood Education in Singapore

Singapore is a small island nation-state in Southeast Asia with a population of approximately four million. The country was a British colony in 1819 and became an independent state in 1963. Singapore is made up of three main ethnic groups: Chinese, Malay and Indian. Chinese is the dominant cultural group and makes up more than 80% of the population. Singapore in the twenty-first century is a multicultural society with a stable government and competitive financial economy. In recent years, education has an become an important public policy, as is evident from national strategies such as the "Towards Excellence in Schools" scheme in 1987 and the "Thinking Schools, Learning Nation" framework (Gopinathan 2001) initiated by the government in a bid to motivate and educate its citizens. This drive towards excellence in education has implications for the way preschool education in Singapore is shaped, and the way children and their education, care, and overall development are perceived.

Preschools in Singapore have become core institutions. A recent population census indicates that there are approximately 144,000 children at preschool age (UNESCO Institute for Statistics 2006), making up 3.3 per cent of the population. It is estimated that at least 90 per cent of children attend some form of preschool (UNESCO Policy Brief 2007). The term "preschool" in Singapore refers generally to two main types of provision: childcare centres and kindergartens. The compulsory school age for children is 7 years old, and preschools cater for children from 2 to 6 years old. Childcare centres and kindergartens differ mainly in their function and provision. Kindergartens cater to children aged 3 to 6 years old and offer daily sessional educational programs, that 2 to 4 hours each. Childcare centres, on the other hand, generally provide full or partial day care for children aged 2 months old and above.

The types of childcare and kindergarten settings available are considerably diverse: there are religious-based childcare centres and kindergartens (e.g. a kindergarten affiliated to a Methodist church or a childcare centre attached to a mosque), workplace childcare centres, private kindergartens (e.g. a Montessori kindergarten), government subsidized kindergartens, and private childcare centres. The pedagogical models and practices of these settings are varied, offering different types of programs that vary in terms of their content, curriculum aims, and overall teaching and learning approaches (Retas and Kwan 2000, Fan-Eng and Sharpe 2000).

Historically, the care and education of preschool children in Singapore has been largely a private concern for the family. Strong family ties and values prescribe that children are often looked after at home by their grandparents or members of the extended family. However, in recent years, the country has undergone demographic and social changes, with more mothers choosing to work in order to supplement the family income and pursue a career. In the last decade, for instance, the participation rate of females in the labour force increased from 48.8 per cent in 1990 to 50.2 per cent in 2000 (Department of Statistics 2005).

Given these demographic changes, there has been a virtual explosion of preschools in the country. The rise in preschool participation is evidence of a radical departure from the traditional modes of caring for young children. With the middle class population continuing to expand, the demand for early education provisions is high. There were 483 kindergartens registered in 2008 with the Ministry of Education (MOE) (Department of Statistics, Ministry of Education). In 2006, the number of childcare centres alone was 725, offering full time care for children aged 7 years and below; an almost 10 per cent increase from the 653 centres registered in 2003. This expansion of childcare centres is indicative of the rise of working professionals, who regard preschools as the way to offer their children the best chance of being educated and integrated into society while they are at work. As suggested in a statement by the Ministry of Education, "parents have become more well-educated, and have higher expectations of the standard of preschool education for their children" (MOE, 2008). As perceptions of work, marriage, and family change, the early childhood care and education sectors in Singapore are expected to be responsive to the changing needs of society, and preschools are regarded as places that can provide stability and guidance to children's lives.

Saint Catherine's: A Singaporean Kindergarten

Saint Catherine's Kindergarten[1] is a preschool in Singapore affiliated with an Anglican church. The kindergarten opened in 1953 catering to children aged 2½ to 6 years old. There are approximately 290 children and 24 staff, headed by the principal, Rina.[2] The average class size is 20 pupils, and every classroom has a teacher and assistant teacher. Like most kindergartens in Singapore, Saint Catherine's operates two daily sessions. The sessions run from 8:15 to 11:15 in the morning and 11:30 to 2:30 in the afternoon.

For Vygotsky, the effective implementation of any early childhood curriculum is very much dependent on the socio-cultural context of the child. At Saint Catherine's, the religious ethos and philosophy provide a unique context to the school's provision and practice. The name of each class is based on the Anglican tradition. There are six nursery school classes: Faith, Charis, Kindness, Joy, Goodness, and Patience; and six kindergarten classes: Jereh, Shalom, Grace, Wisdom, Glory, and Strength. The first view of Saint Catherine's is the adjoining church, which faces a busy main road and is backed by a private residential estate. The kindergarten occupies a separate building at the far end of the church grounds. The setting's daily assembly epitomizes the philosophy of Saint Catherine's:

8:10 a.m.: The children begin to arrive. They make their way to the class-rooms, leaving their belongings, are led to the hall by the teachers for an assembly.

8:30 a.m.: The morning session begins. Rina is at the front of the hall waiting for the children. When everyone assembles, Rina moves to the piano and enthusiastically greets the children over the microphone: "Morning children! Let's start the day with worshipping the Lord, is everyone ready?" Rina's voice and manner are lively and animated. She plays the piano, music resonates through the hall as the children and teachers sing in chorus and perform the actions to the song: "It's a great day to praise the Lord, walking in the light of the Lord," the children sing with excitement and enthusiasm. For the next 20 minutes or so, the hall resonates with music of the children's singing and clapping.

---

1   The name of the setting has been changed for ethical reasons.
2   All personal names have been changed for ethical reasons.

8:55 a.m.: At the end of the last song, Rina leads the children in a short prayer: "Dear Heavenly Father, we praise your name with our singing. Thank you for bringing us together again." The prayer ends with a chorus of "Amen" and the children leave in groups with their teachers and head to the classrooms.

The children begin each day with hymns and devotion. It is clear that Christianity is a strong element that underpins life at the kindergarten. Yet, as much as religion is the core philosophy of Saint Catherine's, there is also an interesting corollary to this attribute. While the school is steeped in its Anglican faith, Rina revealed that less than ten per cent of the children are Christians or share a Christian upbringing. The majority of the children come from diverse cultural and religious backgrounds. I asked if this was an issue with parents. But as Rina pointed out, the majority of parents who come to Saint Catherine's are aware of its Christian values, but are nonetheless content for their children to be there, because they are also aware of how inclusive the setting is. The kindergarten has always catered its provisions to the diverse and multicultural local community. It offers a bilingual curriculum, with English as the first language, and Tamil and Mandarin as second languages. Rina explained that the ethos of Saint Catherine's, such as kindness, respecting your parents, and filial piety, are also highly valued principles in the Asian society. Hence, parents view the philosophy of the kindergarten as complementary to the values that they wish to instil in their children.

Saint Catherine's presents an interesting example of the unique ethos and philosophy that underpins much of early childhood education. The practices of the setting seem to be characterized by the coexistence of different voices, beliefs, and values. What seems to emerge from the setting is an understanding of what it means to live in a multicultural country like Singapore, in a society that is full of contrasts and contradictions, with the mix of Christians and non-Christians, the juxtaposition of traditional and modern, and the assimilation of Chinese, Indian, Malay, and other ethnicities. Saint Catherine's epitomizes the inherent contradictions and complexities that coexist in such a society. Apple (2001) argues that the curriculum is bound to the histories of class, ethnicity, and race. Early childhood institutions are microcosms of the broader society, and it is essential that they are understood within the socio-cultural contexts in which they are situated. If, as Vygotsky argues, children learn best in their social environment, then this contextualization is crucial in facilitating all aspects of the children's early childhood experience at Saint Catherine's.

A Multi-Dimensional Learning Environment

An appropriate word to describe the curriculum at Saint Catherine's is "multi-dimensional." During my visit, I observed a nursery class of 3 to 4-year-olds, led by Sofia, a newly qualified teacher in her twenties. There were 22 children in the class. The session I observed was scheduled as "directed time" as indicated on the timetable:

12.15 p.m.: The children have just finished their lunch. Sofia asks the children to return to their desks. As Sofia gets the children ready, the Chinese teacher Lee Loa shi enters the classroom. The children greet her in Chinese. After a quick exchange and banter with Sofia, Lao shi picks ups some worksheets from the shelf and sits with a group of five children around a table in the language corner. They converse in Mandarin as Lao shi engages the children in writing the Chinese characters on the worksheet.

12.20 p.m.: The children and Lao shi chat with each other in Mandarin. Sofia sits with two children at the green table. The children at the green table are writing alphabets. Some are drawing and colouring pictures. Sofia goes around the table guiding the children individually. The other children are engaged with play activities around the class. There are for children in the "home corner" playing with the cooking set. Two children are by the book corner reading and another four are sitting on the mat playing with Legos, puzzles, trucks, and blocks. Ying, the assistant teacher, supervises the children who are playing, and interacts with them. She encourages each child to try different activities. A couple of the children move on to the tables to work with Lao shi on the Chinese worksheet.

12.30 p.m.: At the green table, as each child completes the worksheet, they leave the table and join the others in an activity. The children choose to engage with different activities. Sofia moves to the "home corner," then to the mat, asking the children questions about what they are doing as she goes. In the language corner, as some of the children complete their writing with Lao shi, they wander over to join the rest of the children in their different activities, while Lao shi continues working with the other children that join her table. There is an active buzz in the classroom as the children move around to the different activities. The atmosphere is lively and the group is chatty.

The session seemed initially confusing, as the time table states, "12 to 1 p.m. directed time," and my expectation of the session was that it would be mostly directed by adults, with didactic teaching and children at their desks, engaged in literacy or numeracy activities. But it was far from my expectations. The session was unstructured, and the children were active and engaged in many different activities simultaneously. The children were also making decisions about which activities they wanted to be involved in and with whom they wanted to engage. It seemed almost bizarre that many of the activities the children were doing did not correlate to what was scheduled on the time table, and they were carrying out many different activities at once, some of which were completely contrasting, such as playing with Legos and colouring rather than learning Chinese characters and writing the alphabets.

Amid what can best be described as a free-flowing, mixed-activity session, there was a definite vigour and energy. The children were engaged in their play, language, and interaction. They were playing alongside one another, watching and listening to each other. Although the children were engaged in some directed learning with Sofia and Lao shi, they were also free to move around and express themselves as they worked. While some did their worksheets and were individually supported by Sofia and Lao shi, others were free to use the time to play, chat, read, or do whatever they chose.

Academic debates still continue about what type of curriculum is ideal for children's learning, and what is the appropriate pedagogy for a quality program. Perhaps some would maintain that Sofia should have provided a more carefully planned curriculum rather than one that offered a "free-flow" session with a variety of contrasting activities all taking place at once. Yet, these multi-activity sessions seemed to be very much a part of the normal daily routine at Saint Catherine's. Learning the alphabet was as much a part of the curriculum as playing, eating, and singing, and these activities occurred simultaneously, not necessarily at set times or in routines. Sofia's and Lao shi's class demonstrated that, functioning within a unique cultural context, there is more than one pedagogical approach.

For Vygotsky, how children are encouraged to learn, and the context for their learning, is critical, and is indeed inseparable, from the content of the curriculum, or what they learn. The vignette exemplifies Vygotsky's theory about the importance of socialization and the social interactions that take place within the classroom. In his concept of the Zone of Proximal Development (ZPD), Vygotsky argues that the role of the adult is critical in enhancing children's learning and in helping children achieve new levels of learning and thinking (Vygotsky, cited in Trudge J., 1990). The same can also be said of the importance of children's socialization through play and peer interactions. The children who play alongside each other are likely to gain from the experience of watching and listening to each other, and paying attention to what is said and done in their interactions.

Increasingly, early childhood educators are expected to work toward learning and educational outcomes, but the way this is achieved is the challenge. Sofia and Lao shi seem to have constructed an environment based on the view that children are active learners, and that their role as adults is, primarily, to engage the children in ways that extend their learning. An effective curriculum is not just about meeting educational outcomes, setting clear aims, or carefully planning. It is equally important to enable children to take ownership of their learning, independently as well as collaboratively, and to create contexts in which their learning is sustained in an environment where they can create and co-construct their own experiences. In essence, the key processes of early childhood education are derived not just from developing carefully planned curriculums or programs, but from the giving children opportunities to undertake tasks, make choices, and partake in activities with the adults and peers around them.

A Socio-Cultural Perspective: How Best Do Children Learn?

Throughout my time at Saint Catherine's, there was a pervading sense of ownership on the part of Rina and her teachers to determine their own curriculum, and to decide what they thought was the best way to help children learn. The excerpt below is from a music and movement session of a nursery school class of 4-year-olds, which was led by its teacher Alice:

8:55 a.m.: Alice and the assistant teacher Mar, are with their class of 4-year-olds. Alice prepares the tape recorder and musical instruments.

9:00 a.m.: Alice explains to me that she will be playing a medley of action songs and that there would be specific actions to accompany each part of the song. She explains that the children have had a few sessions and are familiar with the lyrics and actions. As Alice explains this to me, Mary gets the children to form a circle and hold each others' hands.

9:05 a.m.: Alice says enthusiastically to the children, *"We are going to listen carefully to the music and do the actions. You've done this before, yes? We are going to swing and tap! Are we ready?"* Alice plays the tape.

The song is a lively number with instructions for the children to dance to the rhythm: *"swing and tap, swing and tap, swing your arms, bend them back."* Alice stands outside the circle, singing along and doing the actions. The children move enthusiastically to the music. As the music plays, Alice calls out to the children to listen and follow the music. She repeats her instruction to listen a couple of times.

9:15 a.m.: About 10 minutes into the session, a few children start to stray, breaking away from the circle and doing their own movements. Alice stops the tape and says firmly to children: *"Children, follow the music, listen carefully to the words."* Alice demonstrates to the children the "swing and tap" action again and then asks them, *"are you ready?"*

9:20 a.m.: *Alice starts the tape again. She joins in and the children continue with the actions.*

9:25 a.m.: The song ends five minutes later. Alice stops the tape. She asks the children, *"did you like that?"* There is a chorus of *"yes,"* and Alice continues, saying *"okay, we are now going to use our hand bells."* Alice explains to me that the next song is performed with musical instruments and requires the children to shake their hand bells. Mary gives out two hand bells to each child, keeping them in a circle.

9:30 a.m.: Alice gets ready to start the tape again, but not before repeating her instructions to the children. *"Everyone, we are going to use our hand bells now,"* she says. *"You can shake to the music. You have to listen carefully. I want to see who is listening and who is not listening."* Alice starts the tape and joins in with the children. Like before, as the music plays she reminds the children, *"everyone, listen to the tape, follow the words."*

At the end of the session, Alice admitted that she found it challenging to teach a group of 19 children under the age of five the movements and words to the music. Although I did not say this to Alice at the time, my immediate thought was that Alice's constant instructions and reminders to the children to "listen and follow the words" somewhat undermined the essence of the session. On a couple of occasions, when the children moved to the music without doing the appropriate actions, they were stopped and asked to repeat the correct movement. I thought that surely the aim of a music class is for the children to enjoy the activity, and that whether they knew the appropriate actions was less important than their enjoyment of the session.

However, in my conversation with Alice, it became clear that her ideas and purpose for that session were different than what I had in mind. She tried to further explain.

> "*I think it went ok, but not everyone was following the music. I think the children enjoyed themselves, but not everyone was listening,*" She said. As if to prove her point, Alice explained. "*You see, Wei xiang, Daniel, and Stephanie, they were not listening to the first part of the music, they were doing their own thing. They are not focused enough. Five minutes okay, but ten minutes ... they get distracted.*"

Alice's response suggested that she expected the children not only to enjoy the music, but to learn the actions as well; and the only way to do this was to listen. When I probed further why she thought listening was important, Alice looked almost incredulous that I could be asking a question to which the answer was so obvious.

> "*Listening is important. Of course it is very important, because when they learn, if they listen, they can be focused. Listening is so important. In the primary school, if you don't listen, you will lose out, you won't know what is going on. How will you know what the teacher is saying? In Singapore, it is a race.*"

Alice paused for a while, and as if to emphasize her point further, she continued

> "*Also, listening is important, because in our culture, we are brought up to listen. From [a young age], we have to listen to our parents, our grand-parents, the older generation,*" she said. "*Of course listening is important; a good child is one who listens.*"

Through speaking with Alice, it was evident that listening was something she took very seriously. Alice's notion of listening is a central part of learning. Her belief in the importance of listening comes from the best of intentions: if the children listen, they will be more focused and therefore able to learn and comprehend better what is going on around them. For Alice, listening is an essential part of a wider set of social and cultural values: "*we are brought up to listen; a good child is one who listens.*" Thus, while it was difficult initially to appreciate the essence of Alice's music and movement class without some understanding of this cultural context, the episode nonetheless serves as a reminder to us to respect all forms of knowledge and all perspectives on the best ways children learn.

Cultural values and experiences are integral to early childhood education. Alice's perception of the importance of listening highlights the need to problematize our own understanding of how children learn and highlights the importance of challenging dominant constructions of children's development. As Alice asserts: *"if only the children will listen better, who knows how much more they will learn?"* The plethora of literature that has emerged about children's learning is largely rooted in the official knowledge of child development, which suggests that children's learning takes place through stages of development and that these are more or less universal: all children progress through similar stages, although each at their own pace. Attempts to understand how children learn have also been heavily influenced by the work of developmental psychologists such as Piaget, Bruner, and Erikson, who argue that children learn best by exploring and experimenting. Piaget's theory likens children to budding scientists who learn through discovery, activity, and problem solving (Piaget, 1962). Indeed, the concept of the "enquiring child" is common currency in early childhood education. In the book *Enquiring Children, Challenging Teaching* (2001), Boo defines the term "enquiry" as "a situation where there is curiosity and a desire to find something out by exploration, investigation and research" (p.2). He maintains that children are innately inquisitive, and that they learn essentially through questioning and "initiating and pursuing enquiries." Early Childhood educators often cite the importance of providing an educational environment where children can learn through experimenting and exploring (Devereux J. and Miller L. 2003(ed.); Abbott (2006); Trawick-Smith J. (2006); Tassoni and Beith K (2005); Berk L.E. (2006). However, the danger with this discourse is its pervasive influence on a normalizing and universal notion of children. In a cross-cultural context, this notion of the "inquiring child" can be disempowering when in one instance, the child is constructed in theory as an active learner who is encouraged to experiment and explore, but in another instance, the child is expected in practice to listen and learn the skills of social and cultural negotiation.

The practices at Saint Catherine's reinforce the notion that there are different and multiple ways in which children learn and flourish. Vygotsky's views about the centrality of the social and cultural context of young children's learning become more crucial. The vignette shows that an appropriate curriculum for children is often determined by the milieu of cultural values embedded within their society. Thus, an important prerequisite for effective early childhood education is not only to assist children in meeting specific educational outcomes, but also to understand the cultural and social mores that underpin the world they live in. It is this social constructivist approach that provides a strong foundation for a quality early childhood practice.

Conclusion
Early Childhood Education as Culture-Bound

It is inevitable that within the confines of one chapter, the vignettes represent only a brief picture of the overall ethnographic landscape of Saint Catherine's. Yet, what is reinforced is the centrality of the socio-cultural context of the child. This chapter demonstrates the importance of maintaining a cross-cultural perspective in early childhood education, because children, as well as educators, are contextualized in their local culture and society. With its distinct ethos and curriculum, the practices of Saint Catherine's offer a unique example of how Vygotskian theory informs thinking and practices in different cultural and geographical settings, sustained by the setting's own philosophy of childhood and learning. The narrative shows that perceptions of how children develop and learn are culture-bound, and these multiple perspectives have a pervasive influence on the way we construct our own understanding of early childhood education.

References

Apple, M.W.A. 2001. *Educating the "right" way: Markets, standards, God, and inequality*, New York: Routledge Falmer.

Berk, L.E. 2006. *Child development* (7th edition). United States: Pearson Education.

Boo, M.D. 2001. *Enquiring children, challenging teaching*. Buckingham: Open University Press.

Devereux, J. and L. Miller, eds. 2003. *Early childhood development* (4th edition). New Jersey: Pearson Education.

Gopinathan, S. 2001. Globalisation, the state and education policy in Singapore. In *Challenges facing the Singapore education system today*, eds. J. Tan, S. Gopinathan, and W.K. Ho: 3–17. Singapore: Prentice Hall.

Retas, S. and C. Kwan. 2000. Preschool quality and staff characteristics in Singapore. In *Investing in our future: The early years*, eds. C. Tan-Niam and M.L. Quah: 53–65. Singapore: McGraw-Hill.

Riley, J. 2005. The child, the context and early childhood education. In *Learning in the early years*, ed. J. Riley. London: Paul Chapman Publishing.

Sharpe, P. 2000. Features of pre-school education in Singapore. In *Investing in our future: The early years*, eds. C. Tan-Niam and M.L. Quah. Singapore: McGraw-Hill.

Singapore Department of Statistics (SDS). Singapore's Population Trends; Population Statistics Section. http://www.singtate.gov.sg/ssn/feat.oct2002/pg2-6.pdf. Accessed 20 May 2009.

Singapore Ministry of Education (MOE). 2008. Press release. http://www.moe.gov.sg/media/press/2008/03/improving-the-quality-of-presc.php. Accessed 21 May 2009.

Trudge, J. 1990. Vygotsky, the zone of proximal development, and peer collaboration: implications for classroom practice. In *Instructional implications and applications for sociohistorical psychology*, ed. L.C. Moll. Cambridge: Cambridge University Press.

UNESCO. 2004. Policy Brief on early childhood. Inter-Ministerial Collaboration in Early Childhood Training in Singapore, No. 24, http://unesdoc.unesco.org/images/0013/001374/137413e.pdf. Accessed May 20, 2009.

———. 2007. Policy Brief on early childhood. Partnership with Non-Public Actors: Singapore's Early Childhood Policy. No. 36, http://unesdoc.unesco.org/images/0014/001494/149486E.pdf. Accessed May 20, 2009.

Vygotsky, L.S. 1978. *Mind in Society: the development of higher psychological processes*. Cambridge: Harvard University Press.

CHAPTER FOUR

THE TEACHER'S POSITION IN ADULT–CHILD INTERACTION IN RELATION TO A CHILD'S ZONE OF PROXIMAL DEVELOPMENT[1]

ELENA YUDINA

The Notion of a Zone of Proximal Development in the Context of Child–Adult Interaction

A Zone of Proximal Development (ZPD) is one of the most important and widely known concepts introduced by Vygotsky in psychology. This term is widely used in both textbooks and studies on educational issues; fairly often the concept itself becomes the focus of modern research. It has become exceptionally popular in Western psychological and pedagogical literature; quite often we can see that for both researchers and teachers the immediate association with Vygotsky's theory is ZPD and related concepts, e.g., "scaffolding." Meanwhile, it is really difficult to find a concept as vaguely defined and implying as many myths as ZPD in the entire array of modern educational psychology. The meaning of this term is vague, and its use is obviously metaphorical, hence the danger of its oversimplification, which has been discussed in several publications (see Wertsch 1984, 7–18, Chaiklin 2003, 39–64, Zukerman 2006, etc.).

There is a clear explanation for this: Vygotsky only managed to delineate the contours of the notion of ZPD and describe it very briefly; and his description illustrates the term rather than clarifies its meaning. Here is one of the most well-known definitions that Vygotsky gave to ZPD: "A Zone of Proximal Development of a child is the distance between his/her actual developmental level as determined by independent problem

---

[1] This work was financially supported by Russian Foundation of Humanities, Project No. 07-06-00871a.

solving and the level of potential development as determined through problem solving under adult guidance or in collaboration with more capable peers" (Vygotsky 1991). In the research discussed below, this very definition has proven to be most popular among the English speaking audience (see: Vygotsky 1978).

At the first glance at this definition, it becomes evident that the ZPD of a child is determined by the complexity of tasks that this child solves, either independently or with the help of an adult. Does this mean that the ZPD equals the "range of tasks?" The answer is definitely "no." If we use such a unit of measure for ZPD, we can say nothing of the ZPD of a particular child, because how the child does certain tasks (in other words, testing) can only demonstrate the child's current possibilities, but not the level of his or her potential development.

The notion of ZPD contains an idea that is crucially important for modern psychology and educational practice: if we want to diagnose the real state of a child's cognitive development, we can't just define the level of his/her actual development, i.e., what this child can do now. It is much more important to understand what the child's potential possibilities are; in other words, to mark the space for this particular child's development. If we want education to really lead to learning, we should arrange the education process *in the zone of the child's proximal development*, which makes it necessary to identify this zone. However, this is possible only during the interaction of an adult with the child, because only child-adult interaction identifies the child's ZPD. At the same time, we must keep in mind that education leading to learning should not only *use* the existing ZPD of the child, but also *create* the next zone of the child's proximal development (or extend the current one), and this is also possible only in a certain type of child-adult interaction. Therefore, when we try to identify or create the ZPD, we should not only focus on the complexity of a task solved by a child independently or together with an adult, but rather on the issue of **child-teacher interaction.**

Concerning child-adult interaction, we follow the view that the interaction between an adult and a child is a very important context of a child's development. This view can obviously be considered classical for cultural-historical psychology (L.S. Vygotsky, D.B. Elkonin, A.V. Zaporozhets, and others). Research conducted both within and outside cultural-historical tradition indicates that interactions between children and teachers in class-rooms crucially affect the main direction and quality of child development; this impact being the highest for younger children. In other words, while for Vygotskians the teacher in general is one of the critical mediators for children's internalization of cultural tools (see, e.g., Wertsch 1998), this role becomes even more important in the context of early childhood education.

We can see that the notion of the ZPD covers a certain type of relationship between the teacher's instructions and the child development, i.e. between an adult and a child. However, quite a few problems remain unsolved, and each of them is important for both theory and practice. What is the nature and the scope of adult "guidance" mentioned by Vygotsky in joint problem solving that will really create the child's ZPD? In other words, what kind of assistance should a teacher render to a child in order to create the ZPD? Who is the subject (the master) of the ZPD? What is the relationship between ZPD and the personal learning initiative of a child? Such questions are important for both theory and practice of education.

The practical focus of the issues is: how can cultural-historical psychology and especially the notion of ZPD help teachers in the classroom to promote child development? The notion of ZPD implies the idea of the important role of an intimate adult in learning that will impact the development of a child, i.e., will create and extend his or her ZPD. However, we should always remember that in the ZPD there should be *joint activity* of two people—that of a teacher and a child, and it is essential to have a clear idea of the responsibilities of the two. There are practical questions to be answered in the classroom: Who chooses the appropriate activity for a child, and what is the range for this choice? Who sets the tasks that will create the widest ZPD possible to ensure its developing effect? What kind of teacher assistance will be effective for the creation of the ZPD appropriate to the child, on the one hand, and to the teacher's educational tasks, on the other?

These questions are crucially important for preschool education, since the younger the child, the wider his or her ZPD can be. However, the child's age restricts to some extent the independence in the choice of activity.

In summary, we can say the following:

- The Vygotskian concept of ZPD suggests that the role of an intimate adult is very important for the creation of ZPDs.

- The ZPD can only be reached through joint adult-child activities.

- Interaction in the ZPD always takes place between competent (skilled) and incompetent partners, and the younger the child, the wider the gap between his/her level of competence and that of the skilled partner.

Since every question is not only theoretical but implies practical use, it is evident that the answers depend on a *teacher's position* when he or she "manages" a child's ZPD. Since the ZPD is possible only as the outcome of a child-adult joint activity, the independence and initiative given to a child by the teacher will determine both the appearance of the ZPD and the general direction and quality of a child's development. There can be child-adult common actions where the adult domineers and the child passively follows the adult's instructions. At the opposite extreme, we see no guidance from the adult at all, which prevents the child from acquiring human cultural experience. In both the former and the latter cases, there is no real joint activity, which means there are no conditions for significant extension of the child's ZPD.

Following Erich Fromm, by "authoritarianism" I mean a system of values opposed to humanism and based on irrational authority of power: "I should like to differentiate between two kinds of authority. One is objective, based on the *competency* of the person in authority to function properly with respect to the task of guidance he has to perform. This kind of authority may be called rational authority. In contrast to this is what may be called *irrational authority*, which is based on the power which the authority has over those subjected to it and on the fear and awe with which the latter reciprocate" (Fromm 1994, 16, italics in the original).

The authoritarian system of values implies rigid hierarchy where the one who is above (a stronger one) never hesitates to define what is good for a weaker one, giving no room for criticism or doubt; dictates what the norms are; is supported by the feeling of fear and dependence; and considers obedience as the main virtue. The person whose power is based on irrational authority lives with a permanent feeling of fear that his/her incompetence will be revealed, which makes fear and power the attributes of everyone involved in the system.

As Theodor W. Adorno showed (Adorno 1994, 506), an authoritative ethic generates a certain type of personality that has its own place in this hierarchy and is ready to suppress and to be suppressed. Hence, the main norms studied in my survey were the norms of the teachers' position defining the attitude towards the partner in interactions (interactions with a child, in our particular case) as a subject of education, or as raw material in a teacher's hands only able to follow instructions set by this teacher. The last one relates to the viewing of the child as an object of the teacher's actions.

Interaction between preschool children and teachers in different cultures, which is the subject of our research on the cultural-historical framework, is the focus of this chapter. I have observed that there is a fundamental difference between Western and Eastern teachers' views on this issue: in general, Western teachers hesitate to intervene in children's development, whereas Eastern teachers try to lead the developmental process. For example, one of the myths of educational practice in Russia is that *any kind* of instruction creates or extends the ZPD of a child. Meanwhile, the real teacher's work in the ZPD of a child (it can be classroom evaluation, instruction, or classroom management) demands some special efforts in building adult-child interactions. As stated previously, a teacher's position toward a child is the main factor impacting the nature of the interaction.

Cross-Cultural Studies of a Teacher's Position in Interaction with Children

This sub-chapter describes two cross-cultural studies of the concept of "teacher's position," in relation to early childhood classroom interactions. The purpose of these studies were to reveal the position of preschool teachers working with children of the same age in different countries, and then to compare the outcomes for both groups.

Some time ago, I indicated the special position that a teacher forms during his/her interaction with children. I defined this position as the "position above" (Yudina 1998). Such a position implies regarding a child as a *tabula rasa* that a teacher must fill in and considering the teacher's own actions, knowledge, and evaluations as a model. There is a question about the origin of such a position. Cross-cultural comparative study makes it possible to define the main sources and conditions to form the position (standpoint) of the teacher in teacher-child interaction. Among other things, it becomes possible to answer the crucial question: when a teacher's position is formed, what is the role of general cultural context, compared with the specific features of professional training and with the teaching practice typical for this particular culture?

It is possible that the "above" position is rooted in a traditionally paternal attitude towards children. It is also possible that the very nature of teaching provokes the "above" position. To clarify which of the two assumptions is closer to reality, I conducted a comparative study of Russian and American preschool teachers (Yudina 2005), as well as a sample from Russia and Lithuania (Yudina 1998). In the United States, the author observed that there is practically no paternalism in the relations between different generations, which makes it possible to verify the assumption about the impact of culturally inherent paternalism on a teacher's position. On the other hand, Russian and Lithuanian preschool teachers belonged to the same educational system for more than half a century, but are influenced by different cultural contexts.

The Position of the Teachers in USA and Russia

In the teacher's position towards a child, I point out the following categories: "The goals of teaching activity," "the perception of the child," "the aspects/ kinds of the teacher's activity," "planning," and "the means of correcting a child's behaviour."

The choice of the first three is obvious: teachers' views on these issues mainly define their position in their professional activity. The means of correcting a child's behaviour are closely connected with everyday classroom practice and define the specific features of child-adult interaction. For example, if a teacher is inclined to simply stop or forbid inappropriate types of child behaviour, this very inclination will provoke a lot of conflict (or potential conflict) situations in their interaction with the children. If a teacher uses other means as well (explanation, negotiation, the method of imminent outcomes, support, redirection), and uses direct forbidding only when nothing else works, the interaction will be completely different.

Viewing a child as an object or a subject of his/her own action is presented most clearly in the category "the perception of the child." It is this particular category that crucially influences the strategy of creating interactions between teachers and children. I included in this category teachers' attitudes about the development of a preschool child, age appropriate child-adult interaction, the balance between individual and age-specific stages of development, and the child being the subject of the education process.

Planning as a part of a teacher's professional activity is a very special issue. In most Russian schools and kindergartens, according to systemic regulations, every teacher must submit a detailed plan for every lesson (or activity) outlining every single step. Normally, such a plan begins with setting the goals and objectives of the work. Surprisingly, evidence shows that Russian teachers are sometimes unable to set the goals and objectives of their work by themselves: frequently these are simply substituted for by the clichés imported from the standard methodology of teaching (Yudina 2005). Of course, these clichés shouldn't be regarded as goals, since setting goals requires the teacher's deliberate choice of teaching priorities based on the actual needs of children in his or her classroom.

One possible explanation is that teachers in their planning activity strive to meet the requirements of the teaching methodology, rather than care about children's development or education. Teachers consider methodology not as a means of education, but as an end in itself, even though it is obvious that the teacher should always remember that every methodology is of limited applicability. The process of education regularly demands that teachers reconsider and revisit the methodology, taking the children's interests and conditions into account. At the same time, empirical findings suggest that for Russian teachers the only real goal often consists in following the methodology, so the teacher (and those who come to observe her performance) cares mainly about the process, not actual goals (Yudina 2005).

A teacher's plan dominates the process of interaction with a child, thus replacing the substantive educational aims that might have been previously set. Paradoxically, in this situation, often the child turns into an obstacle that prevents the teacher from implementing the plan. This is why a teacher's attitude to planning is a decisive factor influencing her interaction with the children. In a comparative cross-cultural study it was crucial to define whether this factor is typical for all teachers or culturally specific in forming the teacher's position (Yudina 2005).

I have compared the categories of American preschool teachers' position with those of Russian teachers working with children of the same age, using the same questionnaire that was translated and adapted for American teachers.

As the result, the teachers who had completely different professional training and working experience in different educational systems consider the same categories significant for child-adult interaction. From the study (Yudina 2005), it follows that the overall the level of authoritarianism among preschool teachers in the USA is lower than in Russia, but if analysing each category separately, some discrepancies are found. For example, in the category "Goals of Teaching Activity," the level of authoritarianism is higher with American teachers than with Russian, but in the category "Perception of the Child," a higher level of authoritarianism for Russian teachers compared with American teachers is observed. This means that when interacting with a child, Russian teachers mainly treat him or her not as a participant in an interaction, but as an object, which is the opposite attitude from the teachers in America. This means that the probability of creating a wider ZPD for the American teachers is, to a certain extent, higher than for the Russian teachers.

As mentioned previously, teachers from both countries used different curricula. It seems fairly important to notice that the level of authoritarianism significantly depends on the curriculum the teacher uses. Nevertheless, the curricula factor has a relatively small impact on the level of authoritarianism in child-adult interaction as compared to the country factor. It is evident that no matter how considerable the difference in curricula within a country might be, the gap between the cultures is much more significant (Yudina 2005). This is true for the category "Perception of the Child," in which we can observe a real gap in the attitude towards a child between the two cultures. The set of attitudes towards the child as the key participant of the educational process are extremely important characteristics of the educational system in general. Thus, one can expect that these differences in attitudes might easily lead to the dramatic essential differences between the two systems of education.

Russian—Lithuanian Comparative Study

In the previous study of preschool teachers (Yudina 1998), the distinction between the declared norms and values and their manifestations in real practice were observed. In discussions concerning the children's education and development, teachers mainly present accepted norms and values, and often seem unaware that their practice differs from these declarations. This discrepancy becomes obvious during the direct observation of the teachers' interactions with the children. It is worth pointing out that the teachers' declarations of the values are always strong, clear, and constantly present, while in a normal cognitive process, these values are dynamic—they can disappear, appear again, turn into real action, etc.

Content-wise, these declarations are usually the combination of pseudo-humanistic clichés from the notion of a child-centred approach. As the author's previous studies have shown, these declarations are fairly restricted and stable (Yudina 1998).

The declarations form an outer, or surface layer of the teachers' professional thinking, which often differs significantly from the next layer, that of the actual working norms. If, in the study of teachers' position, this fact is not taken into account, the final picture can be distorted, particularly if the respondents deal with straightforward questions and the wording of these questions corresponds to the established declarations. If this happens, the risk is to analyse the level of declarations, rather than the actual professional attitude, of a teacher to a child in their interaction.

When it is necessary to determine the difference between what is declared by a teacher as a norm and what is actually happening in the teacher's practice, one can compare the outcomes of the observations. In my previous surveys, I studied several groups of people; therefore it would have been impossible to observe each member of the sample. Twenty-eight people took part in this particular survey, so I compared the outcomes of the questionnaire with the findings from the structured observation.

Twelve teachers from Moscow kindergartens and 16 teachers from Russian kindergartens in Visaginas, Lithuania, took part in the survey. All the teachers from Lithuania were native Russians, so both groups of teachers were equal as far as the language factor was concerned. Moreover, the majority of teachers in both groups were trained in the same teacher training system (former Soviet teacher training colleges).

The same questionnaire, as well as the special observation procedure, was used for each country's representatives. During the observation process, I directly observed teachers' actions using a special scheme. These actions referred to the categories of the questionnaire.[1] After the expert evaluation, all the indicators from different categories were ranked, so that every indicator should have a certain weight, which was the same for the indicator both in the questionnaire and in the observation. It made it much easier to compare the two. Teachers gave their evaluation marks to the statements of the questionnaire, and these marks received a certain score; these teacher's real actions were scored, too. These scores were tallied both for the evaluation marks and for the actions for every category. The higher the final score, the higher the level of authoritarianism of a teacher in a certain category. Thus, I could diagnose the *authoritarianism level* of the teachers in their interactions with young children in two positions: *in their declared position* (based on the survey) and *in their actual position* (based on the observations in a kindergarten).

I had the opportunity to compare the declared and actual positions of teachers belonging to two different social and cultural environments, where not long ago, both cultures were parts of the same state. Twenty years have passed since these two cultures separated completely and started developing independently, which obviously widened the gap between them.

The initial assumption was that the authoritarianism level of the teachers' actual positions would differ from that of their declared ones. It would be merely logical if real actions were mainly more authoritarian than the declarations. However, such an assumption was not necessarily accurate, because some teachers could have turned out to have really authoritarian beliefs, interacting with children in a most authoritarian way and never wishing to

---

[1] To facilitate observation in this particular study, I made some general categories more detailed, introducing such additional categories as "discipline," "encouragement and punishment," and "individual approach." These categories were used both for the analysis of the survey data and at the structured observations.

conceal it.[2] The same could have been true for those teachers who prefer and declare real partnership. In such cases, one can't see a clear difference between the authoritarianism level of the real and the declared position.

In addition, it could not be ignored that some teachers' declarations would be more authoritarian than their real actions. Of course, the expectation was that such cases would be quite rare, and probably unique, because it is the declarative norm that is usually approved socially, and I have never encountered official support for authoritarianism in modern education systems. Hence, the declared norm *should* have had a child-centred nature.

First and foremost, the experiment showed that all teachers had two positions: a declared and an actual one. In the whole group there was not a single case in which the declared norm was completely identical to the norm underlying the teacher's real actions, although in some specific categories, such cases could be seen fairly often.

After I had compared the categorical structure and the authoritarianism level for both positions, all the preschool teachers both in Russia (Moscow) and in Lithuania (Visaginas) were divided into three groups. For the outcomes see Figures 4-1–4-3.

Figure 4-1 shows an example of when the authoritarianism level of the position that the teacher has declared for her interaction with a child is somewhat lower than that of her real actions. We can see that in this particular teacher's case, both positions in some of the categories are equal. However, her real actions are mainly more authoritarian than her declared attitudes. Such a ratio is typical for the first group of teachers.

It is important to highlight that the categorical structure of both positions is mainly identical with this particular teacher and the whole group, i.e., the categories that are more authoritarian in one position are mainly more authoritarian in the other. Still, it is not necessarily true for the comparison of all the variants of the positions; I'll discuss this difference later.

---

[2]   A teacher's declaration should not always be interpreted as a lie. It is simply different from what really makes him or her act this way. This is why we can't use the "lie or sincerity scale" that are usual for psychological questionnaires. Very often, teachers conceal their real position subconsciously; often this behavior is dictated by social approval. Still, we can't but realize that some teachers taking part in this survey could have been less influenced by social approval.

Figure 4-1

*The example of a teacher's actual position being more authoritarian
than the declared position*

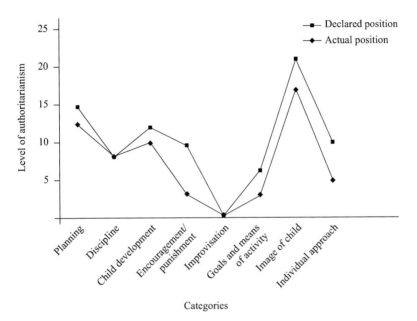

Figure 4-2 shows the second type of discrepancy, namely, when the teacher's position declared for his or her interaction with the children has turned out to be *more* authoritarian than what I observed in practice. Teachers from this group were much less authoritarian in real interactions with children than they were when they filled in the questionnaire.

Figure 4-2

An example of authoritarianism level being higher in the declared position than in real interaction with a child

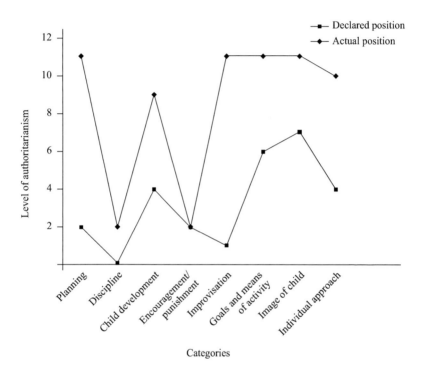

I did find this type of discrepancy between the declared and the actual position, although before the experiment started, I thought it would hardly be possible. The format of this article does not allow us to analyse absolute meanings of authoritarianism of the teachers' actual position in both groups. Still, it is worth mentioning that the teachers from this group demonstrated an authoritarianism level in their real actions that was significantly lower than that of the first group.

Finally, there is a third group, consisting of teachers whose authoritarianism levels for both positions crisscross each other; i.e., within one category the teachers are more authoritarian in declarations and within another category, they are more authoritarian in *real actions* (Figure 4-3).

Figure 4-3

An example of authoritarianism levels of the declared and the actual position crossing each other

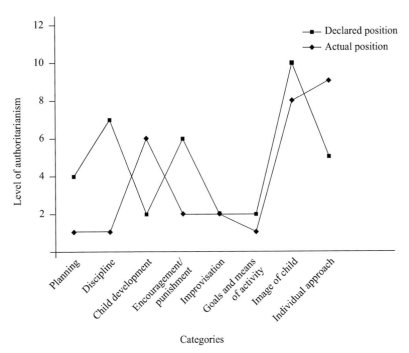

Categories

In some categories, the teachers from the group three show higher levels of authoritarianism in the declared position, while in other categories they demonstrate the opposite. Therefore, group three, unlike the previous two groups, demonstrates the discrepancy in categorical structure between both positions for authoritarianism level, which makes it possible to conclude that the categorical structure of both positions depends on the type of their discrepancy.

However, from my perspective the most interesting outcome of this study is the data on how Russian and Lithuanian teachers split into the three groups. For this data see Table 4-1.

Table 4-1

The distribution of Russian and Lithuanian kindergarten teachers according to the
correlation between the declared and the actual position in their interaction with a child

Group number	Correlation between declared and real position of teachers in interaction with child (authoritarianism level)	Percent of the teachers in groups	
		Russian kindergartens	Lithuanian kindergartens
Group 1	Authoritarianism level in the actual position is higher than in declared one	67	13
Group 2	Authoritarianism level in the declared position is higher than in the actual one	9	50
Group 3	"Crisscrossing"	24	37

First, I would like to highlight the number of teachers participating in
the survey who fell into groups one and two in both countries. It is clear that
majority of Russian teachers (67%) demonstrated that the authoritarianism
level in the actual position is higher than in declared one and that was higher
than we have been anticipated. Their real actions toward children are much
more authoritarian than what they present as a norm in their answers in the
questionnaire. The content of their declarations has been formed according
to the wording of the child-centred approach as it is understood, and is influenced partly by the system of pre-service training and partly by local educational authorities, etc.

Special study of the reasons causing teachers to declare the principles
they never use in real life could have clarified the situation. However, the
data obtained are enough to conclude that the general social and cultural
context (cultural norms, such as dominant norms of interaction with
children, images of the desired future for the child, or cultural peculiarities
of social institutions, etc.) has contributed too, because the percentage of
preschool teachers simply declaring the child-centred approach in Lithuania
in its Russian-speaking kindergartens differs dramatically from its Russian
counterparts. Table 4-1 shows that the percentage of such teachers from
Lithuanian kindergartens is only 13 per cent. At the same time, a higher
percentage of the teachers from Lithuania are much less authoritarian in their
real actions than their declarations (50 per cent of the Lithuanian teachers,
compared to 9 per cent of Russian teachers). The relationship considered
to be the least possible turned out to be impossible for Russian teachers,
unlike Lithuanian teachers, where 50 per cent declared themselves to be
more authoritarian than they are. This could also be explained by elevated

expectations of the teachers, due to their general assumptions about good practice.

Conclusions and Discussion

The outcomes of the two studies can be summarized in three main conclusions.

First, the research revealed a difference between Russian and American teachers in their position on interaction with children. In some categories American teachers were more authoritarian than Russian teachers, while in other categories they were less authoritarian. However, the most significant difference related to the category "Perception of the Child," which reflects the attitude of the teachers towards children. This category indicates whether the child is perceived by the teacher as a participant in the education process in his own right. Clearly, the Russian culture leads more teachers to see the child as an object to be filled with knowledge, (a more authoritarian stance), while the American culture leads teachers to view the child more as a partner in the child's own development.

Second, the data collected revealed discrepancies between the declared and actual positions of teachers in their interaction with children as far as the level of authoritarianism is concerned. In Russia, in most cases, the real action of preschool teachers is more authoritarian than the norms they declare. At the same time, half of Lithuanian teachers are less authoritarian in their real actions than the norms they declare.

Third, the social and cultural context has a great impact on the formation of teachers' attitudes towards children. This is demonstrated by the fact that the level of authoritarianism of the observed Lithuanian teachers in real interactions with children was much lower than that of their observed Russian colleagues.

Further cross-cultural research might additionally clarify the outcomes presented here. To describe the culturally accepted approach of the country to the children, a wider study would be necessary, involving not only the teachers but also representatives of other social groups with frequent interactions with children. For example, it would be essential to study parents' beliefs, particularly those beliefs that go beyond the limits of the "parenting style" that is usually the focus of surveys. However, in these surveys I restricted myself to reveal the differences in the attitudes toward children demonstrated by preschool teachers of different countries, and did not aim at describing the cultural norms of adult-child interaction in different societies.

At least two additional questions arise concerning these outcomes: the first one is about the teacher training system's impact on the teacher's position toward the child. Does this system influence this teacher's position? For example, in previous research (Yudina 2003) it was shown that the norms of interaction with children are translated to teachers directly from teacher training colleges. Can we regard this influence as a separate factor, irreducible to cultural context? I think that the teacher training system can be considered as a part of culture and reflect many cultural attitudes of the society in which it is located.

The second question is: if the teacher's position is culturally determined to such a high extent, does this mean that there is no way to change it? It's important to mention that even if it is true that "culture matters," I am far from implying that the impact of cultural context should be regarded as compulsory for the teacher. One should never forget that every culture leaves some room for professional development. Moreover, culture is not the only factor to affect the teacher's position; it's obvious that people's beliefs depend on their own will and vary even within the same culture. Hence, it is of crucial importance to make significant efforts to develop the professional thinking of teachers, and this holds for all cultures. However, when doing this, we need to take into account some knowledge about how this or that particular culture works with these beliefs. We can even use this knowledge to create appropriate conditions for professional development in a particular culture, knowing how to overcome the problems which exist in this cultural context.

Introducing the concept of the Zone of Proximal Development, Lev Vygotsky described *the special character* of the child-adult joint activity that ensures that education leads to real learning and development. Otherwise, as Galina Zukerman (2006) states, the very notion of the ZPD turns into something ordinary: any type of education, not necessarily dealing with the real interests of the child, implies adult support. Moreover, no one will ever teach a child what he or she already can do. Does this mean that any kind of teaching works within the child's ZPD? The answer is, of course, no. Only the interaction between an adult and a child where each partner has equal rights holds the possibility to first reveal the child's ZPD and then to try and extend it. Only a teacher who allocates the child the right to his or her own decisions in their joint activity can reveal the child's ZPD and promote the child's real development.

As previously established, it is the teacher in the classroom who decides what level of freedom a child should have during their joint activity. This level of freedom is defined by the teacher's beliefs concerning young children: what they are capable of, how they develop, and, consequently, what is the teacher's role in a child's education. The authoritarian position of a teacher in his/her relation to the child (in the survey it is mainly represented by the "Perception of the Child" category) will most likely lead to the teacher taking all of the responsibility for what he/she is doing with the child, leaving no space for the child's decision making. Actually, this kind of action is not a joint activity: the adult is the subject, and the child is but a raw material in the adult's activity.

What is the general level of authoritarianism in an adult's position that we could define as too high or low for education leading to development? There is no numerical criterion. The adequate level of authoritarianism seems to be generated by the whole of culture, and not only by its current state, but also by the vision of the desired future. One thing is obvious: the position of a teacher towards a child in adult-child interaction in developmental education shouldn't be highly authoritarian. But there is still a need for a particular position, because it is clear that not *all* teachers' activities lead to creation of the ZPD; the teacher has to be fully aware of the child's abilities and consciously lead activities into the ZPD. In the ZPD, each partner has their own role; that of the teacher is mainly to follow the child's initiative and produce the appropriate content for their joint activity. This can be done only if teacher takes the partnership position towards children.

References

Adorno, T.W. 1994. *The authoritarian personality (studies in prejudice), abridged edition.* New York: WW Norton & Co.

Chaiklin, S. 2003. The zone of proximal development in Vygotsky's analysis of learning and instruction. In *Vygotsky's educational theory in cultural context*, eds. A. Kozulin, B. Gindis, et al. Cambridge: Cambridge University Press.

Elkonin, D.B. 1989. Zametki o razvitii predmetnykh dejstvij v rannem ontogeneze. In *Izbrannye psychologicheskie trudy*, D.B. Elkonin. Moscow: Pedagogika.

Fromm, E. 1994. *Escape from freedom.* New York: Henry Holt & Co.

Vygotsky, L.S. 1978. *Mind and society: The development of higher psychological processes.* Cambridge: Harvard University Press.

———. 1991. Dynamika umstvennogo razvitija rebenka v sbiazy s obucheniem. *Pedagogicheskaja psychologija.* Moscow: Pedagogika.

Wertsch, J.V. 1984. The zone of proximal development: some conceptual issues. In *New directions for child development. No.23. Children's learning in the "zone of proximal development,"* eds. B. Rogoff and J.V. Wertsch: 7–18. San Francisco: Jossey-Bass.

——. 1998. *Mind as action.* New York, Oxford: Oxford University Press.

Yudina, E.G. 1998. Pedagogicheskaja etika i professionalnoje soznanije pedagoga. *Chelovek,* No. 2. Moscow.

——. 2005. Pozitsija pedagoga: avtoritarism i partnerstvo. *Voprosy psychologii,* No. 4. Moscow.

——. 2003. Issledovanije professionalnogo soznanija prepodavatelej pedagogi-cheskykh colledgej (doshkolnyje otdelenija). *Psichologicheskaja nauka i obrazovanije,* No. 2. Moscow.

Zukerman, G.A. 2006. Vzaimodejstvije pebenka i vzroslogo, tvoriaschee zonu blizhajshego razvitija. *Cultural-historical psychology,* No. 4. Moscow.

CHAPTER FIVE

VYGOTSKY AND THE EARLY YEARS OF ECEC IN ITALY

SUSANNA MANTOVANI

How many languages are mediating our communication in the writing and the reading of this paper? Vygotsky wrote in *Thought and Language* that the first function of language is communication and that language—including word meanings—is the most important means of social relationships.

I wonder which language we are understanding here, and what is the sense the expressed concepts make to the reader: I am an Italian who, over the years, has read Vygotsky in Italian, first translated from English and later from Russian, and I am now writing in English. So the sharing of our thoughts, my writing and your reading, requires not only an effort of patience and endurance, but also of interpretation. It calls for comprehension of and affection towards our theme.

I would like to sketch a parallel between the publication of Vygotsky's works and some landmarks in the development of early childhood education services in Italy from the late 60s through to the late 80s, a time of expansion and flourishing of early childhood education and care (ECEC). I will try to make visible the encounters, the traces, and some of the main themes in which Vygotsky has been influential on the key persons who contributed to the creation of Italy's best preschool experiences. I'll refer to the culture and discourse of grassroots early education experiences in Italy, rather than to the work of academics. In those years, the two met and at times influenced each other, but this influence worked from the bottom up, rather than top down. This seems to be a specific feature of Italian early childhood pedagogy: community practice becoming method or theory, rather than vice versa. This happened with Montessori and the Agazzi sisters, the two most influential approaches of the recent past. It continues to happen with the Reggio Emilia approach and, more widely, through the *"cultura dell'infanzia*" that germinated and bloomed through the networking of the *Gruppo Nazionale Nidi Infanzia*[1] (Mantovani 2007).

At the beginning of my academic career in the early 70s, after a first degree in philosophy and a second in child development, I developed an interest in early childhood educational policies which combined my scientific and political engagement. Over the years, I have had the opportunity to witness and to participate in the development of a system of early childhood educational institutions: *scuole materne* (i.e., "maternal schools" using the same metaphor as the French *école maternelle*, already named in those days *scuole dell'infanzia,* i.e., "schools for childhood," the official denomination since 2003) and *asili nido* (today *nidi d'infanzia* with *nido* meaning "nest") in some of the cities which were most active and successful in developing community services in Northern Italy. Trust in the competence and richness of children, an approach where social, artistic, and verbal learning were progressively combined in projects, and a strong link to the local environment and family participation were features common in these sites in Northern Italy. In the 80s, these features came to be known to the world through Reggio Emilia and *The Hundred Languages of Childhood*.

Pedagogy in this period was studied at the university level only, within philosophy departments, and mainly dealt with either epistemological questions or mere didactics. The general dissatisfaction with the educational system and a stronger need for a link between theory and practice was strong in the late 60s and early 70s in universities and in the student movement. The approach to children's education, shaped in Italy by Montessori and the Agazzi sisters, was influenced and widened by many influences: Libertarian pedagogies such as Neill's, the experience of the German Kinderlaeden, communitarian kibbutz education, psychoanalytical experiences old and new alike, Vera Schmidt's psychoanalytic Kindergarten, and the experiences carried out by the Italian psychoanalyst Elvio Fachinelli (1971) described in the widely read booklet *L'erba voglio* and in community crèches (Mantovani, 1975). Freinet's theories and experiences, embodied in Italy by the M.C.E. (*Movimento di cooperazione educativa*) through leading figures such as Bruno Ciari and Margherita Zebedy were translated from primary schools into the new early childhood contexts.

---

[1]   The association founded in the late seventies where practitioners, administrators, and scholars were equally represented and active, and where the early childhood practitioner, rather than apply or translate into practice theories and methods, invited and involved scholars to do research *with and in* rather than *on* existing early childhood services.

Developmental theories and research were published. Piaget, Vygotsky, and other authors relevant to early childhood development and education (Henri Wallon, Irène Lèzine, René Zazzo, and Susan Isaacs for example), were extensively read by both early childhood practitioners and researchers. Services developed quickly and new regulations were developed, requiring new training and better understanding of children's growth and educational possibilities in social environments other than the family, through the engagement and contribution of researchers. We had the chance to extensively observe children in nursery schools and in the first new crèches. This meant seeing theory coming to life and gaining new life and meaning. Naturalistic, participant observation was necessary to measure the pertinence of academic knowledge on child development in the new educational contexts, to experiment with and evaluate new approaches and practice, and to imagine new professional development paths.

We knew little of children in peer groups and in the care of teachers and non-parental caregivers, so we looked for tools. We observed them daily within social settings, in specific places and spaces, and in particular cities. Documentation, later developed as a fundamental tool for communication, reflection, professional development, and for constructing an integrated representation of children's potential, started as a necessary instrument to form our own living textbooks. The contextualization of development in its cultural and historical setting was an important perspective, and Vygotsky's approach immediately made sense to people engaged in the effort of developing practice intertwined with understanding.

While *Thought and Language* was Vygotsky's best known work in educational and psychological research circles in this period, in my opinion it was the ideas first expressed by Vygotsky in *Psychology of Art* and the works exploring art, including theatre and creativity, that mainly found echoes and matching sensitivities in our early childhood culture "in the field."

Vygotsky's strong impact on the development of early childhood pedagogy in Italy lays the link, emphasized in his works, between pedagogy, psychology, aesthetical thinking, and drama, and the combination of intellectual, social, and emotional components in learning and development. I will try to give some examples of how his works inspired the new ECEC pedagogy, enriching an approach which was already sensitive, not only to the intellectual dimensions of learning and the active role of the child as expressed by the Montessori approach, but also to the social and emotional themes through social experiences, fantasy, and art or "*imagination and creativity*," as the title of one of the works of Vygotsky was translated into Italian in 1972.

I prefer to describe the educational philosophy which inspires early childhood education in Italy—the framework within which we think about education, its means, methodology, and goals, and what we have come to call our "culture" of children (*cultura dell'infanzia*)—as "community experiences which meet theories," rather than as "doing Piaget," or "doing Vygotsky," or "doing Reggio Emilia."

The latter phrase 'to "do" a theorist' sounds strange to Italian practitioners and scholars in the field, and does not reflect the story and development of Italian ECEC. Rather, we conceptualise that each community experience shares common ideas and traditions, while at the same time each community experience reflects cultural peculiarities, and, thus, each experience is culturally and historically situated and within its particular ecological niche (New 1994).

The consciousness of cultural embeddedness exists from the early years of ECEC development in Italy, and this can explain both the early appeal and the influence of Vygotsky's ideas.

Nursery schools first appeared in Italy, at the end of the 18th century. They flourished in many municipalities and around the parishes of the North at the beginning of the 20th century. Montessori's first *Case dei Bambini* were in municipal public houses in Rome. After the war these programs were established in the municipalities governed by the Socialist administration. Teachers only had a vocational high school degree. Some of them came from different fields. All of them were politically engaged either in the Catholic Democratic movement or in the Left parties, in particular the Italian Communist Party which had connections with the Soviet Union, but, in Italy, had its roots in Libertarian Socialism and with thinkers like Antonio Gramsci.

Mecacci, an Italian psychologist, started translating Vygotsky from Russian in 1982; the complete reconstruction of *Thought and Language* appeared in Italy in 1990 in his translation. This translation is considered one of the most complete ever made, certainly closer to the corpus of Vygotsky's writings than the original first Russian edition by Kolbanovsky in 1936. Many parts of Vygotsky's original, Mecacci writes, were considered inspired by bourgeois ideas and influenced by western authors and therefore eliminated in the 1936 translation.

In 1962 the first English edition was published in the U.S. Many passages referring to Marx and Engels, considered too far from Western sensitivity or not connected with the core psychological theme, were left out of this translation. This English translation was then translated into French, Italian, and German in the later 1960s.

Mecacci's edition doubles the number of pages. Vygotsky, argues Mecacci, was a Russian, a Marxist free thinker, and an intellectual embedded in the Jewish culture and tradition and in the cultural atmosphere of his times, in his words, a "refined writer, friend of Eizenstein, Ehrenburg, Mandelstam, Pasternak, Stanislavsky, the educator who respected the right of national minorities to maintain their culture, engaged in the rehabilitation of blind and deaf children… Vygotsky is not a couch psychologist nor a laboratory psychologist, but an intellectual confronting praxis and specific problems in specific cultural-historical contexts" (Mecacci 1990, 23). Such a free thinker is bound to be disturbing and not easily boxed and labelled!

The protagonists behind the development of the ECEC system in Italy read Vygotsky as they had read the other pedagogical literature and matched it to the pedagogical movement stemming from Freinet's work, which was also rooted in a strong political engagement within the Marxist circles.

The late 60s and early 70s were important years for ECEC in Italy. State nursery schools were established in 1968, the first National Guidelines were published, and a bill on municipal infant crèches was passed shortly thereafter. During these years, Malaguzzi (along with Bruno Ciari) organized two key conferences on the new experiences in nursery schools and on "*gestione sociale*" (social management). It was at these conferences that the notion of "*partecipazione*" was presented: a key concept in which pedagogy and civic and political engagement are strictly linked. In 1973 Gianni Rodari, one of the best known writers for children wrote his only essay, dedicated to Reggio Emilia, clearly influenced by Vygotsky, and in 1976 the *Gruppo Nazionale Nidi Infanzia* was founded.

The introductions written by the translators and editors of Vygotsky's works from Russian published by *Editori Riuniti*, the official publisher of the Italian communist party those days, strike the reader today for their uncritical and naive ideology which contrasts sharply with the style of discourse, metaphors, and contents of Vygotsky's writings.

It is important nevertheless to remember that Vygotsky's thought was praxis oriented, influenced by the historical method, truly political in a deep sense, and attributing to school and education a fundamental role for understanding and changing society. The early childhood educators who were active in the municipal schools in Italy shared these values.

The language, the metaphors, and many of the concepts which have today become familiar to many early childhood educators of the world through the diffusion of the Reggio approach, were common culture in Italian nursery schools long ago. The Vygotskian approach had already infiltrated much

Italian pedagogy by the 1970s. Indeed, they had been prominent long before
the popularity of cultural psychology.

Box 5-1

Vygotsky's Publications vis a vis Landmarks of ECEC in Italy

1966: Vygotsky, *Pensiero e linguaggio* (*Thought and language*), translated
into Italian from the 1962 American edition

1968: Bill n. 444 establishing *Scuola Materna Statale* (*State Nursery
School*)

1969: *Orientamenti della Scuola Materna* (*National Guidelines*)

1970: Vygotsky, *Pedagogia e psicologia* (*Pedagogy and Psychology*),
with Lurjia and Leontjiev, translated from Russian

1971: Bill n. 1044 establishing public municipal crèches (Asili Nido)

1972: Vygotsky, Psicologia dell'arte (*Psychology of Art*), translated from
Russian

1973: Vygotsky, *Immaginazione e creatività nell'età infantile* (*Imagination
and Creativity*), translated from Russian

1973: Conference *Esperienze per la nuova scuola dell'infanzia*, organized
by Loris Maguzzi and Bruno Ciari

1973: Gianni Rodari, *La grammatica della fantasia*

1973: Vygotsky, *Lo sviluppo psichico* (*Mental Development*), translated
from Russian

1974: Vygotsky, *Storia delle funzioni psichiche superiori* (*History of
Superior Mental Functions*), translated from Russian

1974: Conference *La gestione sociale nella scuola dell'infanzia* organized
by Loris Malaguzzi

1976: Journal *Zerosei*, later *Bambini*, Formal foundation of *Gruppo
Nazionale Nidi-Infanzia*

1981: First exhibit *The Hundred Languages of Children*

Malaguzzi had read philosophy and psychology, theatre and cinema: Benjamin, Gombrich, Nelson Goodman and Gestalt psychology, Piaget and Wallon, as well as Vygotsky (Hoyuelos Planillo 2004). He was developing, through direct experience with children and in dialogue with other Italian intellectuals and educators, the idea that verbal language is crucial but not the only language children can explore. Drama and other forms of art are crucial in allowing the child to experiment and build well formed concepts and rich gratifying experiences.

Some of the terms Vygotsky uses when discussing art, catharsis and its links with the child's development as a whole, for example, are the same or very close to the language, style, and metaphors which have become well known through *The Hundred Languages of Children*.

Malaguzzi wrote:

"Before...we could suppose with some grounded reasons that the child's thought develops from a concrete stage to a stage of action in the same way as a leaf develops from a bud. We know today that the process is the real drama of development...Where we thought we have a simple movement on a flat surface, we have leaps ...We talked about cooperation and now we talk about conflict...The old theory led us to teach the child to walk calmly and slowly and now the new theory tells us to teach him to jump" (1981).

Compare this to Vygotsky:

"Art is a very special emotional dialectic process for the construction of life...development happens in leaps and you can reach a feeling of lightness...and triumph."

(*Psicologia dell'arte*, 333)

Pedagogical and aesthetical ideas are strictly connected in Italian nursery school culture, and so is the dramatic idea of "conflict" and "leaps," words often used by Malaguzzi in his metaphors. He also affirmed the interesting role of some conflict and chaos, "because interesting ideas could come out of [them]." Drama and theatre in the form of representation, or at least as emotional dialogue, are some of the ways through which the emerging thought and emotional intelligence of children are revealed.

In those same years, a book was published by one of the best known Italian authors in children's literature, *La grammatica della fantasia* by Gianni Rodari (1973). The key concept in this book is the "*binomio fantastico*," the coupling of unusual words and concepts as play, as an intellectual exercise, as a practice of creativity.

"In the 'binomio fantastico' words are not taken in their daily meaning. They are liberated from the verbal chains they belong to every day. They are 'estranged,' disoriented, thrown one against the other in a sky they have never seen before. Then they are in the best condition to generate a story... Children can master this technique with amusement. This exercise has a real cognitive importance, but we should not forget the fun it generates. In our schools we do not laugh enough..."

(Rodari 1973, 19).

Rodari refers to Klee (who stated that concepts are impossible without their opposite) and to Wallon, who wrote that thoughts form in couples (ibid.). We know that Rodari had read Vygotsky's *Imagination and Creativity* and that he shared with Vygotsky (and many other Italian early childhood educators) the idea of a strong link between pedagogy, learning, and aesthetic thinking.

"Every activity...whose result is not the mere reproduction of already experienced impressions of actions, rather the creation of new images of actions, belongs to a creative and combinatory behaviour...The child combines (experiences) and constructs a new reality, corresponding to his needs and curiosity. So, like in play, the children's attitude to composition becomes a creative activity"

(Vygotsky, *Immaginazione e creatività nell'età infantile*, 21).

Rodari comments on this work of Vygotsky's, calling it:

"a booklet all gold and silver...that describes clearly imagination as a form of activity of the human mind and entitles each human being to sharing a common talent and attitude to be creative, and differences in creativity are, to a great extent, due to social and economical factors"

(*Grammatica della fantasia* 1973, 169).

Play is another issue. Rodari is sceptical of the naïve vision of play; for him:

"The symbolic function allows the child to change at his pleasure the meaning of significance: he wants to ride, he does not have a horse, but he does not need magic; he has a broom and the broom is a horse, a train, an aeroplane..."

This clearly echoes his reading of Vygotsky. Rodari describes play as a creative function of our imagination, shared by artists, scientists, and technicians and recalls that Vygotsky thinks that:

> "germs" of creative imagination can be found anywhere, but that to become play these germs need a process through which the child reconstructs reality. "But since imagination can build only though materials taken from reality… the child, in order to nourish his own imagination and using it for adequate goals that reinforce its structure and widen its horizons, should be granted the possibility to grow in an environment rich in impulses and stimula, in all possible directions."
>
> (*Grammatica della fantasia*, 169–170)

Play is not only considered as fun free activity, but also as theatre, drama, and conflict, and as a way of reasoning and combining new meanings.

Rodari was one of the most read authors for children in Italy, and was very active in the pedagogical world. He worked with many nursery schools, in Reggio Emilia and other cities. His book, *Grammatical della Fantasia*, was common reading in the field. In dialogue with schools, Rodari developed all of these thoughts, particularly the idea of a rich child, in a rich environment full of "provocations" (a typical expression of Malaguzzi to define the hints and proposals to children in Reggio's schools) where "*Se la fantasia cavalca con la ragione*" (If fantasy rides with reason), wonderful things can happen.

This was miles and decades away from Montessori's mistrust for play and children's art, but we are also far away from an irrational and anti-cognitivistic idea of play and imagination.

The zone of proximal development and the idea of scaffolding, the two main Vygotskian themes discussed by educational psychologists in Italy, emerged later in widespread education and were mainly connected to learning at the primary school level. In the early years of ECEC, Malaguzzi wrote about these themes and expressed a veiled critique of Vygotsky:

> "Vygotsky reminds us that language and thought operate together to give course to ideas and to produce an anticipated trace of action, to produce and control it, to describe and argue about it. It is an important precious idea we have to keep in mind in education…"

Within this conceptualization of the relationship between adult and child and going back to the theme of learning and teaching, he points out the advantages of the Zone of Proximal Development (ZPD).

This question is not without ambiguity...can you give competence to somebody who does not have it? "Circularity sets an active link between who is learning and who is teaching, but this concept is not used by Vygotsky" (Malaguzzi 1995). "Our Vygotsky," he states in the same text, "is the Vygotsky of imagination and art."

Art, theatre, fantasy, fun, creativity, leaps, drama: all this life is biologically rooted, but governed by consciousness, it can be developed and sustained in a school which is culturally situated: a concrete, political view of education, but also the idea that children are *rich*. We are quite far from the idea of compensatory education that was also discussed in Italy in those years (for example, through publication of the work of Bereiter and Engelmann). Italian nursery schools have always refused the compensatory and deficit approach, aiming to become rich and inclusive through ways not confined in specific "interventions" or "programmes," but rather by creating environments where discovery, learning, and pleasure are possible.

The programs are implemented through prepared, rich, provocative environments where the adult can observe and document children's ideas and promote social confrontation, discussion, and negotiation. William Corsaro sees *discussione* as a peculiar Italian feature among children in nursery school (Corsaro 1997), sustaining them to achieve projects where fantasy can ride with reason, as when building an amusement park for birds in the Villetta school.

Another strong Vygotskian idea that had echoes in the Italian schools for the very young was the idea of learning as an originally social experience. In Italian nursery schools the *peer group* (more than the adult or the more expert and older child) has long been considered the main vehicle of learning. In the 70s, the idea of "small groups" within classrooms and the spatial organization in corners where the children could group freely or be guided for different activities was debated and experimented with and became a predominant option, versus an individualised organization. *Piazzas* and other spaces for meeting and engaging in social activities appeared in most schools and crèches.

Children can learn if competent, sensitive, and creative adults observe, mediate, expand, *document,* and engage with children (rather than with one child) in activity: their ideas can be provoked and challenged and can become projects. What is added (again Malaguzzi quoted, appreciated, and expanded Vygotsky in this respect) is circularity: everybody engaged in the process negotiates, changes, and learns. Nowadays, these ideas look familiar, but the humus for their growth was prepared in the 70s in nursery schools, promoting the idea of a culturally situated learning, of schools themselves as cultural niches, and of participatory experiences and learning.

Partecipazione is another key concept where echoes of Vygotsky can be found. *Partecipazione* is intended in Italian municipal nursery schools and developed in Reggio Emilia from the original "political" idea of *gestione sociale* into something more complex. This participation does not just mean taking part in the complex social experience through which adults and children in school engage, communicate, negotiate, decide, and act. It also means listening, talking, and understanding with agency, and the taking and sharing of responsibilities. It is the experience that makes significant learning possible for all members of the school community in a circular movement and probably with sudden leaps.

Most of my students are future teachers. When I ask them in their first year what they know about Vygotsky, many seem to think that Piaget lived first, then Piaget died, and Vygotsky followed with his ideas. They are immensely surprised when they discover that Piaget and Vygotsky were born in the same year, that Vygotsky died in 1934 and Piaget some fifty years later. I used to be frustrated by this, but perhaps I was wrong. In their effort to make sense of what they read and studied, they perceive the potential, the openness, the inspiring, and the stimulating features of an extraordinarily modern a thinker who was a true scientist and a true humanist, a man of thought and an educator in action, a man whose ideas and writings can still give insights, provocation, and challenges in this complex world where languages and cultures mix. The drama of development is in front of us every day; it can become Babel or a dramatic, but cathartic challenge to our creativity. Children deserve brave educators who can become creative thinkers.

How can we make our schools better equipped to give sense to the experience of the learning process and capable of creating stimulating environments which reflect the values of childhood and where self-initiative, collaborative learning, and active research can take place? Is it possible to set and keep fixed goals and expected outcomes in such a complex and fast changing global scene? In such a complex scenario it is essential to reconsider and reread the authors, philosophers, pedagogues, and psychologists who have been the foundations of our pedagogical tradition and practices to find new meanings and inspirations.

Vygotsky is certainly one of them.

References

Corsaro, W.A. 1997. *The Sociology of Childhood*. Thousand Oaks: Pine Forge Press.

Edwards, C., L. Gandini, and G. Forman, eds. 1993. *The Hundred Languages of Children: The Reggio Emilia Approach to Early Childhood Education*. Norwood: Ablex.

Fachinelli, E., L.M. Vaiani, and G. Sartori, eds. 1971. *L'Erba voglio: pratica non autoritaria nella scuola*. Torino: Einaudi.

Hoyuelos Planillos, A. 2004. *La ética en el pensamiento y obra pedagógica de Loris Malaguzzi*. Barcelona: Rosa Sensat-Octaedro.

Malaguzzi, L. 1995. *I cento linguaggi dei bambini*. [The hundred languages of children]. eds. C. Edwards, L. Gandini, and G. Foreman. Bergamo, Italy: Edizioni Junior.

Mantovani, S. 1976. *Asilo nido, psicologia e pedagogia*. Milan: Bruno Mondadori.

———. 2007. Italian References, in *Early Childhood Education (Four Volumes): An International Encyclopedia,* eds. M. Cochran, and R.S. New. Santa Barbara: Praeger.

Rodari, Gianni. 1973. *Grammatica della Fantasia*. Torino: Einaudi.

Vygotsky, L.S. 1962. *Thought and Language*. Ed. and trans. E. Haufmann and G. Vakar. Cambridge: MIT Press. (Idem. 1962. New York, London: Wiley; Idem. 1986. Ed. A. Kozulin. Cambridge: MIT Press.)

———. 1966. *Pensiero e linguaggio*. Florence: Giunti.

———. 1973. *Immaginazione e creatività nelletà infantile*. Rome: Editori Riuniti.

———. 1990. *Pensiero e linguaggio—ricerche psicologiche, collana Biblioteca Universale Laterza*, translated by Luciano Mecacci, Roma-Bari: Laterza.

Part III

Vygotsky and Classroom Practice

CHAPTER SIX

FICTION, DRAWING, AND PLAY IN A VYGOTSKIAN PERSPECTIVE

STIG BROSTRÖM

Introduction

Reading fiction, drawing, and playing are seen as integral parts of both the original kindergarten tradition and current conceptions of early childhood education and care. However, in many countries, there is an increasing tendency to place a lower priority on aesthetic activities and to focus, instead, on introducing the "three r's"—reading, writing, and arithmetic—skills traditionally introduced in the primary school years.

The introduction of early literacy in preschool is challenging, especially from a Nordic perspective, and it has also been criticized as "schoolification" (OECD 2006). However, nowadays, practitioners, parents, and researchers from the field of early childhood generally perceive preschool as a learning environment, and are willing to adopt the practice of early literacy, as long as it complements the original kindergarten tradition.

A research review by Scarborough and Dobrich (1994) enumerated 31 published investigations into the efficacy of reading to preschoolers, and found a relationship between reading aloud to children and children's later general reading abilities. Correspondingly, a number of other research results (e.g. Robbins and Ehri 1994, Sénéchal and LeFevre 2002, Silvén et al. 2003) show a link between the role of joint reading by parents and children and children's language competencies and later development of reading skills.

Findings also indicate that joint reading in preschool has a positive effect on children's storytelling if it includes dialogues on the books and working with the literature via role-play and drawing (Anning 2003, Pellegrini and Galda 1998, Silvén et al. 2003). Another study by Pellegrini and Galda (1993) shows that children's storytelling skills achieve a higher level of quality when children in small groups reflect on the stories through role-play and drawing activities.

One might think that the above findings and the generally positive views on literature and reading aloud expressed by educators should result in a high occurrence of literature activities in preschool, after-school leisure-time centres, and the first years of school. However, a Danish study (Broström, Frandsen and Vilhelmsen 2008) carried out in 212 educational school settings with children aged six to eight years old shows a less optimistic picture: to a large degree, teachers do not include literature in literacy teaching, and their use of aesthetic activities such as play and drawing is rather limited. These findings are in agreement with research conducted by Anning and Ring (2004), which point out that teachers do not pay much attention to children's drawings.

In order to stimulate a conscious and increased use of literature and aesthetic activities as a means of developing early literacy competencies, this chapter provides a theoretical platform that is based on a cultural-historical understanding of Vygotsky's work.

Basic Concepts

Three Cornerstones in Vygotsky's Theory

Two of Vygotsky's books, *Mind and Society* (1978) and *Thinking and Speech* (1997), focus on the relationship between learning and development. By analysing three basic paradigms, which researchers Fred Newman and Lois Holzman (1993, 57) call "mistaken paradigms"—the separatist perspective (no relation between learning and development), the identity perspective (learning is development), and the unified process (learning and development have mutual influence on each other)—Vygotsky establishes a new understanding of the relationship between learning and development: learning and development as a dialectical unity in which learning leads to development. According to Vygotsky, "learning is not development; however, properly organized learning results in mental development and sets in motion a variety of developmental processes that would be impossible apart from learning" (Vygotsky 1978d, 90).

The thesis that learning leads to development forms the basis of the construction of three concepts which, with reference to Stetsenko (1999), make up the learning landscape of the cultural-historical school: 1) adult-child interaction as a source of development of mental processes; 2) cultural tools as mediating factors for the development of higher psychological functions; 3) the concept and theory of a Zone of Proximal Development

(ZPD) as the main path for learning and development. The three concepts are embedded in each other and united together via the child's activity. The activity is the crank for their mental development.

Social Interaction

Vygotsky argues that social interaction between children and adults is the main source for the development of advanced mental functions. Cognitive functions are first seen as an outward appearance between the child and the adult and then, step by step, become internalized and a part of the child's own mind. This understanding is expressed in the following often-used quotation: "An interpersonal process is transformed into an intrapersonal one. Every function in the child's cultural development appears twice: first, on the social level, and later, on the individual level; first, *between* people (*interpsychological*), and then *inside* the child (*intrapsychological*). This applies equally to voluntary attention, to logical memory and to the formation of concepts. All the higher functions originate as actual relations between human individuals" (Vygotsky 1978c, 57).

Since the human mind originates in and from social interactions in a specific culture, the educator has to not only highlight the social interaction between teacher and child, but also, in general, to ensure the occurrence of social and shared situations, in which children construct meaning and individual cognitive development takes place. Thus, Barbara Rogoff (1990, 1993) argues that an important form of interaction is guided participation in culturally organized activities, which results in children's cognitive learning and development. In guided participation the adult and child have a shared perspective on the activity, and they have a shared role in socio-cultural structural activities (Rogoff 1993, 134); however, the adult takes responsibility and ensures that each child is challenged in an appropriate manner and is introduced to shared developing activities. The idea behind the guiding concept is that the adult leads the child in accordance with the child's perspective. If an adult takes too much responsibility, there is a risk that the child's own initiative, motive, and interest will be overlooked. The claim is to establish a shared and joint interaction, to stress the mutual complementarity; in short, to make up an activity and relationship characterized by dialogue and *intersubjectivity.*

The American scholar James Wertsch (1985) illustrates the concept of intersubjectivity in an analysis of an interactive dialogue between a mother and child who are doing a puzzle together. Although the mother adjusted her communication to the child's capacity to learn, at the same time, she also challenged the child. Thus, intersubjectivity is not only a symmetrical dialogue (Wertsch 1998; Rogoff 1990). Inspired by Bakhtin (1981), Wertsch (1985, 225) states that intersubjectivity reaches a new quality when the dialogue contains voices in conflict.

Following the educational approach with reading and aesthetic activities seems useful while children are constantly involved in social interaction, both with the adults and with other children.

Cultural Tools—Symbols and Signs

The second component, cultural tools or signs and symbols, helps the individual to master his or her own mental processes, just as technical tools help to master the work process. Vygotsky (1985, 310) mentions a number of examples of cultural tools: language, numbering, algebraic signs, art, writing, drawings, and so on. In *Internalization of Higher Psychological Functions* and in *Tool and Symbols in Child Development* (both in Vygotsky, 1978) the mediating functions of cultural tools are described. Through the child's meeting with and use of the cultural tools, higher mental functions are mediated, for example, thinking and perception (Vygotsky, 1978c, 52–7).

Thus, in the reading activity, drawing, and play, the teacher has the opportunity to support children's active work with signs and symbols.

Zone of Proximal Development

The third cornerstone of Vygotsky's theory is the idea of the ZPD. In social interaction with adults and more developed peers the child is able to imitate a variety of actions which go beyond the borders of his or her own capacity (Vygotsky, 1978d, 88). In other words, the child surpasses his or her actual level of development, which is defined as mastering specific mental functions. Going beyond this level, the child constructs a ZPD, which is defined not as his developed functions, but his functions under development. For that reason Vygotsky very poetically uses the word "flowers" of development, and not "fruits" of development. The educational interest is focused on the adult's ability to define the distance between activities that the child is able to handle independently and those that he or she can manage with more competent partners. This is what Vygotsky names the ZPD, defined as "the distance between the actual developmental level as determined by independent problem solving and the level of potential development as determined through problem solving under adult guidance or in collaboration with more capable peers" (Vygotsky 1978d, 86). This well-known quotation suggests an educational approach in which the children are given opportunities to be confronted with situations and activities that they cannot handle or master alone, but that they can master through social interaction. Such interactions lead to learning and development. In Vygotsky's words, "We propose that an essential feature of learning is that it creates the zone of proximal development; that is, learning awakes a variety of internal developmental processes that are able to operate only when the child is interacting with people in his environment and in cooperation with peers" (Vygotsky 1978d, 90).

Though the idea of ZPD has resulted in many forms of creative education, there is also a risk of simplification and using the idea as a mechanic instrument (Holzman 1997, 60). Here Holzman warns us by saying this is not at all a zone but a "life space," in which human beings are involved, and through which higher mental functions arise and develop. Also, Cole and Griffin (1984), Engeström (1987), and Stetsenko (1999) warn against regarding ZPD just as a tool for learning existing knowledge.

Together with the two aforementioned cornerstones, ZPD can be seen as a tool for creating educational strategies which not only support children's acceptance of culture, but also give children a tool for creating the "new." Engeström (1987) uses the concept of learning by expanding learning processes which result in something new, or in unexpected and creative changes. Taking an aesthetic and narrative educational approach and arranging a challenging life space ZPD might give children the possibility to be creative individuals capable of developing quite new dimensions to themselves (content, knowledge, and methods) in both their lives and activities.

Aesthetics

To support children's literacy competence, including their reading ability, fiction marks a pivotal point. Fiction contains an aesthetic dimension, and most children reflect on the stories via aesthetical activities: their own story-telling, drawing, and play. Here, the concept of aesthetics is defined as an activity based on sense perception and emotions, where children receive and adapt impressions in a creative, interpretive and imaginative way, and their expression makes use of figures of speech, symbolic language, and consciously reflected idioms.

The concept of aesthetic is rooted in antiquity, where the Greek word *aisthesis* stands for sense, feeling, emotions, and knowledge about the beautiful; however, in today's pedagogy, aesthetic is much more representative of form, the expression symbolizing emotions and senses.

Aesthetics is closely connected with fantasy and creativity. Vygotsky (1971, 2004) argues that *imagination* or *fantasy* is constructed on the basis of elements from reality assembled in new ways. In agreement with Vygotsky's (1978c, 57) idea of the movement from interpersonal (inter-psychological) to intrapersonal (intra-psychological), fantasy becomes an inner process inside the individual. The extent of the fantasy depends on the richness of the child's experiences, because these experiences are the material that makes up the construction of fantasy (Vygotsky 2004). Thus, fantasy or imagination has a material basis and takes the form of mental constructions inside the individual. Then the individual takes the route back again, from the internal to the external. To conceptualize the process toward a transformation and external expression of the fantasy, for example in a visible aesthetical expression or product, one can use the concept of creativity or Vygotsky's concept of *crystallized imagination* (Vygotsky 2004, 11–20).

When children express their experiences through individual or collective activity, we can interpret this as a form of aesthetical production. In one way this expression is a reproduction, or, in other words, an imitation of the world (the heard story, the seen action, and so on). However the child's storytelling, drawing, or playing is not a mechanical and precise reproduction, but a subjective and emotional reproduction, and in many cases the child has added quite new dimensions.

Mimesis

The Vygotskian dialectical materialistic view understands the material world as a source for epistemological cognition; and logical thinking, drawing, and playing as a reflection of the external world, or a kind of representation. On the other hand, however, the individual person's own mental processes allow room for his or her creative activity and thinking. Thus, the reflection is a dynamic and creative representation. Describing such a reproduction or representation of aesthetics in literature, one often borrows the Greek word adopted by Aristotle—*mimieshai*—which translates into English as *mimicry* (Diamond 1997). Mimicry has two meanings, namely *imitation* and *mimesis*. In this understanding, imitation implies a copy of the original (which is in contradiction to the Vygotskian understanding of the concept imitation), and mimesis implies a change and transformation of the original starting point into an interpretative form. In short, one might say that in imitation the original model will be recognizable in the expression, but in mimesis, the original form may no longer be visible in the new form. The Marxist critic Georg Lukács (1971) made use of the mimesis concept, and so does Jerome Bruner (1990), who describes mimesis as a metaphor that refers to reality, not in order to make a copy but in order to create new content. Diamond (1997) writes that in artistic representation mimesis represents a sensual, critical receptivity to, and transformation of, the object. In other words, we see not only a rational reproduction, but also a sensuous moment of discovery, and a critical movement away from traditional norms and standards.

In line with Diamond, one might say that children's role-play or dramatic fantasy play often involves the above characteristic (Broström 1999b). Thus, the Norwegian play researcher Faith Guss (2005) contributes to this "understanding of playing as an aesthetic and critically reflective cultural activity among children of day care age" (Guss 2005, 234). This corresponds with Vygotsky's (1978b; 2004) view on play. Here, children create an imaginative situation and not only an echo of what they have seen and heard, but also a creative transformation of their impressions and, with that, creation of a new reality (Vygotsky 2004).

The American Vygotskian researcher Lois Holzman (1997) also understands imitation as a process characterized by dynamic and creative dimensions, for which reason she uses the concept *creative imitation*. Referring to a dialogue with a 21-month-old boy, she claims that "the babbling baby's rudimentary speech is a creative imitation of the more developed speaker. It is not, Vygotsky warns us, to be understood as the kind of mimicry that some parrots and monkeys do. It is creative, relational revolutionary activity… In imitation in the linguistic zone of proximal development, the child is *performing* (beyond himself) as a speaker" (Holzman 1997, 62). Continuing with the concept of creative imitation, she adds Vygotsky's term *completion* (Vygotsky 1997, 251) in order to emphasize that when we speak, we are not only expressing our thoughts, but also, the thoughts are completed in the words.

In children's storytelling, drawing, and play we see such a creative imitation resulting in a "completely new content, which is not seen in human experience and does not correspond to existing conditions" (Vygotsky 2004). Through such exceeding and expanding activities new learning processes often arise, which Engeström (1987, 174) calls learning by expanding. Because play (and also storytelling and drawing) sometimes contains such intense moments we can use the concept of expanding play (Broström 1999b).

Educational Practice

A number of developmental research projects were carried out in preschools and schools (Broström 2005a and 2005b; Broström 2006) based on the hypothesis that children's storytelling, drawing, and play—as reading of fiction combined with aesthetic reflections and expression—might be useful tools in developing children's literacy competence in early years.

A brief glimpse into this work following the seven phases below illustrates a possible way of using an aesthetic and narrative dimension related to early literacy:

1. A teacher reads aloud a short story of high literary quality.

2. Based on the story, the teacher and children can engage in a structured conversation, (Chambers 1994) called a *literature dialogue.*

3. After the dialogue the children *make drawings* to illustrate their understanding of the text.

4. Arranged in formal groups, the children are challenged to turn their literature experiences into *playing.* The teacher performs the role of observer and also participates as 'teacher-in-role.'

5. Sometimes the teacher asks the children to present their version of the story for their classmates and other teachers.

6. After the presentation, the teachers and each play group hold a structured conversation called a *learning dialogue.*

7. During all phases, the teacher and the children engage in *philosophical dialogues* reflecting their ideas.

Selection of Books

From an early age, children must be exposed to literature, and step-by-step they will create their own literature competence: they will experience the structure of a story and composition, learn to understand the world through another person's observations, and discover a number of symbols and symbolic expressions.

In a school class with children aged five to seven, teachers selected five short books from the series *Miss Ignora in the Water Tower.* All five books display strong emotions that all children experience: friendship, anger, happiness, sorrow, shyness, disappointment, and love. The books make up a series with a recognizable structure and a permanent gallery of characters. The series differs from traditional series for young children, because the main character develops over the course of the books. Each book contains 21 pages dominated by vigorous and expressive illustrations that support and expand on the text. The pivotal element in the stories is the daily life of a school girl, "Miss Ignora." The stories are told in simple, rhythmical, and unsentimental language, and the children are able to identify with Miss Ignora. The titles of the books reflect Miss Ignora's development:

- Miss Ignora Explodes
- Miss Ignora in the Schoolyard
- Miss Ignora and the Starry Sky
- Miss Ignora Falls in Love
- Miss Ignora and George Influence their World

In the first two books, Miss Ignora and her daily life are presented. When she loses her temper and explodes in front of her teacher, her best friend Nina becomes afraid, and Ignora is sorry. Ignora sometimes speaks with her neighbour, a fishmonger, from whom she also occasionally steals fish, which she feeds to the cats. The second book takes place in the schoolyard, where Miss Ignora is scolded and bullied by a boy, George. In the third book Ignora is alone: her mother has left her, and her father has died in a traffic accident. However, at night, when she is sitting on top of the water tower, she is able to speak to him. In the fourth book her problems with George are overcome and she develops a friendship with him. The fifth book describes how Ignora and George come to the assistance of a dog in distress, and later they reflect on the theme of being people who make a difference in the world.

Reading Aloud

A successful session in which a teacher reads aloud has a mutually-reinforcing structure, in which teacher and children establish an atmosphere of positive expectations. Then, the teacher presents the book (the author, title, cover, etc.).

In determining how to carry out the reading, some researchers and teachers argue for having a running dialogue throughout the reading

(National Institute for Literacy 2000) in order to retain children's attention, while other experts on reading argue that children should be encouraged to listen to the whole story without interruption, in order to get an overall impression (Chambers 1994).

Literature Dialogue

After a reading session in the classroom, during which the teachers introduced the first *Miss Ignora* book, they arranged a structured conversation about the stories inspired by Chambers (1994) who proposed that children should be asked a number of questions to which each one should reply:

1. Did you find elements in the story that you liked?
2. Did you find something that you disliked?
3. Did you find something that surprised you?
4. Did you find patterns in the story that you recognised which remind you of other stories?

After reading the first book, *Miss Ignora Explodes*, the children were invited to discuss the book in the light of the four questions above. Answering the first question, *"did you find elements in the story that you liked,"* many of the boys said they thought it "was cool when Miss Ignora exploded," whereas the girls liked it "when Miss Ignora apologised to the teacher" (because of her explosion) and she was "nice to the cats." Responding to the second question, *"did you find something that you disliked,"* many girls mentioned the explosion as a problem. A few of the girls also disliked the fact that Ignora stole from the fishmonger. Some of the boys also expressed reservations about stealing fish and about Miss Ignora's explosion. But a number of other boys said: "There was nothing we disliked."

The children asked a number of moral and philosophical questions which they reflected upon and discussed for a while. The experience provided ideas for the following aesthetical activities.

Children Make Drawings

After the reading session and the dialogue, the children were encouraged to talk about and draw their ideas as they related to the debate over what they liked and disliked in the book.

Some children made collective drawings in small groups, while others made individual drawings. A typical drawing was an isolated episode from the story, such as when Miss Ignora fed the cats (Figure 6-1) or Miss Ignora exploded in front of the teacher (Figure 6-2).

Figure 6-1

Figure 6-2

When the children had finished their drawings, the teachers displayed the results on two bulletin boards, placing similar ideas side-by-side. This enabled the children to view their own answers and reflections and compare them with those of their peers. The session led to a new dialogue, and a third question was asked: *Did you find something that surprised you?* Common answers were as follows:

- Why does she not have a mother?
- Why does she reach the point where she explodes?
- Why does she live in that strange house?
- Why does she not ask for help from the fishmonger?
- Why has Miss Ignora's father died in a traffic accident?

The children's comments formed the basis for fruitful conversations. Most of the children had reached a high level of attention by the time they replied to and reflected upon the fourth question: *Did you find patterns in the story that you recognised, which remind you of other stories?*

Some children were able to compare the stories of Miss Ignora to other well-known children's books. For example, one boy replied, "Pippi Longstocking—both Pippi and Miss Ignora have no father and mother." Another boy said, "It reminds me of Superman," and a number of boys and girls also compared the story to *Sleeping Beauty*.

Play

Continuing the children's interest in the first three books, the teacher read the last *Miss Ignora* story: *Miss Ignora and George Influence their World.* The plot deals with Ignora and George as they become friends and free a dog which is wedged in a door. Then they talk about how, in doing so, this had influenced their world.

After the reading session, the children were encouraged to start their own play events, and they quickly set up different groups to discuss the theme, roles, and actions for playing. One group of boys and girls was inspired by the incident involving the stuck dog, and they spent some time planning a play with many details. The characters were Ignora, George, an angry man, Ignora's friend Nina, a dog, and some cats. An extract from the transcript reads:

Miss Ignora said: *"Hey, would you like to be my boyfriend?"*

George answered: *"Yes."*

Miss Ignora said: *"Then we take a promenade in the park."* Miss Ignora and George danced around.

George: *"Oh, see an old shack, it's ugly,"* and then he continued: *"Something is whining."*

Miss Ignora: *"Yes, it is from over there, inside."*

George looked around and then he said: *"Oh, it is a nice little dog."*

"Come here," Miss Ignora said and then she kissed the dog on the nose.

Suddenly a man showed up from the old shack. He scolded the children and cried: *"Get out, now!"*

Miss Ignora said: *"Sorry, we will ...."* And then she whispered to George: *"What a sour man."*

The sour man cried: *"This is my place; buzz off, stupid children!"*

The two children disappeared quickly, and went away from the place.

Then George said: *"Oh, I am so hungry; let us eat."*

George and Miss Ignora created a place to eat. They set up a table and some chairs illustrating a restaurant in which they sat down.

They sat in front of each other and ate their food. Suddenly Miss Ignora burst out: *"Oh, I forgot my appointment with Nina."*

She left the table and ran over to her best friend Nina who was loudly sniffing. Then Nina sobbed: *"You forgot our appointment."*

"Sorry Nina," Miss Ignora said, *"I was out eating with George. Sorry, should we not all play together?"*

Then they started to play skip. George and Nina swung the skipping rope.

A bit later Nina said: *"I do not like this anymore."* And Miss Ignora agreed.

"Hey," George said, *"look at that nice dog."*

Miss Ignora said: *"It is the sour man's dog. Let's return the dog to him."*

George said: *"I really do not like to do it, but we have to."*

The three children went to the sour man's house and knocked at the door. Then he opened and snapped: *"Pooh...it is you again."*

Nina timidly said: *"We just want to return..."* At this point, however, the sour man interrupted her with a curt 'Buzz off!'

He closed the door, and when the three children were alone with the dog, Nina said: *"Oh, how bad he was."*

"You are right," Miss Ignora replied, *"he was old, big, and fat."*

While the children talked, the sour man arrived and said: *"I just want to apologize because I was so angry. I would like to give you my dog as a present."*

With this remark the children decided to return to their house with the dog and eat rolls and drink cocoa.

Through the example of Miss Ignora, the teachers challenged the children to become storytellers themselves. Inspired by the Miss Ignora books the children were invited to state their own reflections and to discuss moral and philosophical themes, which they then expressed in narratives, drawings, and play.

The above extract from play shows that children actually constructed a plot: the sour man and the smart problem-solving. In the book there was a dog, which was whining, and also an angry man, but the children constructed a completely new plot: the man became nice and gave the dog to them. Independent problem-solving was also expressed, namely in Miss Ignora's conflict between being with her best friend Nina or with George. Thus, their play displayed productive and creative dimensions close to the concept of expanding learning (Engeström 1987) and expanding play (Broström 1999b).

Conclusion

The starting point for this chapter was the hypothesis that the reading of fiction followed by aesthetic reflection (drawing and play) might be a useful tool towards the development of children's literacy competence in the first years of school. The chapter constructs a theoretical basis for such an educational approach. This hypothesis has not been explored in detail, but the components have been described and discussed: reflections about the reading of literature combined with children's drawing and play. The idea was to show that the use of aesthetics, which is part of the original kindergarten tradition and current early childhood education and care, might be an approach that can help children construct the prerequisites for reading.

It is hoped that the different components, Vygotsky's three cornerstones, the concepts of aesthetics, and the idea of fiction, drawing and play, might form the basis of a theoretical foundation for early literacy in preschool.

References

Anning, A. 2003. Pathways to the graphicacy club: The crossroad of home and preschool. *Journal of Early Childhood Literacy* 3: 5–35.

Anning, A. and K. Ring. 2004. *Making sense of children's drawings.* Buckingham: Open University Press.

Bakhtin, M. Mikhailovich. 1981. *The dialogic imagination: Four essays.* Ed. Michael Holquist. Translated Caryl Emerson and Michael Holquist. Austin and London: University of Texas Press.

Broström, S. 1999b. Drama games with 6-year-old children. Possibilities and limitations. In *Perspectives on Activity Theory,* ed. Y. Engeström and R-L. Punamaki, 250–263. New York: Cambridge University Press.

——. 2005a. Transition problems and play as transitory activity. *Australian Early Childhood Research Journal,* 30, 3: 17–25.

——. Stig. 2005b. *Fuld fart mod skolestart.* Aarhus: Dansk Pædagogisk Forum. Forlaget.

——. Stig. 2006. Transitions in children's thinking. In *Informing transitions in the early years. Research, policy and practice,* ed. H. Fabian and A-W. Dunlop, 61–73. London: Open University Press.

Broström, S., M. Frandsen, and K. Vilhelmsen. 2008. *Læsning og litteratur i skolestarten.* Copenhagen: Nationalt Videncenter for Læsning.

Bruner, J. 1990. *Acts of meaning.* Cambridge: Harvard University Press.

Chambers, A. 1994. *Tell me: Children reading and talk.* Stroud: Thimble Press.

Cole, M. and P. Griffin. 1984. Current activity for the future: The zo-ped. In *Children's learning in the zone of proximal development,* eds. B. Rogoff and J.V. Wertsch, 45–64. San Francisco: Jossey-Bass Inc., Publishers.

Diamond, E. 1997. *Unmaking mimesis.* New York: Routledge.

Engeström, Y. 1987. *Learning by expanding. An activity-theoretical approach to development research.* Helsinki: Orienta-Konsultit.

Guss, F. 2005. Reconceptualising play: Aesthetic self-definitions. *Contemporary Issues in Early Childhood,* 6(3): 233–43.

Holzman, L. 1997. *Schools for growth: Radical alternatives to current educational models.* London: Lawrence Erlbaum.

Lukács, G. 1971. *The theory of the novel: A historico-philosophical essay on the forms of great epic literature.* London: Merlin Press.

Malchiodi, C.A. 1998. *Understanding children's drawings.* London: Jessica Kingsley.

Matthews, J. 1999. *The art of childhood and adolescence: The construction of meaning.* London: Falmer Press.

National Institute for Literacy. 2000. *Report of the National Reading Panel: Teaching children to read.* U.S. Department of Health and Human Services.

Newman, F. and L. Holzman. 1993. *Lev Vygotsky: Revolutionary scientist.* New York: Routledge.

OECD. 2006. *Starting Strong II. Early childhood education and care.* Paris: OECD.

Pellegrini, A.D. and L. Galda. 1993. Ten years after: A re-examination of symbolic play and literacy research. *Reading Research Quarterly, 28,* 163–75.

———. 1998. *The development of school-based literacy. A social ecological perspective.* London: Routledge.

Robbins, C. and L. Ehri. 1994. Reading storybooks to kindergartners helps them learn new vocabulary words. *Journal of Educational Psychology* 86(1): 54–64.

Rogoff, B. 1990. *Apprenticeship in thinking.* New York: Oxford University Press.

———. 1993. Children's guided participation and participatory appropriation in sociocultural activity. In *Development in context. Acting and thinking in specific environments,* ed. R.H. Wozniak and K.V. Fischer, 121–153. New Jersey and London: Lawrence Erlbaum Associates, Publishers.

Scarborough, S.H. and W. Dobrich. 1994. On the efficacy of reading to preschoolers. *Developmental Review* 14: 245–302.

Sénéchal, Monique and J-A. LeFevre. 2002. Parental involvement in the development of children's reading skill: A five-year longitudinal study. *Child Development, 73* (2): 445–60.

Silvén, M., A. Ahtola, and P. Niemi. 2003. Early words, multiword utterances and maternal reading strategies as predictors of mastering word inflections in Finnish. *Journal of Child Language, 30:* 253–79.

Stetsenko, A. 1999. Social interaction, cultural tools and the zone of proximal development: In search of a synthesis. In *Activity theory and social practice: Cultural-historical approaches,* ed. S. Chaiklin, M. Hedegaard, and U.J. Jensen, 235–252. Aarhus: Aarhus University Press.

Vygotsky, L.S. 1971. *The psychology of art.* Cambridge: M.I.T. Press.
————. 1978. *Mind in society. The development of higher psychological processes,* ed. M. Cole et al. Cambridge: Harvard University Press.
————. 1978a. Tool and symbol in child development. In *Mind in society. The development of higher psychological processes,* ed. M. Cole et al., 19–30. Cambridge: Harvard University Press.
————. 1978b. The role of play in development. In *Mind in society. The development of higher psychological processes,* ed. M. Cole et al., 92–104. Cambridge: Harvard University Press.
————. 1978c. Internalization of higher psychological functions. In *Mind in society. The development of higher psychological processes,* ed. M. Cole et al., 54–7. Cambridge: Harvard University Press.
————. 1978d. Interaction between learning and development. In *Mind in society. The development of higher psychological processes,* ed. M. Cole et al., 79–91. Cambridge: Harvard University Press.
————. 1985. Die instrumentelle methode in der psychologie. *Ausgewälhlte schriften,* Bd. 1, 309–317. Berlin: Volk und Wissen.
————. 1997. Thinking and speech. In *The collected works of L.S. Vygotsky. Problems of general psychology,* ed. R. SW. Rieber and A.S. Carton, 143–285. New York: Plenum.
————. 2004. Imagination and creativity in childhood. *Journal of Russian and East European Psychology,* 42 (1): 7–97.
Wertsch, J.V. 1985. *Vygotsky and the social formation of the mind.* Cambridge: Harvard University Press.
————. 1998. *Mind in action.* New York: Oxford University Press.

CHAPTER SEVEN

HEARING CHILDREN'S VOICES —EMULATING VYGOTSKY'S THEORIES IN GOOD EVALUATION PRACTICE

LINDA E. LEE

Introduction

The evaluation field has experienced a shift toward inclusion of a "broader epistemological perspective and wider array of empirical methods— qualitative and mixed methods, responsive case studies, participatory and empowerment action research, and interpretive and constructivist versions of knowledge" (McClintock 2004, nab.). Evaluation practice has also begun to value different "ways of knowing." Consequently, a move toward more qualitative methods is due, in large part, to the critique that traditional research and evaluation methods often act to impose external judgment without including the voices of participants and stakeholders in a meaningful manner and taking into account their different ways of under-standing the world.

When making choices about policies and resources for programs, researchers, policy makers, and decision makers often undertake evalua-tions which include the opinions and perspectives of people involved in designing and implementing programs, as well as those who are the clients, participants, or beneficiaries of the programs. However, the opinions and experiences of children—particularly young children—are often omitted in research and evaluation processes. This paper will illustrate how Vygotsky's theories are relevant to the move toward using innovative research and evaluation methods to include the diverse perspectives of children, a constituency whose insights, voices, and world views are often missing from the discourse.

Trends in Program Evaluation

Despite a re-awakened debate over whether randomized control trials constitute the gold standard in evaluation, a solely quantitative approach has given way, in large measure, to the use of mixed methods. From a program evaluation perspective, Patton (1997, 290) has argued the importance of taking context and purpose into account:

> Using both qualitative and quantitative approaches can permit the evaluator to address questions about quantitative differences on standardized variables and qualitative differences reflecting individual and program uniqueness. The more a program aims at individualized outcomes, the greater the appropriateness of qualitative methods. The more a program emphasizes common outcomes for all participants, the greater the appropriateness of standardized measures of performance and change.

The dynamics and realities of the educational setting are factors which create difficulties for randomized experiments, as well as for other experimental and quasi-experimental research methodologies. Educational systems are complex, and classrooms, with their unpredictability, are not clinical laboratories. According to Luntley (2000, 205); "classrooms (and other educational units) share a common structural feature with other social and natural systems—namely, nonlinearity. Ignore this and you get faulty logic of understanding of the system at issue." Similarly, Shavelson and Towne (2002, iii) propose that:

> A wide variety of legitimate scientific designs are available for education research. They range from randomized experiments of voucher programs to in-depth ethnographic case studies of teachers to neurocognitive investigations of number learning using positive emission tomography brain imaging.

While evaluation utilizes a range of approaches, recently Freeman and Mathison (2009, 12–13) have focused on the importance of "constructivism" and "constructionism" in researching children's experiences, the former being the individual's construction of their world experience, as compared to the latter, which emphasizes the influence of culture on how people see their world. Vygotsky's idea that socialization is a process of cultural transmission and that learning takes place within a social environment is central to this concept: "it was never the teacher or the tutor who did the teaching, but the particular social environment in the school which was created for each individual instance" (Vygotsky 1997, 47). As summarized by Freeman and Mathison (2009, 13), Vygotsky's "belief that individual learning is the result of one's engagement in a social and cultural world has done much to advance the importance of context in constructivist theories."

Another consideration gaining traction in the evaluation community concerns the notion that "there are different ways of knowing the world, and thereby, investigating it" (Adams St. Pierre 2002, 26). In the transformative paradigm a central focus is placed on the experiences of marginalized groups where the researcher "links the results of the inquiry to wider questions of social inequity and social justice ... transformative research has the potential to contribute to the enhanced ability to assert rigor in the sense that ignored or misrepresented views are included" (Mertens and McLaughlin 2004, 4). Consequently, the inclusion of those groups traditionally disenfranchised within evaluation becomes a priority. Such populations include children and youth, those with emerging literacy (particularly in national official languages), and persons with disabilities. House and Howe (2000, 5) in their 'deliberative democratic' approach to evaluation place great emphasis on efforts to include diverse standpoints in evaluative practice: "the *first requirement* of deliberative democratic is inclusion of all relevant interests."

Issues Concerning Young Children's Participation

The inclusion of relevant interests is coherent with the shift from a global needs-based to rights-based perspective in the case of children, as articulated in the United Nations Convention on the Rights of the Child (CRC). The CRC addresses children's rights to survival, right to development to the fullest, rights to protection from harmful influences, abuse, and exploitation, and rights to participation to the fullest in family, culture and social life: "Children's participation in social life in which they are stakeholders is not simply a consideration but a right."[1] One can argue that if children have the right to participate in social life, they indeed should have the right to express their opinions regarding their participation. While this may be understood in certain contexts, the inclusion of children's own voices in research and evaluation practice have often been muted or indeed absent.

---

1   The United Nations Convention on the Rights of the Child in English can be found at http://www.unhchr.ch/html/menu3/b/k2crc.htm.

While children should have the right to participate and express their views, a number of issues need to be addressed, including adult acceptance of the legitimacy of children's views. Researchers and evaluators may express concerns about reliability, particularly because they question children's ability to express their understanding of the world in credible ways. Other barriers to children's participation in research and evaluation activities concern children's vulnerability, safety, and comfort. Certainly, while there are ethical and legal considerations regarding children's participation, a variety of strategies have been employed by researchers to overcome these barriers as research into children's lives becomes more frequent.[2]

If the right of children to have voice is acknowledged, the question then becomes which methods are most suitable for their inclusion, particularly in the case of young children. As Article 13 of the Convention on the Rights of the Child states: "The child shall have the right to freedom of expression; this right shall include freedom to seek, receive, and impart information and ideas of all kinds, regardless of frontiers, either orally, in writing or in print, in the form of art, or through any other media of the child's choice." Regarding the issues of how children can express their views, researchers and evaluators are moving towards embracing alternative methods as suggested in Article 13. As Vygotsky would argue, the first step is to build the child's interest and then actively engage the child in an appropriate task.

While the UN Convention on the Rights of the Child recognizes the usefulness of various media in conveying children's perspectives, Leavy (2009, 13) speaks to the power of arts-based approaches more broadly in offering new pathways to create knowledge within and across disciplinary boundaries. "Arts-based practices can be employed as a means of creating critical awareness or raising consciousness. This is important in "social justice-oriented research that seeks to reveal power relations ... and challenge dominant ideologies." Therefore, as a population with emerging literacy skills that has a right to participate and express their views, arts based, visual, and graphic methods, often coupled with children's verbal explanation of their products, provide suitable vehicles for children's voices. Interestingly, visual methods of researching young people's experiences have generated increased attention over the last few years.[3]

---

[2]   A discussion of ethical issues specific to research with young people can be found in both Freeman and Mathison (2009) and in Heath, Brooks, Cleaver, and Ireland (2009).

[3]   For example, see: Freeman and Mathison (2009), Heath, Brooks, Cleaver, and Ireland (2009), and Thompson ed. (2008).

Successful Evaluation Methods Used with Young Children

A number of methods have been successful in engaging young children. In the visual realm, methods can be categorized into drawing, photographs, and graphic representations, including mapping and webs. While older children and youth may move into videography or computer and Internet applications, the examples in this paper address children in the early years of their lives, in the age range of four to seven years.

The first example is a project that used multiple methods to assess an initiative testing a model that focused on creating conditions that foster educational success for Roma children in the early years of school. Roma children have often been mislabelled as mentally handicapped and segregated into special education settings, reflecting the racism and bias that has too often been directed at Roma populations. Therefore, this pilot project, supported by the *Open Society Institute*, operated in special schools in Bulgaria, Czech Republic, and Slovakia and in special schools and remedial mainstream classes in Hungary, under the auspices of the national non-governmental organizations implementing the Step by Step Program.[4] The fundamental purpose of this experiment was to test, through the use of an objective and systematic evaluation process, the hypothesis that Roma students can succeed to the standards of mainstream education given the appropriate conditions for learning. While students remained in the segregated settings, regular curricula were used and learning conditions were enhanced. The intention was that by grade four students would be capable of entering mainstream classes. In summary, learnings from the project confirm the hypotheses that Roma children are misplaced and that many Roma children in special education settings can academically successful to achieve mainstream standards. Project results also provide insight into conditions that support school success for Roma children.

One of the methods used to collect data was interviews with children aged five, six, and seven in both the pilot and comparison classes regarding their school experience. As part of the interview, children were asked to draw something that they liked about school. In this instance the visual was combined with another method; that of a semi-structured interview where children were asked, among other things, to explain their drawings. As argued by Pink (2005), "visual methods are not purely visual. Rather, they

---

4   See Chapter 13 for a detailed description of the Step by Step Program and its origins.

pay particular attention to visual aspects of culture. Similarly, they cannot be used independently of other methods."

Figure 7-1

Drawing by girl in Hungary

In the first drawing, the girl showed herself peer-teaching the alphabet to classmates. Everyone was smiling; the classroom was bright and colourful. The girl explained that she liked school, particularly reading. Other data confirmed that children in the pilot classes were significantly more likely than children in the comparison classes to say that they liked academic subjects.

In the second drawing, a boy in Bulgaria was asked to do the same thing. His drawing depicted a man in front of a house, not in a school setting. He explained that: "In my picture there are flowers, a man, and a coloured house with a chimney, windows, and a lamp coloured in blue and green. I like to look at the flowers… but it is a little bit sad because someone has beaten the man; he is crying and there are tears." In this case, the realities of the boy's life overpowered the question he had been given. While his response did not answer the question asked, it spoke deeply to the realities that affect Roma children and that, indeed, have an impact on their school success. Only through his drawing were his realities and their impact on him brought to the fore.

Figure 7-2

Drawing by boy in Bulgaria

Another tool for children's self-expression is the use of graphic representations. For example, one elementary school was implementing an early years numeracy initiative at the kindergarten to fourth-grade level. Teachers received professional development sessions and classroom support to broaden their own understanding of mathematics and learn new methods for teaching mathematics to young children. In an evaluation of the initiative, the author wanted to find out from the children themselves how they viewed mathematics. Were they being taught that mathematics was more than addition and subtraction? Were teachers using manipulative materials in their teaching of mathematics? As part of the evaluation students were placed in groups of three. They were given a sheet of graph paper and markers and asked to answer the question: "what does math look like?" The children's work confirmed that they conceived of mathematics not just as numbers but also as shapes, graphs, Venn diagrams, time, number lines, and so on. While the detail of the creations varied from group to group (which could have been used as an assessment tool for student understanding), the fact that the representations in all groups contained more than simply numbers illustrated that teachers were indeed using a variety of tools and strategies to teach mathematics. They had moved beyond the rote teaching of arithmetic, and this was amply demonstrated by the children's drawings and representations.

Chapter Seven

Figure 7-3

Representations of mathematics

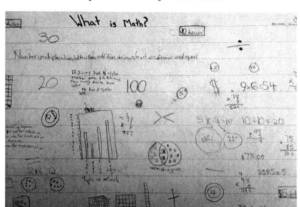

Young children can also be engaged in using photography as a tool for expression. The use of photography can be categorized into two dimensions: children respond to photographs taken by others or children take the photographs themselves. In terms of responding to photos, this can be accomplished through showing a variety of images to stimulate thinking and remembrance about a particular time or issue ("photo-elicitation") or through categorization of images followed by reflection ("photo-sorts"). As noted by Schwartz (1998) people respond to photographs "without hesitation. By providing informants with a task fairly similar to viewing a family album, the strangeness of the interview situation is averted."

In the development of a new gallery at a Canadian museum, a photo-sort technique was developed and used to elicit responses from visitors, including children as young as five or six and adult visitors for whom English was a second language.[5] The researchers took approximately 40 photographs of the existing galleries showing glass cases, walls of explanatory text, small and large dioramas, and areas of the gallery where the visitor actually boards a full-size sailing ship. Then, as visitors left the gallery they were asked, to express their gallery preferences by sorting the photographs. They

---

[5]   The method was developed and termed "photo sort" by Proactive Information Services Inc., Winnipeg, Canada.

were asked to sort the photographs into three piles: what they really liked about the museum, what was all right (they could "take or leave"), and what they did not like. Once they had created the three categories of photographs, they were asked to talk about the photographs of the exhibits they really liked and then about the exhibits they did not like. In total, the process took approximately five to seven minutes per person. Through the process, many views were accommodated, including individuals for whom a traditional questionnaire would not have been effective because of their English or French literacy levels, such as young children.

In cases where people take photographs themselves, they are more actively engaged in a process of thinking about their world, collecting "data" that illustrates their perceptions of the world, and then reflecting on what they have assembled. Paulo Freire pioneered this work in Peru while conducting a literacy project when he asked people questions about their lives and requested that they answer through photographs. In one case, when asked about child exploitation, a young child produced a photograph of a nail on a wall. Through dialogue it was discovered that the nail was used to hold children's shoe-shine boxes.[6]

Hurworth (2003, n.a), in thinking about the use of photography (although not specifically with children), sets out three categories of photography: reflexive photography, photo novella, and photo voice. In reflexive photography participants take photographs focused on a certain issue or question. Then, when they are interviewed, the photographs are used to promote reflection and deeper levels of thinking. The photo novella is created when participants use photographs to tell a story in pictures, usually a story about their daily lives. "Photo novella is meant to be a tool of empowerment enabling those with little money, power, or status to communicate to policymakers where change should occur" (Hurworth 2003, n.a.). Photo voice, similar to photo novella, is used in participatory action research to enable personal and community change and includes the dimension of critical dialogue through group discussion of photographs.

One example of photographs taken by young people is a case where a school administration wanted to determine how safe students felt when they were at school.[7] The staff included students from kindergarten

---

6   As told by Burke, Catherine (2008), p.26.

7   Thanks are extended to Sargent Park School, The Winnipeg School Division, Manitoba, Canada for giving the researcher permission to share their process and the photograph of their "hot spot" map.

(age 5) to ninth-grade (age 14). While there was no incident that created fears over student safety, the staff wanted to ensure that their students were in a comfortable and welcoming school environment. Students were put into teams which combined students in the early elementary grades with those from higher grades. They were given cameras and the task of taking photographs of areas in the school and on the school grounds where they felt unsafe or uncomfortable. The teams then came together to compare photographs. They selected common photographs of 'unsafe' places and put captions on them explaining each situation. For example, older students from other schools come to this building for particular courses because of the industrial arts facilities. The door where they enter the school was seen as a scary place for the younger children because of the "big kids" who were not familiar to them. Another area of the school was a poorly lit hallway. Working together, the students connected the photos with the areas which were illustrated on a map of the school. They called the areas "hot spots." The map, with the accompanying photographs and explanations, was placed in the school staff room for all to see. Then at a school meeting which included the school administrators, teachers, educational assistants, secretary, and custodian, the staff developed a plan to address the areas identified as "hot spots" by the children.

Figure 7-4

Map of "Hot Spots" (Sargent Park School, Winnipeg, Canada)

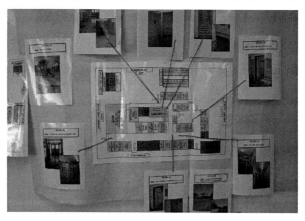

The previous examples illustrate how young children, on their own or working with others, can be given voice through the use of various visual methods. The methods are such that they can be used for various purposes and at any stage of a research or evaluation project. Visual methods provide a means of connecting the psychological, emotional, and physical realities of children's lives, in part because they are familiar and comfortable vehicles for children's expression. Drawing, for example, is clearly a common mechanism used by young children to present their understanding of the world.

In the case of the Roma children, drawing helped to engage them and promote a longer, more detailed interview. As can be the case with visual methods, unpredictable information was conveyed through the drawing by the Bulgarian boy. While it did not answer the question that was posed, it addressed, on a deeper level, the issues that young Roma and their community faced; issues that were germane, and indeed central, to the intentions of the pilot project. In the case of "what does math look like," the children's representations of mathematics were used in combination with other methods to support triangulation. The children's drawings supported teacher self-reporting of the adoption of new methods to extend their teaching of mathematics. The use of a photo-sort in the museum setting engaged people who would not otherwise have been able to participate, making the interview process more stimulating and interesting for respondents. In the photos taken and used by students to present the perceived unsafe places in their school, the technique supported a participatory research process that also helped to build trusting relationships between older and younger students.

In all the examples, the use of visual methods provided a mechanism for the voice of young children to be heard as part of research and evaluation processes. In all cases, children were actively engaged in a task, based on visual images, that was interesting and appropriate to their own culture and context and which had benefits beyond the mere collection of data.

Considerations for Researchers and Policy Makers

Engaging in participatory practices that include and empower all relevant stakeholders, including children, should be in the best interests of both researchers and policy makers. One can argue that it is also the responsibility of researchers working in civil societies to demonstrate the value of people's views whose voices are often silenced or otherwise go unheard. The processes required to give voice often entail methodological innovation and risk taking. As noted by Sparkes (2002):

"Not only do we speak from a particular place but we actually speak from various subjective spaces according to different social roles, gender positions, age differentials, and different positions of sexuality composing multiple subjectivities which include how we view and move around the world."

For researchers, the use of visual methods provides an entry point into the world of a young child and helps provide a richer perspective which may represent otherwise inaccessible information. If used in combination with other methods, researchers have the opportunity both to expand their repertoire using visual methods and to create an environment where such methods are legitimized. The sole use of visually-based methods is not being touted here, but rather, the addition of these methods along with those that are more commonly used and widely accepted. As noted by Banks (2001, 12): "All films, photographs, and art works are the products of human action and are entangled to varying degrees in human social relations; they therefore require a wider frame of analysis in their understanding, a reading of the external narrative that goes beyond the visual text itself." With the on-going debate over what counts as credible evidence in evaluation, it is incumbent upon researchers and evaluators to consider the combination of methods that will provide the richest, most compelling and credible information for decision-makers.

Policy makers must make decisions that are appropriate to their own realities, cultures, and contexts. However, if research and evaluation are viewed from a transformative paradigm, policy makers must begin to understand that knowledge is socially constructed and that different groups experience the world differently. If, as Vygotsky would argue, individual learning is the result of one's engagement in a social and cultural world, policy makers engaged in their own socio-political worlds must recognize other realities and other ways of knowing, if their policies are to be relevant to the intended beneficiaries. For example, if policy makers are to introduce educational policies that support high quality education for all, they must consider the voices of those who are marginalized or otherwise unheard. If these perspectives are not considered, then any new policies and the resultant practices may fail to address the underlying conditions that are obstructing success for marginalized groups.

From a human rights perspective policy makers need to respond to the fact that children have rights; their views need to be considered in any discourse and decision making. However, if their views are to be accurately represented, they must be captured through means that are developmentally and contextually appropriate. Policy makers and research funders need to ask for and value the use of a variety of information gathering methods during research and evaluation processes, rather than being satisfied with traditional methods designed for adult and other dominant populations. By demanding the use of methods that accurately reflect children's voices and realities, funders and policy makers have the opportunity to enhance the skill sets of researchers and expand the mind-sets of those in power, through valuing the voices and lived experiences of children. In so doing, they also contribute to the creation of more inclusive and socially just societies.

References

Adams St. Pierre, E. 2002. 'Science' rejects postmodernism. *Educational Researcher.* 31 (8): 26.

Banks, M. 2001. *Visual methods in social research.* London: Sage Publications.

Burke, C. 2008. "Play in focus: children's visual voice in participative research." *Doing visual research with children and young people*, ed. Pat Thomson, 26. London and New York: Routledge.

Freeman, M. and S. Mathison. 2009. *Researching Children's Experiences.* New York and London: Guildford Press.

Heath, S., R. Brooks, E. Cleaver, and E. Ireland. 2009. *Researching young people's lives.* London: Sage.

House, E.R. and K.R. Howe. 2000. Deliberative democratic evaluation. *Evaluation as a democratic process: promoting inclusion, dialogue and deliberation: New directions for evaluation,* 85: 3–12.

Hurworth, R. 2003. Photo-interviewing for research. *Social research update.* Guildford: University of Surrey. http://sru.soc.ac.uk/SU40.html.

Leavy, P. 2009. *Method meets art: Arts-based research practice.* New York and London: The Guilford Press.

Luntley, M. 2000. *Performance, pay and professionals.* London: Philosophical Association of Great Britain.

McClintock, C. 2004. Using narrative methods to link program evaluation and organization development. *The Evaluation Exchange*, IX: 4.

Mertens, D. and K. McLaughlin. 2004. *Research and evaluation methods in special education.* Thousand Oaks: Corwin Press.

Patton, M.Q. 1997. *Utilization-focused evaluation: The new century text. Edition 3.* Thousand Oaks: Sage.

Pink, S. 2005. *The future of visual anthropology.* London: Routledge.

Schwartz, D. 1989. Visual ethnography: Using photography in qualitative research. *Qualitative Sociology,* 12 (2): 119–154.

Shavelson, R. and L. Towne. 2002. *Scientific research in education.* Washington, D.C.: National Academy Press.

Sparkes, A.C. 2002. Autoethnography: Self-indulgence or something more? In *Ethnographically speaking: Autoethnography, literature, and aesthetics*, eds. A. Bochner and C. Ellis, 209–232. Walnut Creek: AltaMira Press.

Thomas, G. and R. Pring, ed. 2004. Conclusion: evidence-based policy and practice. In *Evidence-based practice in education.* Berkshire: Open University Press

Thomson, P., ed. 2008. *Doing visual research with children and young people.* New York and London: Routledge.

United Nations convention on the rights of the child (English). http://www. unhchr.ch/html/menu3/b/k2crc.htm.

Vygotsky, L.S. 1997. *Educational psychology.* Florida: St. Lucie Press.

CHAPTER EIGHT

PROMOTING LEARNING AND DEVELOPMENT —THE PRESENCE OF VYGOTSKY'S IDEAS IN A PORTUGUESE APPROACH TO ASSESSMENT IN EARLY CHILDHOOD EDUCATION

GABRIELA PORTUGAL, PAULA SANTOS, AIDA FIGUEIREDO, OFÉLIA LIBÓRIO, NATÁLIA ABRANTES, CARLOS SILVA, AND SÓNIA GÓIS

Introduction

In order for the early childhood teacher to attain the highest quality teaching, the teacher must be able to respond to the diversity of childhood experiences, which are evident in different educational contexts. In a successful high quality system, the teacher should have a deep knowledge of the content areas approached and should use documentation and evaluation strategies that can sustain curriculum development and the teaching-learning processes.

Early childhood education aims to organize the experiences and relations through which children learn and develop personal and social competences. All these variables constitute the curriculum, encompassing educational principles, processes, and practices guided by educational goals and development of competences. Individual, social, and cultural characteristics of a certain group of children or of some children in particular must, naturally, be taken into account in the organization of the educational setting.

It is our belief that thinking about curriculum (planned or not planned) in preschool education means reflecting upon 'what each child carries within himself or herself.' What benefits does sharing an environment built for and with the child in contact with other children and specialized professionals, during a certain period of time, bring to a child's development?

How do early childhood Portuguese teachers monitor and evaluate this process, in view of educational principles, practices, and competence development? How do they monitor curricular development, and how do they know 'what each child carries within himself or herself'?

Educational Principles in Practice

The planned curriculum reflects the values or educational principles of its authors with regard to children, education, and the society which is idealized.

When future or current Portuguese early childhood education professionals are questioned or challenged to describe the education principles which guide their teaching practices, they emphasize, in addition to the unique characteristics of each age group, the individuality of each child. They state that children are unique and unrepeatable, and that they develop at different rhythms and in different ways in the emotional, cognitive, social, physical, and motor control areas, all of which are important and relate directly to each other. Along these lines, teachers with whom we have been working agree on the importance of the relationships which the child establishes with others (both children and adults), developing communication and language, experiencing the feeling of cooperation, discovering abilities, and developing autonomy and individual expression (as defended by Vygotsky, assuming social reality as a true source of development). There is also consensus amongst Portuguese teachers concerning the importance of appropriately organizing space, time, materials, and activities; diversifying relational experiences; paying attention to the child's particularities; and emphasising the importance of playing, exploring, discovering, satisfying curiosity, and relaxing. The child is perceived as being active, sensitive, and imaginative; and closeness, empathy, and careful observation of the child are needed if the teacher is to create forms of interacting in a Zone of Proximal Development (ZPD). In this way, teachers value a structure of continuity and connection between children and adult, considered fundamental to the development of relationships based on trust, which allow children to develop a sense of security and self-esteem that will lead them to accept, take risks, and exceed their own expectations. Teachers agree that the children who are confident in themselves and in their abilities are those who bring together better conditions to learn.

In addition, it is essential that all those involved in the child's learning and development process cooperate together. This community of relationships involves teachers, other professionals, families, and members of the broader community, and values an atmosphere in which participants listen, respect, and pay attention to multiple points of view in order to discuss and solve conflicts and generate the mutual enrichment of all involved. In this process, teachers stress the importance of taking into consideration the children's socio-cultural, community, and cultural contexts when developing the curriculum.

With regards to professional development, teachers state that they value joint discussion and reflection as a team, based on pedagogical experiences and observations.

All these education principles or values are, naturally, important, since they will affect many of the decisions made at the level of curriculum organization in childhood education. However, many teachers, on a daily basis, often seem to be unaware of the foundations of educational action, because there is no evidence of it in their practice.

When observing common teaching practices, some features become evident (Portugal, Libório, and Santos 2007): an educational culture in which curriculum development is, frequently, conceived independently of children's needs and interests, where there is a great focus on activities offered and directed by adults. Free activities, routines, relationships, dialogues, and challenges created by children are not educationally valued.

Bennet (2004) refers to many examples of inadequate pedagogical theories and practices which can be observed in early childhood education: insufficient or inadequate interaction with the children; inadequate attention to and value of the horizontal learning which takes place between children; difficulties with group management; lack of stimulating learning environments; insufficient group work and practices based on reflection; excessive focus on academic objects; or, on the other hand, excessive reluctance or even rejection of learning objectives which are valued by families, schools, and society. Many pedagogical practices have not incorporated the results of what research and observation tell us about children: their enormous ability to learn in vast areas and domains (social, emotional, cognitive, linguistic, motor, etc.); the assumption that learning is based on social, affective, and experiential domains; the importance of interaction with families, between children, and between teachers; the windows of opportunities that exist for certain types of learning experiences during the first years of life (emotional control, development of language, social competences, curiosity about the rest of the world, etc.).

In conclusion, quite often in practice we observe a significant distance between what is said and what is actually done.

In this context, it seems crucial that every professional should learn how to observe what is taking place in his/her kindergarten, in an attempt to understand the way in which the principles and values he/she embraces are really present in its organization and dynamics.

The Development of Competences

In Portugal, the Curriculum Guidelines for Preschool Education (CGPSE) (see Appendix A)[1] are defined as a framework of reference which is common to all early childhood teachers allowing for different curricula and options. Vygotsky's ideas can be easily identified within CGPSE: learning takes place within social contexts through interaction with others, adults and children, making it important to start from what the children know concerning their culture and personal knowledge and experiences. According to Vygotsky (1981), "any function in the child's cultural development appears twice, or on two plans…First it appears between people as an interpsychological category, and then within the child as an intrapsychological category." This perspective, in CGPSE, means valuing adult-child interactions, children's interactions and attitudes and strategies such as learning through play, working in the Zone of Proximal Development, promoting significant and differentiated learning, considering social reality as a source of development, etc. In addition, CGPSE points out the importance of taking into consideration the children's cultures of origin, the type of partnership to be established with the family, the mediation between the children's cultures, and the skills and competences the child should be able to appropriate in order to be successful in future learning experiences and development (through the appropriation of pertinent symbolic-cultural instruments around content areas—personal and social development, expression and communication, and knowledge of the world).

CGPSE is an open document. It provides the early childhood teacher with some orientation in the contextualising areas of knowledge and of child development, making the conception and development of different curricula and evaluation practices possible.

Considering preschool education a process which should start from what children already know (the Zone of Actual Development), difficulty arises

---

[1]   Ministry of Education (ed.) (1997): Orientações Curriculares para a Educação Pré-Escolar. Lisboa: Ministério da Educação (*Curriculum Guidelines for Preschool Education*), http://sitio.dgidc.min-edu.pt/recursos/Lists/Repositrio%20 Recursos2/Attachments/25/Orientacoes_curriculares.pdf.

when trying to define with great precision what children aged 3, 4, or 5 years old should learn. The education professional should know how to help the children develop personal and social competences, valuing a holistic approach in the definition of development domains, distanced from a checklist which lists basic, atomized, and normative abilities.

According to CGPSE, personal and social development is an essential part of the entire educational process. Personal and social development encompasses the way the child relates with himself/herself, with others, and the world, in a process which implies the development of attitudes and values. Personal and social development also covers the areas of communication, expression and world knowledge.

Social and personal development underlies all curricular development, and is ascertained by the adult through the observation of the child's involvement and emotional well-being. This is manifested in children's positive dispositions and attitudes regarding learning, interest, motivation, concentration, self-confidence and self-esteem; in the quality of the relationships that children establish with others (children and adults), in the way they are accepted by other children and develop friendships; in the ability to control their behaviour, treat others with respect, understand their own feelings and be sensitive to feelings and perspectives of others; in the way they are able to integrate and participate in the daily life of a group, combining individual and group interests; in the way in which they perceive what is "good" and "bad" and understand the consequences of their words and actions; and in how they function autonomously in different routine activities.

According to the Portuguese Curriculum Guidelines, in order for each child to begin their subsequent school progression, preschool education should aim at developing a set of basic competences for future learning and development. These competences should consider attitudes, behaviour within the group, and essential learning which implies certain indispensible acquisitions for the formal learning of reading, writing, and mathematics.

Attitudes. Education should favour positive attitudes which are at the basis of all learning, namely positive self-esteem, curiosity and the wish to learn, self-organization/initiative, creativity and a feeling of connection to the world.

The child's behaviour in the group. The child should be able to integrate into the daily routine of a group, which includes the ability to connect with others, based on a feeling of mutual respect and understanding, combining individual needs with the needs of others. These are the foundations of cooperative behaviours. The child "should, for example, be able to accept and follow the rules of sociability and social life, collaborating in the organization of the group; know how to listen and take turns to talk; understand and follow orientations and orders, as well as take the initiative without disturbing the group; be able to complete tasks" (CGPSE, 91).

Basic learning/acquisitions. By mediating the child's introduction to the culture, the teacher cannot ignore the child's intentions, knowledge, and comprehension. Rather, the teacher should create culturally and socially useful learning experiences and activities. Nowadays, literacy, numeracy, and technological proficiency are considered indispensable in modern society. The inclusion of these aspects of contemporary culture in the kindergarten curriculum is a challenge which calls for the deconstruction of the antonymic representations about playing and/or free initiative and learning activities, making it important to overcome the preconception that learning, in areas such as numeracy and literacy, presupposes participating in directed/mandatory activities. In fact, the official orientation documents state that the adoption of an organized and structured pedagogy neither means introducing 'traditional' practices which are meaningless to the child, nor disregarding the importance of play in many learning experiences. It is important to recognize that the pleasure of learning and mastering competences also requires concentration and personal effort.

According to the CGPSE, it is expected that the children grow in the dimension of understanding and oral communication. They need to become aware of the different functions of writing, of the correspondence between the oral and written code (understanding that what is said can also be written and read), and to learn that each one of these codes has specific rules. They should also carry out basic learning activities at the level of mathematics, acquiring notions of space, time, and quantity, developing their logical and conceptual thought. Children should also develop technological proficiency and varied knowledge about the physical and social world, as well as experiences in the areas of art and motor control. Along the lines of Vygotsky's thought, it is naturally a process of appropriation of concepts with sociocultural pertinence, of symbolic-cultural instruments which are not used solely in human thinking, but which completely reorganize thought, being at the basis of the complete integration of the child in society as an autonomous, free, and responsible being.

Considering the individual, social, and cultural particularities of a group or individual children that one organizes the education environment, are our education contexts favourable to learning and development? What supervision and evaluation processes exist?

Assessment in Early Childhood Education:
The Official Orientations

In order for preschool education to contribute to more equal opportunities, the Curriculum Guidelines highlight the importance of a structured pedagogy. This implies an intentional and systematic organization of the pedagogical process, requiring that teachers plan their work and evaluate the process and its effects on children's development and learning. Continuing with what is stated in the Curriculum Guidelines, the intention of the education process presupposes observing, planning, acting, evaluating, communicating, and articulating. Teachers must plan according to what they know about the group and about each child, based upon reflection about education intentions and the forms of their materialization/adequacy to the group and to each child. They must create challenging situations, but safeguard against excessively demanding circumstances. Ideally, they will involve the children in the planning process. Teachers then must take action, materializing education intentions through action. They then must evaluate the process and the effects, involving the children and legitimizing future planning. Finally, the teacher must communicate with colleagues, education assistants, parents, and community agents, investing in team work and promoting education continuity and the transition to compulsory schooling.

Other official texts which contextualize childhood education in Portugal refer to the importance of the teacher creating and developing the respective curriculum through planning, organization, and evaluation of the education environment, as well as the importance of the curricula activities and projects, with the purpose of encouraging integrated learning. These documents emphasize the importance of evaluation by the teacher from a formative perspective, concerning their intervention, the environment, and the education processes adopted, as well as the development and learning of each child and of the group. In this process, it is crucial to be aware of and know how to use diverse observation and evaluation procedures, concerning both the processes and the effects.

Despite all these orientations, in Portugal a great heterogeneity of thought and evaluation practices can be observed, stressing their complexity and subjectivity. Teachers frequently invoke lack of time, resources and, quite often, lack of knowledge concerning the use of appropriate observation and evaluation procedures, both of the processes and of the effects.

In fact, our knowledge of some Portuguese early childhood educational experiences tells us that early childhood teachers need clearer competences and training in evaluation practices that allow them to respond to the demands of the next teaching level (primary school) and to the organizational needs of the school. It is therefore essential to develop documentation and evaluation instruments which allow the specificities and diversities of childhood to be accounted for, observable in different education contexts, without forgetting to provide answers to the more generic character of official orientations and scientific consensuses on the quality of education.

The evaluation of each child's learning and development process, being one of the most difficult, is surely one of the most important in the process of education. Evaluation in the context of childhood education is particularly challenging. It is well known that the competences of younger children depend on the situation or context, and do not conform to the constraints imposed by a test or standardized checklist. A continuous monitoring and evaluation within the scope of the kindergarten experience appears to be a more faithful and respectful approach to the children's development and learning. With observation and documentation in the centre of evaluation, the teachers need to know *what* to observe and/or what and *how* to document. In this process, it is crucial to use evaluation systems capable of monitoring the materialization of education principles, identifying the forces and the areas which need differentiated attention and intervention, accompanying the progression/development of competences, and justifying the decision making process concerning the intervention.

The Project: Assessment in Early Childhood Education: Children Follow-up Instrument (CFI)[2]

Reflecting upon these realities of early childhood education in Portugal, both what is expected officially and what is happening in practice, a group of researchers at the Department of Educational Sciences, University of Aveiro, have developed a research project on evaluation and curriculum development in preschool education, involving 13 kindergartens, 24 early childhood teachers and about 40 students in their pedagogical probation training in each school year (from 2007–2008 to 2009–2010). The project focuses on the construction of an instrument to assist pedagogical practice,

---

[2]   Assessment in early childhood education—children follow-up instrument (Project funded by the Portuguese Foundation for Science and Technology—PTDC/ CED/67633/2006), http://www.fct.mctes.pt/projectos/pub/2006/Painel_Result/ vglobal_projecto.asp?idProjecto=67633&idElemConcurso=903.

facilitating the relationship between the practices of documentation, evaluation, and curricular edification. The concrete result of the research will be the Children Follow-up Instrument (CFI) (see Appendix B) and a practical guide to support schools and their early childhood teachers.

Concerning the way children develop and learn, the CFI (1) promotes practices that are guided by humanist and social-constructivist principles, emphasizing developmentally appropriate practices; (2) considers that education occurs in interaction and is a dialogue between children and adults marked by respect, listening, stimulating, scaffolding, and giving autonomy to the learner (permitting action at the ZPD) and (3) assumes that children are competent and full citizens but need the support of adults.

Inspired by Laevers et al. (1997), this instrument is structured around the principle that evaluation should be process-based and should allow the development of practices that are oriented not only to the future benefits or results, but also to the actual participation of children, their levels of involvement and their well-being.

"Responding well" to children was one of the defining goals of our CFI project. Responding well implies considering the living circumstances that characterize children's lives, and recognizing the cultures and sub-cultures of community and family life. This perspective demands attention and acceptance of diversity, as well as curriculum individualization—a "child-centred" perspective. Accomplishing this goal requires constant questioning of practices, critical thinking, and open minds.

According to an experiential approach, the most economic and conclusive way to assess the quality of any educational setting is to focus on two dimensions: (1) emotional well-being and (2) the level of involvement experienced by children (Laevers 2003). The experiential model is a framework that offers a respectful way of feeling, thinking and doing in early childhood education—a "child-centred" way, in which the adult begins, as point of reference, with the child's experience, reconstructing meanings through his/her expressions, words, and gestures. Interventions are based on encouraging a child's initiative (autonomy), creating an enriched environment (stimulation), and developing an experiential dialogue (sensitivity). Promoting the well-being and involvement of the child leads to the ultimate goal of enhancing the child's development and emancipation.

As Laevers writes (2003), "when we want to know how each of the children is doing in a setting, we first have to explore the degree in which children do feel at ease, act spontaneously, show vitality and self-confidence. All this indicates that their emotional well-being is okay and that their physical needs, the need for tenderness and affection, the need for safety and clarity, the need for social recognition, the need to feel competent, and the need for meaning in life and moral value are satisfied. The second criterion is linked to the developmental process and urges the adult to set up a challenging environment favouring involvement." Applying this perspective tells us that children start having problems when the educational setting does not succeed in tuning in to their specific needs. Raising the levels of well-being and involvement become reference points for practitioners who want to improve the quality of their work, who want to improve learning and development.

Laevers (1994) introduced the LIS-YC (Leuven Involvement Scale for Young Children) as the result of efforts to operationalize the concept of involvement, helping teachers observe and assess involvement on a five-point scale. "At level one, there's no activity. The child is mentally absent. If we can see some action it is a purely stereotypic repetition of very elementary movements. Level two doesn't go further than actions with many interruptions. At level three, we can without a doubt label the child's behaviour as an activity. The child is doing something...but we miss concentration, motivation, and pleasure in the activity. In many cases the child is functioning at a routine level. In level four moments of intense mental activity occur. At level five there is total involvement expressed by concentration and absolute implication. Any disturbance or interruption would be experienced as a frustrating rupture of a smoothly running activity" (Laevers 2003, 16).

And Vygotsky's ideas? We assume a very narrow relationship between high involvement and the Zone of Proximal Development. For the child's progress, the relationship between the level of preparation and child's development and the level of demands made by the school is essential (Vygotsky 1933, in van der Veer and Valsiner 1991). For Vygotsky, teachers should collaborate with the children in joint cognitive activities which should be selected in order to adapt to the child's potential level of development. Teaching is only considered good when it is one step ahead of development and awakens those functions which are in the process of becoming mature or in the ZPD (Vygotsky 1956, quoted by Wertsch and Stone 1985). In Bruner's approach, the teacher's task consists of "scaffolding"—reducing the number of steps of freedom which the child has to deal with when carrying out the task (Bruner, 1985). After the child masters the basic aspects of the task, the teacher encourages the child to use those competences in order to develop towards something more complex. This principle, which consists of gradually increasing the level of demand, is what maintains the child in the ZPD ("region of sensitivity to learning"). In this way, the more efficient teachers focus their activity in the region of sensitivity, keeping the level of the child's involvement high. If being involved means moving within the limits of our abilities, even if we do not exactly know what those limits are, it is possible to infer, by the child's level of involvement, if they are making use of their current and potential talents, or not.

Ultimately, we understand, like Vygotsky, that professionals who limit themselves to addressing the child's real level of development are making the same mistake as a farmer who, when calculating the crop of a season, only takes into account the fruit that is ripe. When researching what the child can do alone, the teacher takes into account the development of the previous day. By focusing on what the child can do in interaction with a stimulating physical and relational context, the teacher addresses tomorrow's development. In this way, Vygotsky's evaluative approach includes the determining of the real and potential level of development, as well as the quality of the interactions which are going to allow the level of potential to become a reality. The children follow-up instrument (CFI) adopts these perspectives, considering that the orientation towards emotional well-being and involvement responds well to the essential question: to what extent, in this precise context, does the child develop?

Laevers also presented a scale for the assessment of emotional well-being, which indicates to what degree the educational environment succeeds in helping children to feel at home, to be themselves, and to have their emotional needs (confidence, attention, recognition, and sense of competence) fulfilled (Laevers et. al. 2005). Both involvement and emotional well-being scales are adopted in the CFI.

In the process of observation and documentation it is crucial to use benchmarks which are capable of identifying both the forces and fragilities which need priority attention and intervention, as well as the children's opinions regarding the "things which concern them." Allowing the monitoring of the subsequent progress (immediately addressing the processes of emotional involvement and well-being experienced by the children) and the decision making process concerning the intervention are also crucial.

Laevers, et al. (1997) describes a group of initiatives that may favour well-being and involvement, including action points such as: (a) the organization of the space and the offering of interesting materials and activities; (b) careful observation by the teacher of how children interact with all that they encounter in their environment, in order to identify interests that can be met by more targeted activities; (c) the way an adult supports the on-going activities with stimulating interventions and gives room to an open form of organization that stimulates children to take initiative; (d) the way an adult addresses the field of social relations, investing in a positive group climate and the exploration of behaviours, feelings, thoughts, and values; and (e) attention to children needing special support because they do not reach the levels of well-being and involvement teachers strive for—that is, children with behavioural, emotional or developmental problems.

In parallel, by using the CFI, early childhood teachers are stimulated to think about factors contributing to well-being and involvement: quality and diversity of the educational offerings, interactions, materials, activities, challenges, group climate, and room for initiative. They also can adjust the intention of their intervention considering the development of the competences of the group and of particular children. In CFI, competences development analysis, inspired in Laevers and Bertrands (2006), is focused on attitudes—well-being and self-esteem, self-organization and initiative, group behaviour, and social competence, and basic acquisitions—fine and gross motor skills, art, language, logical, conceptual, and mathematical thinking, and understanding of the physical and social world. Curiosity and the will to learn (exploratory drive), creativity, and a feeling of being linked to the world are considered to be implicit and transversal to all the other competence areas.

The observation and reflection cycles inherent to the CFI encompass different phases or moments: (1) general observation and evaluation of the entire group of children, which involves considering children's levels of emotional involvement and well-being, and immediately identifying the children who generate greater concern due to their low levels of emotional involvement or well-being (at the risk of developmental stagnation, real development coinciding with potential development); (2) analysis and reflection about general observation and evaluation, working on under-standing the relationship between levels of involvement and well-being and the organization of the educational environment, and (3) defining objectives and initiatives for the group in general and for some children in particular (namely those who reveal lower levels of involvement and well-being or who generate questions or concern), according to the previous analyses.

The use of the CFI in this way allows for the activation of a continuous cycle of observation, evaluation, reflection, and action. These actions focus on the children's well-being, involvement, learning, and development, integrating the conception and development of strategies of intervention and the organization of the educational environment in a way which best adapts to the group's characteristics.

Conclusion

The project described as "Assessment in early childhood education—Children Follow-up Instrument" has aimed at furnishing teachers with knowledge about observation, documentation, and evaluation procedures, as well as their effects. After two years of implementation in the field, we can say that the correct use of CFI allows early childhood teachers to have a clear understanding of the way the group functions, considering levels of involvement and well-being; the aspects which require specific interventions, considering educational offerings, group climate, room for initiative, school organization, and adult style; the identification of children who need differentiated attention; the drawing of a trajectory of initiatives that can lead to the solving of problems and to the maximization of educational quality, both towards the group and the individual child; the evaluation of results (development of competences), and the development of the preschool curriculum.

Once developed, the continuous cycle of observation-assessment and actions inherent to CFI, which are the capacities of empathy and of adopting the child's perspective, are reinforced, as is the capacity to reflect and to question the existence of certain habits and routines. This allows the early childhood teacher to feel more inspiration and orientation to try out different approaches and to innovate. If well-being and involvement increase, the teachers knows they are on the right track, and they know they are promoting and developing greater self-confidence, nourishing curiosity and the exploratory drive, and developing competences.

What we have observed in the context of supervision of several pedagogical practices based on CFI supports the idea that its use seems to provide greater consistency, continuity, and coherence in curriculum development, from principles to educational objectives. In addition, the use of CFI sustains professional development in conception and organization of the educational setting; observation, planning, and assessment; relationships and educational intervention; curriculum development; and team work, reflection, and research capacities.

We also have seen evidence that child development, in this context, is intrinsically related with the quality of the educational interaction. The actual level of a child's development is irrelevant if teacher does not unveil the child's potential level of development (in part read by involvement levels), which can be activated in interactions with and through the support of a more capable partner (such as another adult or child).

Naturally, we do not consider the CFI to be an instrument capable of *per se* answering all the challenges of childhood education. However, we believe that it may constitute a possible path for carrying out pedagogical practice which is more respectful and aware of each child's experiences and development within kindergarten. From our experience, we have concluded that the appropriate use of the CFI allows curricular development to be monitored and to reflect "about what each child carries within them" during and at the end of their kindergarten experience.

References

Bennet, J. 2004. Curriculum issues in national policy making, Paris, OECD. Paper presented at Conference at the 14th Annual Conference on Quality in Early Childhood Education, Quality Curricula: the influence of research, policy and praxis. September 1–4, 2004, Malta.

Bruner, J. 1985. Vygotsky: a historical and conceptual perspective. In *Culture, communication and cognition. Vygotskian perspectives*, ed. J. Wertsch, 21–34. Cambridge: Cambridge University Press.

Laevers, F., ed. 1994. *The Leuven involvement scale for young children. Experiential education series,* No. 1. Leuven: Centre for Experiential Education.

———. 2003. Experiential education—Making care and education more effective through well-being and involvement. In *Involvement of children and teacher style, Insights from an international study on experiential education*, ed. F. Laevers and L. Heylen, 13–24. Leuven: University Press.

Laevers, F. et al. 2005. *Observation of well-being and involvement in babies and toddlers.* [A video-training pack. Research Center for Experiential Education—Leuven University] Leuven: CEGO Publishers.

Laevers, F. and E. Bertrands. 2006. *Draft document: basic ideas, principles and process followed during the curriculum development.* Leuven: Research Centre for Experiential Education, Leuven University.

Laevers, F., E. Vandenbussche, M. Kog, and L. Depondt. 1997. *A process-oriented child monitoring system for young children. Experiential Education Series,* No. 2. Leuven: Centre for Experiential Education.

Ministério da Educação, ed. (1997). *Orientações curriculares para a educação pré-Escolar.* Lisboa: Ministry of Education.

Portugal, G. Libório, O., and P. Santos. 2007. Combinando teoria, praxis e reflexão sobre o desenvolvimento de competências na formação de educadores, na Universidade de Aveiro. In *Actas do VIII Congresso da SPCE "Cenários de educação/formação: novos espaços, culturas e saberes*. (org. CD: Ernesto Candeias Martins).

Van der Veer, R. and J. Valsiner. 1991. *Understanding Vygotsky: a quest for synthesis*. Oxford: Blackwell.

Wertsch, J.V. and C.C. Stone. 1985. The concept of internalization in Vygotsky's account of the genesis of higher mental functions. In *Culture, communication and cognition. Vygotskian perspectives,* ed. J. Wertsch, 162–179. Cambridge: Cambridge University Press.

Chapter Nine

Using Scaffolding to Teach Children with Disabilities: Applying Vygotsky's Ideas in Azerbaijan

Ulviya Mikailova and Yulia Karimova

Introduction

Early childhood programs in Western contexts are highly likely to reflect Vygotsky's ideas about how children learn and develop. The literature is rife with recommendations on how to use scaffolding effectively for achieving developmental and educational outcomes.

Even the most superficial survey of Western teacher preparation materials shows a thorough presentation of the theories of Vygotsky, giving Western teachers ample background and opportunity to integrate his ideas on scaffolding and the Zone of Proximal Development (ZPD) into their teaching methods.

The situation is quite different in Azerbaijan. Here, Vygotsky's theories and teaching strategies based on his ideas are completely unknown to Azeri teachers, because neither pre- nor in-service preparation programs include the theories of Vygotsky in their curriculum. We assert that this lack of knowledge is a prime reason for the difficulties Azeri teachers experience in attempting to meet the individual needs of children with disabilities. To fill these gaps, the Center for Innovations in Education, an Azeri non-governmental organization, has created and implemented (and continues to implement) a program of professional development for Azeri teachers and teaching assistants. Through CIE's training and mentoring, teachers and assistants learn and are coached in observing and assessing needs in order to use appropriate scaffolds for each child, teaching them in their ZPD, rather than according to a fixed methodology which is likely to be unsuited to the child's developmental abilities.

Linking with Vygotsky's Theories:
Teaching Children with Disabilities in the International
and National (Azeri) Contexts

Modern Western and contemporary Azeri teaching practices are based on different theories. Western teaching practices are heavily influenced by the theory of social constructivism. The core essence of that theory is that people learn new content and processes through "constructing new knowledge based on what they already know and believe" (Bransford, Brown, and Cocking 2000). In constructivism (Soloway et al.), "the central notion is that understanding and learning are active, constructive, generative processes." Western teaching practices are based on the students' active inquiry, whereas Azeri teaching practices are based on a traditional view of teaching and learning as the passive transmission of knowledge from the teacher to the student.

In developing his concept of social constructivism, Vygotsky emphasized active discovery over passive reception and particularly stressed the role of social interaction—that learning is strongly influenced by social interactions, which take place in meaningful contexts.

In *Mind in Society: Development of Higher Psychological Processes*, Vygotsky describes the ZPD as "the distance between the actual developmental level ... and the level of potential development which the child can attain under adult guidance or in collaboration with more able peers" (Vygotsky 1983). An important key to enhanced development and learning thus is the guidance and support provided by adult modelling and corrective feedback (Byrnes 2001). This is called "scaffolding."

An important aspect of scaffolding instruction is that the scaffolds are temporary. According to Vygotsky, the external scaffolds provided by the educator can be removed because the learner has developed "...more sophisticated cognitive systems, related to fields of learning such as mathematics or language; the system of knowledge itself becomes part of the scaffold or social support for the new learning."

Vygotsky believed that children can be taught any subject effectively through scaffolding techniques applied in the ZPD. "Teachers activate this zone when they teach students concepts that are just above their current skills and knowledge level, which motivates them to excel beyond their current skills level" (Jaramillo 1996, 1).

Implicit in the idea of scaffolding is that the teacher enables learners to participate in complex tasks that they cannot perform adequately without assistance (Reid 1998, 4). The distinguishing feature of scaffolding is the role of dialogue between teacher and student. The purpose of dialogical exchange is to provide the learner with enough guidance and support to accomplish goals that are impossible without assistance (Starr 2000).

Studies have shown that in the absence of guided learning experiences and social interaction, learning and development are hindered (Bransford, Brown, and Cocking 2000).

Overview of Education of Children with Disabilities in Azerbaijan

Throughout the world, children who have special educational needs have traditionally been marginalized within or excluded from mainstream schools. As a result of the 1990 World Conference on Education for All: Meeting Basic Learning Needs, addressing the challenge of exclusion from education has been put on the political agenda in many countries, including Azerbaijan.

The public education systems of the countries of the Commonwealth of Independent States (CIS), including the Republic of Azerbaijan, have undergone significant reforms over the past two decades. Recent studies indicate that there have been some improvements in the access, equality, finance, and governance of education. Still, many of these countries do not fully achieve the Millennium Development Goals and commitments in Education for All. A regional study by the United Nations International Children's Emergency Fund (UNICEF) in 2007 found that "separate education of children with special needs still prevails and wider reforms can encourage exclusion of such children" (UNICEF 2007). Regarding equality in education, the same study reports that "opportunities for children with special needs outside of institutions are limited, and many children with disabilities are not enrolled in schools." The UNICEF study concludes that there is much needed to be done in CIS countries to improve access, equality, governance, and financing of education, including educational arrangements for disabled and otherwise disadvantaged children.

The public education system of the Republic of Azerbaijan is based on the former Soviet education system and offers variety of educational provisions for children with special educational needs. There are different educational provisions such as home education (the school teacher visits the CWD at home and provides education on a specifically designed curriculum), special classrooms within regular schools, and special schools to accommodate the needs of CWD. Including children with disabilities in regular, mainstream classrooms is very new notion and practice in the country, because the system of education is built on the Soviet science of "defectology," which is usually associated with the education of CWD separately from other children. According to Ministry of Education officials, there are sixteen residential schools[1] and seven special day schools under the ministry's administration.[2] Thus, the majority of available government-provided educational provisions facilitate isolation and segregation of CWD from their peers and the society at large. Nonetheless, the Government of Azerbaijan has recently launched initiatives such as the National Program on Development of Inclusive Education (2005–2009) and the National Program on Alternative Care and Deinstitutionalization (2006–2015), which are intended to enable disabled children to receive education together with their non-disabled peers and to have greater access to education across the country. About 200 children with mild and moderate disabilities attend inclusive classrooms which are newly created by the government in collaboration with international and national non-government agencies and piloted in several regions of the country.[3]

A national study by UNICEF in 2009 found that there is a supportive atmosphere among parents and the education community towards inclusive education: more than 96 per cent of surveyed parents and about 95 per cent of surveyed teachers indicated that they support education of disabled children, because it will facilitate better futures for such children (UNICEF 2009). Parents of typically developed children educated in inclusive classrooms with children with disabilities have also expressed support for educational arrangements for children with special needs. The study also revealed that there is *some* support for *inclusive* education among the school community: about 37 per cent of surveyed school directors and the same

---

[1]   3,644 CWD receive education in these institutions, according to official government statistics.

[2]   According to government statistics, there are five additional boarding schools under the administration of other governmental ministries (Ministry of Labor and Social Protection of Population and Ministry of Health), serving 513 CWD. The government policy towards these institutions is not clear, but there are talks of including them in the De-institutionalization Program of the Government of Azerbaijan.

[3]   These classrooms were created under the auspices of *Improving Attitudes, Practices, and Policies*, a pilot project on inclusive education funded by World Vision Azerbaijan and implemented by the Center for Innovations in Education.

percentage of teachers believe that children with disabilities should be enrolled in inclusive classes.

Pilot Project on Inclusive Education: Challenges and Approaches towards Mainstreaming Children with Disabilities

Due to strengthened advocacy efforts of families of children with disabilities, international organizations, and local NGOs during last few years, the public at large and policy makers have started to recognize the need for better care, education, and integration of CWD. The Ministry of Education and The Haydar Aliyev Foundation, a government-supported national foundation, are the major local players, and their interventions have resulted in significant improvements in the field of education of CWD. However, these improvements are limited only to infrastructure and building supplies for physically accessing school facilities, and often ignore issues pertaining to quality of education and availability of services for CWD.

As the previously cited UNICEF study shows, the quality of exclusive home schooling and special education is very poor, and mainstream preschools and schools have little capacity to accommodate CWD in inclusive classrooms. In spite of the variety of educational provisions for CWD, it is important to highlight that these efforts are very often limited to only "giving access," and the quality and outcomes of such educational opportunities are highly questionable, as many of these schools don't have the necessary capacity to teach and educate CWD. Teachers and their assistants (when there are assistants) lack training in methodologies appropriate for individualizing education to meet the needs of children with disabilities.

During observations of the above mentioned study, it was not possible to learn if teachers working in the special and boarding schools were familiar with the child-centred, individualized methods crucial to reaching CWD appropriately and successfully, or if they were provided with opportunities to learn about such methods. Some of the comments from observers follow:

> We observed [the following] approach being used by all teachers with all children in all grade levels, independently of the nature of their learning difficulties and health problems: The same content and same teaching approaches were used for all children.

...We observed teachers using a very limited range of methods to explain new topics and present new concepts. Most of the time, the teacher would talk and ask pupils to repeat what she was saying. Oral questioning was almost the only method to carry on the lesson: asking a concrete question, assuming recollection of the information, and expecting a concrete answer. Oral presentation and questioning was the only method to explain a new topic and reinforce it.

The survey data revealed that the majority of respondents believe that teachers who are directly involved in education of CWD need more intensive training and capacity building. For instance, only 35 per cent of surveyed teachers stated that they have received specialized training in skills specifically related to teaching CWD. Moreover, the overwhelming majority, about 79 per cent of them, expressed the need for additional training. A similarly large majority of surveyed directors—over 85 per cent—expressed the need for additional training for teachers.

International early childhood education experts and consultants have cautioned that the government needs to take serious steps to fill in the gap and allocate necessary resources for professional development and capacity building of teachers and other specialists; otherwise, the Government of Azerbaijan may fail to implement meaningful reforms in the field.[4] In addition, many interviewed teachers stated that there are no teaching methodologies, skills, and strategies available for their perusal, though they are eager to learn them to improve their ability to deliver quality education. Finally, Azerbaijani higher education institutions have limited programs to prepare cadres of new teachers to fill the gaps.

In order to begin addressing these vast needs, the Center for Innovations in Education (CIE) created and implemented the integrated pilot project "Children with Disabilities: Improving Attitudes, Practices and Policies," (2005) with the goal of working toward the development of the professional capacity of educators, which is critical for mainstreaming CWD into general education in regular schools and kindergartens.

---

[4] For instance, about 70% of surveyed teachers acknowledged that it is very or somewhat difficult for them to teach CWD, while only 30% said that they don't have any difficulties. More than a half of the surveyed directors reported having difficulties in teaching disabled children.

The pilot project built on CIE's previous work in building child-centred classrooms as part of the Step by Step (SbS) program.[5] Throughout the project, children with disabilities were mainstreamed into SbS classrooms in regular schools and kindergartens, with CWD making up 10 to 15 per cent of the classroom population. Because the teachers in SbS classrooms had already been trained in child-centred, individualized learning methodologies which included family involvement, their classrooms were considered ideal environments for the inclusion of CWD. These teachers were then provided with intensive trainings on inclusive education, training which included Vygotsky's principles of using temporary scaffolds to help children with disabilities reach their ZPD. On-going assessment and monitoring of teaching practices in these classrooms indicated that training was not enough in itself, and that teachers would need on-going mentoring to help them develop the most appropriate practices to meet the needs of CWD in their classrooms.

So, after initial training, the project developed a three-stage approach for guiding teachers and their assistants—observation of classrooms, needs assessment, and, subsequent mentoring of teachers and TAs.

CIE's Approach to Capacity Building of Practitioners: Observation, Needs Assessment, and Mentorship

After initial training, the professional development process continued with observations of teaching practices in inclusive classrooms. The primary purpose of the systematic observations was to provide project staff and teachers with an on-going examination of the quality of teaching and learning in these classrooms. Another important purpose of the assessment

---

[5]   The Step by Step (SbS) Program began implementation in Azerbaijan in 1998 as a program of the Open Society Institute-Assistance Foundation-Azerbaijan. In 2004, the SbS program staff created their own non-profit, non-governmental organization—Center for Innovations in Education—which continued to implement SbS as its flagship program with continued support from the Open Society Institute and other funders. As a comprehensive education reform program for children birth through age ten, the Step by Step Program introduces child-centered, individualized teaching methodologies and supports community and family involvement in preschools and primary schools.

process was to give insight into the pedagogical approaches taken by teachers in each pilot class, follow the commonalities and differences, if any, and collect the best practices in teaching CWD in Azerbaijan.

Systematic observations and analyses of teaching practices represent an effective tool for improving the teaching in education systems all over the world (Saginor, N. 2008; Fitzpatrick, J., Sanders, J., and Worthen, B. 2004). In Azerbaijan the approach of observing, recording, and analysing classroom practices with the aim of improving teaching was introduced and implemented by the CIE staff as part of the early childhood inclusive education methodology of the SbS program (begun in 2004).

Instrument. Observers used an instrument developed by the project team which served as a guide to gather, discuss, and analyse findings related to inclusive educational provision. Classroom observations were conducted by a team of mentors made up of experienced and motivated teachers and project staff. Initially, staff used a mentoring tool developed by the International Step by Step Association (ISSA 2004), but in 2007, a new observational instrument was developed by the CIE staff members in order to address the complexities of the local school system, which represents a mixture of teacher-centred, curriculum-based, and child-centred classroom practices. The observational instrument was conceptualized as a "diagnostic" tool for the evaluation of classroom instruction, with subsequent analyses of strengths and needs for improvement and mentoring.

The diagnostic assessment tool includes the following areas for observation:

1. *Physical Environment*—Examines the children's working space, class-room organization, equipment, and access to educational facilities and visual aids.

2. *Learning Environment*—Looks at the environment which teachers create to provide opportunities for all children to learn and participate in the learning process, through active engagement in meaningful and collaborative interaction with peers and staff; the issues of acceptance and tolerance are also emphasized. Particular attention is given to motivation and encouragement which teachers provide to help children to take learning risks.

3. *Teaching Methods and Learning Activities*—Examines the methods and activities which teachers plan and implement during the lesson to enhance children's learning. The focus is given to individualization, or the use of differentiated instructional

methods and various accommodations and modifications needed to meet the educational needs of children with disabilities. Are teachers/assistants paying special attention to the abilities and potential for each child in order to ensure that they are able to enter their ZPD? The issue of pupils' assessment is also included into this area.

4. *Social Environment*—Examines the social environment in the classroom and the teachers' abilities to model behaviours which develop the capacity of children to learn and live together, promote and reinforce positive social values, and evaluate children's behaviour. Family involvement is also seen as an important aspect of social environment.

All areas were rated according to three indicators: not observed, rarely observed, and consistently observed. Observers provided comments elaborating their observations on each indicator, recognizing the teachers' need to have evidence of what was happening in their classrooms, and creating a basis for subsequent discussion and mentorship.

Observations and Mentoring. In order to respond to teachers' concrete needs and provide methodological assistance, mentors conducted six to eight hours of diagnostic non-participant observations with the aim of recording the evidence of teacher's and pupils' behaviour and identifying areas for improvement. Teachers were given the instrument at least two weeks prior to the mentors' visit in order to familiarize themselves with the assessment criteria. Before entering the classroom, mentors talked to teachers and TAs to learn their views on what kind of difficulties they experience in teaching CWD. After classroom observations and data analyses, a conference with the teacher and TA was conducted in order to put together the puzzle of the classroom picture and to make recommendations.

Figure 9-1 shows the scheme of the mentoring process provided by the CIE project staff.

Figure 9-1

Scheme of mentoring process

Pre-lesson Interview → Classroom Observation →
→ Post-lesson Interview → Data analyses → Mentor-teacher meeting

What Do Observations Show? The most common and significant concern which teachers and TAs emphasize prior to observation, is that it is too difficult for them to engage CWD in class activities, because their pace does not fit into the pace of the rest of the class. In many classes, CWD rely exclusively on TAs and are rarely involved in formal classroom activities. Observations show that when teachers employ child-centred methods and strategies and try to give an informal start to lessons, for example, with a request to the class to reflect on personal matters, CWD are interested and involved in this informal type of interaction. They participate in discussions of family news or interesting events which happened recently. Much of the positive informal interactions of CWD and their mainstream peers can be observed during such informal reflections.

However, not all teachers were able to keep this pace and continue informal regulation of the classroom. Many times teachers were observed as becoming stricter or more structured after the first five to six minutes, switching to a more traditional lesson. In classes where teachers tried to give a different, non-traditional start to the learning process, they would often end up asking oral questions and concentrating on the information the pupils could recall or reproduce, rather than focusing on giving more freedom and facilitating independent learning. Whenever teachers switched to a more traditionally formatted lesson, (*brief oral check of previously learned material, oral presentation of new material with minor writing on the blackboard, assigning activities for individual or group work to reinforce learning, or assigning homework),* CWD became less involved with the class and started a separate learning process with the TAs.

Happily, there were teachers observed making good steps toward more consistent implementation of child-centred approaches. They facilitated learning through informal conversation between children by giving prompts, asking graduated questions, restating questions when needed, modelling thinking processes, and helping children to give answers using their own words and self-made expressions.

Another positive aspect observed was the positive working relationships built between the teacher, TA, and CWD. Whenever the teacher and TAs worked together as a team and emphasized the importance of a positive and comfortable atmosphere for learning, the CWD acquired new skills, became fully engaged with the class, and learned positive behaviours through interaction with peers.

The individual cases that follow below show some of the best practices implemented in pilot classrooms under the supervision and guidance of CIE mentors. These cases illustrate how CWD can be engaged with their class and how they make progress through guided learning experiences and adult support.

Individual Cases:
Using Scaffolding to Teach Children with Disabilities

Nihad's Story

Nihad, 12-year-old boy, fifth grade, school No. 246, Binagadi District, Baku (Gulnar, Teacher; Sakina, TA)

Nihad was diagnosed with autism. Before coming to school, he used the services of several rehabilitation centers and was involved in sports such as tennis and volleyball.

Modelling Desired Behaviour

Due to local bureaucracy, it took several months for Nihad's parents to negotiate his enrolment in the inclusive education program in one of the mainstream pilot schools in Baku. As a result, Nihad entered first grade after his classmates had already learned basic reading, writing, and math skills and concepts. During his first days of school he was calm and very quiet, and did not show any aggressive behaviour towards his classmates and teachers. His behaviour changed after several days when he started refusing to enter the classroom and stay without his parents. He cried and always tried to run away. The teacher and TA tried to understand the reason for the dramatic change in his behaviour and came to the conclusion that he might have been distressed by understanding that he could not do what his classmates were doing: holding a pen, writing, and reading. Sakina, his TA, urged Nihad to enter the classroom with his mother, watch what his classmates were doing, and try to learn to do the same, but Nihad kept refusing to go into the class and behaved very aggressively.

In order not to further exacerbate the situation, either for Nihad or for the class, the CIE mentor recommended that Sakina, the teaching assistant, take Nihad for a walk outside the school building. She talked to him about something other than his behaviour and their duties. She hoped to gain his trust, because she felt this was an important step toward his inclusion: if he trusted and accepted her, he would eventually accept and trust the whole class. She also hoped, through talking, to gain some insights into Nihad's current likes, dislikes, strengths, abilities, and weaknesses, in order to use this knowledge to help model appropriate behaviours. The knowledge Sakina gained during the walk would be built upon later to help Sakina create appropriate scaffolds to help Nihad enter his ZPD.

Finally, Nihad stopped pushing Sakina away and agreed to listen to and play with her. Then Sakina's goal became to get him into the classroom. For this purpose, understanding that Nihad needed visual reinforcement for verbal instructions, Sakina made and used a series of cards—graphic organizers—where the route to the classroom and Nihad's classroom space were illustrated. She started showing the cards, explaining the meaning of pictures, and continuing to talk about each detail on the cards, because she thought it was important not only to narrate, but also to show what was on the cards, and to illustrate how to follow the instructions given on the cards. She kept doing this until he agreed to come into the class and took his seat. It took several days to explain to Nihad what to do using the graphic cards.

When Sakina successfully got Nihad inside the classroom, she developed another series of cards which addressed other needs and topics: an illustration of how to behave during the break, a picture with a hamburger for when it was time to eat, a picture of house and a woman for when it was time to go home, etc. Sakina also used cards to help Nihad understand concepts such as synonyms and antonyms. In time, Nihad learned to understand the teacher by gestures and mimicry; he did not always need Sakina's *pictures and cards*, but still he needed her to *show* before he could do whatever he was asked to do.

Writing Strategies and Scaffolding

In order to help Nihad learn how to hold a pen and write, Sakina started with writing a letter per day. She always showed an example of what was expected from Nihad. She wrote, pretending that she was doing it for herself, so that Nihad would not think that she was pushing him to do it. Then, she decided to draw out the letter using a pencil, and asked him to draw the letter by pen. Using this method, Nihad learned writing by the end of his first year in school.

Sakina said she never gets tired of Nihad. She said that it is very gratifying to work with him, because he always reciprocates by successfully learning; but it is always at his own pace, and his own time and manner. Through her observations of Nihad's specific learning abilities and needs,

Sakina was able to create scaffolds that helped Nihad enter his Zone of Proximal Development. Clearly, if she had used more traditional Azeri teaching methods, expecting Nihad to learn at the same pace and through the same methods as his mainstream peers, the opportunity for Nihad to learn would have been lost.

Shamkhal's Story

Shamkhal, 9-year-old boy, fourth grade, school No. 153, Yasamal District, Baku (Sevinj, Teacher; Aysel, TA)

Shamkhal was diagnosed as a child with autism and speech impairment. He is two years older than his classmates. He did not attend preschool before entering primary school, and inclusive education was his first formal educational experience. His parents are well-educated and very supportive of Shamkhal's education. They are good partners for his teacher and TA.

Before the school year started, Sevinj (the teacher) and Aysel (the TA) had several meetings with Shamkhal's parents to discuss his habits, behaviour, attitudes, what he likes/dislikes, and what he can do, etc. His mother was concerned about whether or not he could be educated alongside typical children. She said that Shamkhal displayed only two attitudes toward other people: he either accepted them or not. She believed that if he liked Aysel, he would like school, and recommended that Aysel try to build a friendly relationship with her son from the outset. Aysel was lucky—Shamkhal liked her immediately.

Our observations showed that Shamkhal was exceptionally calm and quiet when he came to school. He never attempted to communicate with children and adults and would never make eye contact. He seemed to be indifferent to what happened around him, and never showed any reaction, but sometimes could become unexpectedly angry and aggressive. Aysel told us that she did not believe he would ever communicate with her or react to classroom activities and classmates.

Writing Strategies

With her team of mentors, Aysel developed several scaffolding strategies to teach Shamkhal how to write. Through observations, she noted that he liked playing with modelling clay. She invented an instrument: a big table with big letters on it where Shamkhal could easily place pieces of modelling clay onto the contour of the letters. The first time it was not easy, because Shamkhal could not make pieces that were small enough to fit into the given contours. Aysel noted that his fine motor skills were not developed at all; he could not even hold a pencil. When Shamkhal learned to make small enough pieces and fit them onto the letters, Aysel started writing on paper. She drew pictures of letters in chain lines and asked him to draw out the letters by pen. When he learned to do this, Aysel switched to a dotted line and continued asking him to draw on her writing. She taught Shamkhal writing by holding and leading his hand, first on the big table and then on the paper. Once she realized that Shamkhal had learned writing, she attempted to take her hand away to let him write independently. She started doing this gradually, first by taking his hand for a while, and then by extending the time that she allowed him to do it on his own. Shamkhal has now learned to write and does it quite successfully, but still asks her to hold his hand for a while for support, so she holds her finger on his elbow.

When Shamkhal experienced difficulty controlling the size of his letters, Aysel created another scaffold to meet his need—she created guidelines from paper and attached them to Shamkhal's paper helping him to see and physically feel that his writing must fit into these homemade borders. When Shamkhal was able to consistently fit his writing between the paper borders, Shamkhal decreased their size, and eventually remove the paper borders when his letters reached the size of the lines on the paper.

Reading Strategies

As noted earlier, during his first days of school Shamkhal did not show any interest in the activities of the other children in the class. In reading lessons, children were learning sounds, letters, and syllables. Shamkhal did not respond to requests to repeat after the teacher or answer any of her questions. To help Shamkhal, Aysel first tried to talk to herself out loud, so that he could hear her and repeat if he wanted, but this was unsuccessful. One time, she noticed that Shamkhal was trying to repeat another pupil's gestures and mimic when he was reading words by syllable. Shamkhal was not looking at that pupil but continued to move his lips as if he was also reading. Aysel tried to build on this slight interest, and started to pronounce sounds and letters clearly while making eye contact. She held his hand in order to keep his attention, a technique which had sometimes proven successful in the past. Aysel and the teacher re-arranged tables in the classroom so that Shamkhal could see his classmates faces when they read and could concentrate on the same activity that they were doing. This worked very well, catching his attention and interest, and getting him involved with the rest of class. Step by step, Shamkhal started making sounds and imitating whatever he heard from his classmates. In the beginning, he could make only unclear sounds and croaks, while Aysel held his hand (an important component, without which he would stop paying attention or responding). Aysel was also able to gain Shamkhal's interest when the class was singing together, which Shamkhal found very inspiring. Through imitating other children singing, and with great joy, Shamkhal began to make sounds and progressed greatly with his speech. Slowly, using rewards suited to Shamkhal's interests and passions, Aysel was able to help Shamkhal improve his pronunciation and ability to repeat, and eventually even to read. Now Shamkhal reads short texts in textbooks. While he continues to work on his pronunciation, Shamkhal is very good in learning short poems and reciting them from memory. He is happy when he can recite a poem in front of the class and receive good grades from his teacher. By paying close attention to Shamkhal's interests and learning abilities, Aysel was able to build temporary scaffolds to help him learn to write, speak, and eventually read. Constant cooperation and willingness to step outside usual traditional teaching methods enabled the teacher and Aysel to build trust with Shamkhal, fully engage his interest, and guide him into his ZPD, a feat which seemed impossible during his first days of school.

Scaffolding Strategies Used by Azeri Teachers and TAs

Our brief overview of the theoretical underpinning and practical implications of scaffolding strategies influenced by Vygotsky's theories and used in the different parts of the world gives some framework for analysis of how those strategies were employed by Azeri teachers and TAs in pilot inclusive classrooms. In general, we can observe some common features in the Azeri TAs' approach to scaffolding.

Motivating the Learner by Establishing a Positive Relationship

Analyses of theory and research on the role of motivation in learning indicate that, in general, higher motivation leads to better learning (Lepper and Malone 1987). This complies with Vygotsky's theory of ZPD, because it is hard to imagine a teacher able to help a child enter their ZPD without first establishing a positive relationship. In our observations, teachers began building positive emotional relations with children prior to the implementation of scaffolding strategies. Teachers underlined good relations and trust as key conditions for development of children's motivation to learn and to create the conditions in which children take their own initiative to learn. Teachers also were constantly providing positive feedback at the end of each step of the learning process to keep motivation to learn high and to eliminate frustration and disappointment. The positive relationships and motivation to learn created situations in which learning became a pleasure and joy for both the child and teacher (case of Shamkhal and Aysel).

Assessment, Scaffolding, and Monitoring

An initial, mostly informal, diagnostic assessment of the child took place during the relationship-building phase. The scaffolding strategies presented were developed to teach the child based on his or her specific needs and were constantly adjusted to better direct the child toward learning goals. The decisions to gradually adjust and remove old scaffolds and develop new ones were based on on-going evaluation and monitoring of the child's comprehension and growing abilities.

Modelling as a Strategy for Scaffolding

Modelling, and specifically performance modelling, along with verbal expla-nation, was the main scaffolding strategy used by teachers. In individual cases, teachers modelled an activity (writing, for example), demonstrated examples of good performance, and then assisted and guided the child in practicing each step of the task. The teachers initially demonstrated the entire task, and then simplified it, bringing it into the child's ZPD, where it was a challenge for the child, but not beyond the child's developmental ability. In the cases of Shamkhal and Nihad, the entire task (writing a letter) was performed part by part, starting from simpler components and working towards the entire task with continuously increasing difficulty.

An example of tiered scaffolding was provided in the case of Shamkhal learning how to write letters. Aysel's scaffolds fostered Shamkhal through different stages of writing ability, from emergence (writing letters and single words; understanding that we write in one line, line by line) to early writer status (recognizing words and sentences, understanding mistakes, writing words pronounced by the teacher) (Dorn and Soffos 2001). Shamkhal learned through the modelling provided by Aysel, interactions, verbal communication, and even physical contact with her.

The scaffolding strategies were mainly developed and implemented by adults, rather than children, and this practice closely agrees with Vygotsky's findings that children can only enter the ZPD through interaction with an adult (Lawson 2002). Scaffolding strategies were implemented using external representations developed by TAs such as tables, graphic organizers, visual diagrams, memory cards, etc.

The scaffolding strategies which teachers and TAs designed and used in the classrooms were recommended and implemented with the help of the project staff and mentors, but all hands-on materials and instruments were thought of and developed by the TAs, with some help from parents. Our experience in the provision of mentoring clearly shows that mentoring with a strong grounding in Vygotsky's theories is important to the successful implementation of inclusion of CWD in Azeri general education schools, and it helps to teachers and TAs achieve their professional development capacity. The most successful TAs are now trained to become mentors for other new teachers and TAs. As the cases show, despite the variability in strategies and approaches, it is *interaction* and *constructive dialogue* between an adult and a child that lead to progress and personal development which would not be possible without the professional knowledge and experience provided by project staff and mentors.

Conclusion

Assessment and monitoring of CIE's piloting of inclusion of CWD in mainstream classrooms in Azerbaijan, shows that mentoring teachers and TAs to apply the theories of Vygotsky is an invaluable component of ensuring that such children are not only included, but grow, learn, and achieve educational goals. With reinforcement and prompting from their mentors, teaching assistants and teachers were able to work together to take a step back from traditional Azeri teaching methods. They learned to focus on the individual needs of the child with disabilities in their classroom and to mold a learning environment best suited to the child's needs. By building relationships and observing the child carefully, teaching assistants were able to create scaffolds which helped the CWD enter the ZPD. It is foreseen that replication of this program in more and more classrooms will help Azerbaijan dramatically improve both access to education and social inclusion of CWDs, bringing Azerbaijan closer to reaching the goals of the international community to providing every child, regardless of ability, the right to development and

education, as stated in the UN Convention on the Rights of the Child, as well
as the more recent UN Convention on the Rights of Persons with Disabilities.

References

Bransford, J.D., A.L. Brown, and R.R. Cocking, ed. 2000. *How people learn: brain, mind, experience, and school, expanded edition.* Washington: The National Academies Press.

Byrnes, B. 2001. *Cognitive development and learning in instructional contexts, second edition.* Needham Heights: Allyn and Bacon.

Dorn, Linda J. and C. Soffos. 2001. *Scaffolding young writers: A writers' workshop approach.* Portland, Maine: Stenhouse Publishing.

Fitzpatrick, J., J. Sanders, and B. Worthen. 2004. *Program evaluation: alternative approaches and practical guidelines, Third edition.* Boston: Pearson Education, Inc.

ISSA. 2004. *Step by Step mentoring guide for quality improvement: A master teacher trainer handbook.* Budapest: International Step by Step Association.

Jaramillo, J. 1996. Vygotsky's sociocultural theory and contributions to the development of constructivist curricula. *Education* 117: 1.

Lawson, L. 2002. Scaffolding as a teaching strategy. Paper presented at City College, EDUC 0500, November, 2002.

Lepper, M.R. and T.W. Malone. 1987. Intrinsic motivation and instructional effectiveness in computer-based education. In *Aptitude, learning, and instruction III. Cognitive and affective process analysis*, eds. R.E. Snow and M.J. Farr. Hillsdale, NJ: Erlbaum

Reid, D.K. 1998. Scaffolding: A broader view. *Journal of Learning Disabilities*, 31: 4.

Saginor, N. 2008. *Diagnostic classroom observation: moving beyond best practice.* Thousand Oaks: Corwin Press.

Soloway, E. S.L. Jackson, J. Klein, C. Quintana, J. Reed, J. Spitulnik, S.J. Stratford, S. Studer, S. Jul, J. Eng, and N. Scala. *Learning theory in practice: case studies of learner-centered design.* Retrieved November 16, 2002, from http://www.acm.org/sigchi/chi96/proceedings/papers/Soloway/es_txt.htm.

Starr, L. 2000. *Teaching the American revolution: scaffolding to success.* From Education World Curriculum Article Website. http://www.educationworld.com/a_curr/curr218.shtml. [Retrieved November 14, 2002].

UNICEF. 2007. *Education for some more than others?* Geneva: UNICEF Regional Office for Central and Eastern Europe and Commonwealth of Independent States.

————. 2009. *Education of children with disabilities in Azerbaijan: barriers and opportunities.* Baku: UNICEF Azerbaijan Country Office.

Vygotsky, L.S. 1983. *Sobraniye Sochinenii [Collected Works]*, Vol. 5. Moscow: Pedagogika.

CHAPTER TEN

IMPLEMENTING A PLAY-BASED CURRICULUM
IN PRIMARY SCHOOL:
AN ATTEMPT AT SUSTAINABLE INNOVATION

BERT VAN OERS

An Attempt at Sustainable Innovation

School improvement is essentially a complex and contestable matter. It is *complex* because of its multidimensional dynamics and the great number of stakeholders and interests involved. Any proposal for educational improvement is, however, also essentially *contestable*, due to the implied notions of quality. This very nature of educational improvement makes the claims for sustainable school improvement tricky and extremely difficult to address. Nevertheless, in the Netherlands a group of teachers, teacher educators, curriculum developers, and researchers, have been involved for two decades in a joint attempt to innovate primary school education in ways that address this complexity systematically, so that sustainable improvements eventually may turn out (van Oers 2009). This chapter discusses a part of this enterprise.

An important starting point for our collaborative work is the developmental approach to cultural practices, based on the Vygotskian cultural-historical theory of human development.

The innovation project discussed here took place in the Netherlands in a number of schools since the 1980s. In this article I will discuss only a part of this theory-driven innovation project. Initially, the project focused on the early grades of primary school. It was an innovative approach to Dutch early childhood education, as it tried to break away from the traditional form of early years education (4 to 8-year-olds), by raising the standards of the curriculum without, at the same time, importing "direct transmission of cultural abilities" into the early years classrooms.

In the following sections I will briefly explain the developmental theory that underpins this work. The educational concept based on this theory is now called *Developmental Education* (in Dutch: "Ontwikkelingsgericht Onderwijs") and the curriculum strategy for the junior grades of primary school is called *Basic Development* (Basisontwikkeling). This educational concept and its related work plan serve as tools for teachers, which empower them to implement and maintain the curriculum in their everyday teaching practices (van Oers 2003, especially Part II). Furthermore, I will describe in this article how this educational concept was implemented in a primary school, and report on a three year longitudinal study that demonstrates the sustainability of this innovation in a real school practice.

The Promotion of Development in Primary Schools

One of the lessons that educators learned from Vygotsky's theory of development is that educators are responsible to a great extent for the pace and course of development of their children. In their attempts at promoting children's development, a growing number of teachers and educational researchers is trying to implement Vygotsky's idea that "good learning is in advance of pupils' development" (Vygotsky 1978, 89). Good teaching takes place in what Vygotsky defined as the Zone of Proximal Development (ZPD).

In our attempt to use Vygotsky's theory for the innovation of a primary school curriculum, we were forced to develop the notion of the ZPD further in order to use it as a starting point for concrete curriculum development. In our interpretation, we started with Vygotsky's remarks, in different places in his work (among others in 'Thinking and Speech', Vygotsky 1982, 250; see also Vygotsky 1978, 87–88), where he states that the notion of *imitation* constitutes the core of ZPD. In his explanation of this statement Vygotsky added that he doesn't mean to say that directly copying actions of others should be seen as the basis of ZPD. Vygotsky makes it sufficiently clear that, for him, imitation implies getting involved in pre-given (historically developed) activities. He writes (1978, 88): "Using imitation, children are capable of doing much more in collective activity or under the guidance of adults." Hence, it is the *participation in socio-cultural activities* that he refers to as the essence of ZPD.

However, it is not the participation per se that promotes children's development, because there are numerous different ways of legitimate participation, ranging from peripheral forms of participation to participation from a leadership position. Rather, it seems plausible to assume that it must be the kind of interactions evoked (and allowed) within the context of these activities which actually promotes the development of children. The quality of the guidance given to the children, and the inherent meaning of this activity (including its roles, tools and rules) for the children, are expected to be one of the major determining factors in the promotion of development of the children (see, among others, Rogoff 1990, 2003; Daniels 2001).

Play as a Format of Activities

Vygotsky also pointed out that the learning of four to seven-year-old children manifests special characteristics that relate to the stage of development of the children. In his view, these children are related to reality in a playful way; they tend to be predominantly focused on role-play and they learn most easily and meaningfully in the context of play (Vygotsky 1978, 102–103). He dubbed the term "leading activity" (vedujuščaja dejatel'nost') to refer to this characteristic. Later, Elkonin (1972) adopted this same term and further elaborated on this notion by employing it as a basis for a cultural-historical developmental theory.   In his view, role-play is the leading activity for children aged four to seven years old (Smirnova 1997; Karpov 2005).

Following Elkonin's analysis of role play, I have argued elsewhere (van Oers 2003a, 2009), that play is not a special type of activity that should be distinguished from work or learning. Rather, *every* activity can be accomplished in a playful way, when the *format* of this activity adopts the following characteristics:

1. *rule-governed*: the activity follows explicitly or implicitly specific rules that constitute the nature of the activity, and regulate the use of the tools and the interpersonal relationships;

2. *engaging:* this means that children should be personally involved in the activity; the decision to participate (or end participation) is principally theirs; the format of the activity essentially allows for voluntary decision-making. An outstanding condition for the occurrence of such engaged activity is giving the children permission to follow their personal interests or interpretations;

3. *degrees of freedom:* the activity permits the participants to make personal choices. Every participant is to some extent free in the choice of actions, or in the choice of how to perform an action; this is an existential quality of the play activity, resulting in the condition that uniform and obligatory prescriptions of actions or methods can never be reconciled with play activity.

Hence, every rule-governed activity that allows participants to take part in an engaged and relatively free manner can be characterized as a playful activity. Due to this format, children can playfully make their own versions of cultural activities and can have meaningful access to them. At the same time, this allows adults also to take part in children's play and to introduce new tools, rules, and roles. In the following sections I will describe an outline of a play-based curriculum and how it was implemented in practice, following the above-described conception of play.

Implementing a Play-Based Curriculum

Construction of the Curriculum Strategy

From a Vygotskian perspective, a group of innovators and teacher educators began to develop a curriculum *strategy* in the 1980s for four to seven-year-olds in Dutch primary school (Janssen-Vos 1997). A main starting point for the developers was that education should be sensitive both to the *personal meanings* of the pupils, as well as to the *cultural meanings* that schools as cultural institutions ought to promote in children. Therefore, the standards (official goals) defined by the government were accepted as valuable goals, but the routes toward these goals could never be uniform, but, rather, should be fitted to the interests, attitudes, and abilities of the child. As a consequence, the developers did not want to construct a strict and uniform curriculum document that specifies on a day-to-day basis what should be done in early years classrooms. The goal for the developers was to describe theoretically well-founded ideas and activities that could be used strategically by individual teachers in order to bring all pupils meaningfully to the required aims.

In collaboration with practitioners, a curriculum strategy was developed over the years, in which the basic ideas of teaching young children were described, general guidelines for contents were explained, and several examples of good practice were elaborated. The major idea in these proposals was that teachers in their classrooms should offer young children ample opportunities for learning basic cultural abilities (like literacy abilities, numeracy, social relations, normative behavior, etc.) in the context of a diverse range of role-play activities. When the teacher participates and assists the pupils at those tasks they cannot accomplish independently, these role-play activities instantiate a ZPD for the children. The teacher must be sensitive to the teaching opportunities that emerge in such play (van Oers 1999b; 2003). Likewise, peers can also serve as assistants to each other in order to make the play activity a joint enterprise that promotes learning.

The construction of the teaching strategy was closely connected to a practical implementation of these ideas in classrooms. This work finally resulted in a play-based "curriculum" (called "basisontwikkeling"), which is now being implemented in several primary schools in the Netherlands. However, it soon became obvious that the application of this teaching strategy in early years classrooms required an intensive learning process for the teachers themselves. Therefore, the process of implementation was always set up as a collaborative enterprise of a teacher and a teacher educator, who assisted the teacher in her classroom. Teacher educators who were also committed to the Vygotskian theory established a meaningful support system for teachers who worked with this play-based curriculum. The educators offered in-service assistance, addressing the teachers' problems in their daily work, and collaboratively trying to find solutions that were consistent with the theory involved. The teacher educators basically applied the same theoretical view on learning to their collaboration with teachers as the teachers themselves were supposed to apply to their relationships with their pupils.

It was assumed that the external support system would serve as a teaching scaffold that would be "internalized" in the school in due time. In the innovation process, the school is expected to internalize the support system and to become self-supportive in the permanent optimization of the learning conditions for pupils and teachers.

Outline of the Play-Based Curriculum

Due to the non-standardized character of the curriculum, it is impossible to describe here in comlpete detail the play-based curriculum, with all its variations in the classroom (exemplary descriptions can be found in van Oers 1999a and b; van Oers 2003, part II). One of the key tenets of the curriculum is that activities in this play format are readily accessible to children. When children are playing "post office," "museum," "hospital," "construction builder," etc., they make their own versions of the cultural (adult) life activities, dealing with the associated tools in their own way, sometimes introducing new rules into the play, but also discussing in the group whether these rules are justified, how they should be implied, etc.

Taking the post office as an example, we can describe a good specimen of a playful activity of this play-based curriculum. At first the children constructed the post office together, and as it progressed the children began to accomplish some of the activities that they thought were associated with a post office: they sat behind a window, pretended to perform some important work with telephones, calculators, and letters, etc. They imagined that the post office needed all kinds of stuff like stamps, letters, checks, and credit cards, etc. Sometimes, they brought these props in from their homes, but most of the time the children started producing these things themselves. They often wanted them to look real. The children often asked for help from the teacher: "How do I write 'five' on this stamp?" "How do I write 'hundred' on this check?" At these moments the teacher herself could decide to give help or to suggest that the child seek help from a more knowledgeable peer. Engaged in this activity, the children had to accomplish many actions that required cultural abilities like reading, writing, communicating, and calcu-lating. These moments were used by the teacher as opportunities to help children in the performance of these actions. Such assisted performances were the basis of the children's cultural learning. By participating in the play, the teacher could also introduce special requests. In the post office, for example, the teacher could ask: "Don't you need a time table that says when the office is open?" Or: "Don't we need letters that can be distributed by the mailman?" "Who wants to write a letter?" Addressing a particular child (grade three), the teacher suggested: "Why don't we write a letter to your friend in grade four? Would you like to do that?" The child accepted the idea, and the teacher continued: "What do you want to write to your friend? Can you do it? When it is finished, we can bring your letter to the post office and ask the mailman to bring it to your friend's class." Then some children started writing letters, addressing envelopes, making (or buying) stamps, etc. When there were a significant number of letters produced, there was always a pupil who volunteered to be the mailman.

In this way the role-play of "post office" evolved. New actions emerged from the activity, including those that required the cultural abilities of writing, reading, calculating with money, etc. When the children encoun-tered actions that they could not do on their own, they got help from the teacher or from a more knowledgeable pupil. By definition, this help was relevant to the children's needs, and the learning of these actions most of the time resulted in meaningful learning. So the children gradually learned the abilities of reading, writing, calculation, social abilities, etc. (For a description of the evolution of another activity, see van Oers 1998a.)

From grades one through four, pupils are engaged in these kinds of role-play activities, including–of course–not only the post office, but all kinds of other activities as well. Often a number of role-play activities occur in parallel in one classroom. Sometimes these role-plays are suggested by the children, sometimes by the teacher. It is obvious that these activities follow particular rules that are closely linked to the interests of the children (so they lead to engaging activities). Obviously, the children enjoy some degree of freedom in the performance of their actions, as well as in the construction of a personalized version of the cultural activity.

Implementing the Program in a School Context

It probably doesn't come as a surprise that this curriculum strategy is not an easy way of teaching a classroom of young children. The average number of children in a Dutch classroom is about 25, and all of them deserve the right to learn the cultural abilities in their own way, by practicing different words or calculations related to meaningful play activities. Of course, in these contexts, the teacher can steer the activity to a certain degree and suggest particular actions in order to achieve certain cultural aims. The teacher constantly has to invent new appropriate activities for all pupils and accordingly get them involved in new culturally relevant activities and actions that call for appropriating the use of new cultural tools (like writing, counting, reading, etc).

In order to master this form of "developmental teaching," the teachers in our experimental schools get intensive help, feedback, and supervision for a long time from a teacher educator (for an extensive treatment of the procedure see van Oers et al. 2003). After basic acquaintance with the general idea of the theoretical background of the program, teachers are engaged in a discussion about their own classroom practices, and are invited to articulate what they find problematic. The teacher educator assists the teachers with the analysis of these problems and encourages discussions about these problems and their possible solutions with the team. At this stage of the teachers' education, it is important to start from the teachers' own practices, help them to reflect on this practice, and recognize the problems and potentials of developmental teaching. When a provisional solution is found (i.e. a solution that is accepted by both the teacher and the teacher educator), the teacher transfers this into her classroom and tries to implement that solution for weeks or months. During that period, the teacher educator also visits the teacher in her classroom and observes her working with the children.

Sometimes video footage is made that can be discussed with the teacher afterwards. The main objective for this initial stage of teacher development is recognizing the moments of developmental teaching and recognizing the value of the approach for solving the teachers' problems.

In the next stage, the teachers implement more elements of developmental teaching in their classroom practices. In particular, they adopt the observational strategy that underpins the planning and evaluation of the developmental courses of the children. The same strategy is followed as the one described above, with a major focus on the use of the observation strategy. Observing children and registering their progress is guided by an observation manual, called "HOREB," which gives an overview of observation points related to general development and progress in the subject matter areas, reading, writing, and numeracy. In relation to these observations the teacher must learn to make decisions about appropriate follow-up for the individual pupils. Although the conjectured developmental courses are basically individual, it is still possible (and often necessary) to encourage pupils to work together in (heterogeneous) groups.

Finally, teachers learn step-by-step to implement this play-based curriculum on their own, although teachers in a team mostly continue to help each other long after the initial training process is finished. When the team takes over the role of the teacher educator, by collaboratively reflecting on the curriculum, one can say that the external support system, initially embodied in the teacher educator, is internalized in the school.

The Play-Based Curriculum: A Sustainable Innovation?

Sustainable school innovation is assumed to be a process of permanent improvement of teaching practices and conditions. The sustainability of an innovation is dependent on different conditions, which partly have to do with the acceptability of the innovation for external stake-holders like parents and the government. In the discussion with external stake holders, but also for the maintenance of a positive attitude in the teachers, the achievements (learning outcomes) of the program are often a major argument. On the other hand, the sustainability of an innovation also depends on the level of self-dependence a school can maintain with regard to the ongoing innovation and the constant improvement of the learning conditions for pupils and teachers.

In the following passage, I will discuss some learning outcomes both at the school (team) level and at the level of learning outcomes in the pupils. Both should be seen as necessary arguments for a stable implementation of the play-based curriculum.

Brief Review of Some Learning Outcomes of a Play-Based Curriculum

The development and implementation of the play-based curriculum described above has been assessed from different perspectives: evaluations have been made by teachers themselves on the basis of their daily classroom observations, by innovators/teacher educators, researchers committed to the Vygotskian paradigm, and researchers from a more distanced point of view (Harskamp and Suhre 2000; Suhre 2003; Edelebos 2003).

From the beginning, the development and implementation were monitored by the innovators and teacher educators. They stimulated the teachers to appropriate a specially developed monitoring strategy for their daily observations of the pupils in role-play activities (for details, see van Oers et al. 2003). The outcomes of these observations were mainly used for planning purposes, but these data also reflect parts of the personal developments of the pupils in the different subject domains. An evaluative study (van Oers 1999a) demonstrated that the teachers' daily observations with regard to literacy development with the help of this observation strategy (HOREB) turned out to be as reliable as a standardized test for emergent literacy. The teachers, in general, performed as well as the standardized tests at identifying pupils that could be considered "at risk" and pupils that could be considered "advanced." Hence, there was no reason to administer those standardized tests in addition to the teachers' (trained) observations, as both produce the same kind of information.

Over the years, several positive evaluation studies have been conducted with regard to learning outcomes in pupils related to literacy and mathematics in the early grades. Many of these outcomes have been summarized in previous publications (van Oers, 1999a, 2002, 2003b; 2007, 2009, 2010; Poland, 2007a and b). There is no space to repeat the outcomes of these studies here in detail. A general conclusion, however, is warranted, saying that the play-based curriculum as implemented in our Developmental Education approach in the early grades is a reliable learning context for young children to appropriate cultural abilities in the areas of mathematical thinking and literacy (reading and writing).

Internalization of the Support System

One of the main conditions for the maintenance of innovation is the extent of integration of the external support system (scaffolds in the form of in-service teacher educators) for the ordinary habits and professionalism of the school. In a longitudinal study of a target group (two teachers) that we followed for three years, we could study this aspect of the innovation process. The two teachers in this target group were both experienced with regard to the developmental education concept. They had received guidance from teacher educators for several years on the appropriation and application of this concept in their classrooms. When I started this research the teachers in the target class were no longer involved in an intensive in-service program, although the teacher educator still visited the school on a regular basis (about every three months) for evaluation of progress, for consultancy reasons (if needed), or for support of new teachers that were at the beginning stage of the appropriation of the education concept. In general, we can say that the school could be expected to arrange to an increasing extent its own course of development.

As the main indicator of the internalization of the developmental education concept in the school, we took the maintenance of the observation system HOREB. This was quite an intensive and time consuming procedure because it required the teachers to keep diaries of all individual pupils in the class on a daily basis, in order to document these pupils' developmental progress and plan their future activities. Furthermore, the teachers were also expected to write on a regular basis developmental reports about the pupils. For our research the teachers were expected to write these individual reports twice a year (even three times in the first year). These diaries and reports were taken as core elements of the developmental teaching, because they are seen as essential tools for setting up teaching arrangements that are sensitive to the pupils' topical interests, attitudes, and abilities. Losing this habit would be an indication of the loss of the developmental education concept in the system.

Given that the target group had 34 pupils, who were described twice a year, we can calculate that the teachers in the target group had to write 68 developmental reports a year (102 in the first year), addressing both numeracy and literacy development. Each report was about one or one and a half pages. Since we also needed a group to compare to the target group, we also asked the teachers from the two proximal grades to hand over the developmental reports about their pupils (when the target group was in grade two, we also collected reports from grade three and four of that year;

when the target group was in grade three we asked for reports from grades two and four; when the target group was in grade four, we asked for reports from grades two and three). So, in total, the school produced over three years more than 200 developmental reports about their pupils, despite the fact that it is time-consuming and painstaking work. Most of the time, the teachers sent in their work on time and without solicitation. We take this as evidence of the teachers' commitment to the school's professional culture. The project was finished in the year 2000; currently, the school is still applying this observational strategy. Combined with team meetings, conferences, and publication of their practices as paradigms for other schools, we may say that this school has really internalized the support system for the maintenance and development of the developmental education concept as a practical strategy. Moreover, the school started to be a supporter of innovations at other schools as well.

The teachers of the lower grades of primary school (grades one through four; ages four to eight) continued applying a play-based curriculum, and embedding their teaching in activities that make sense for the children. That allows them substantial degrees of freedom with regard to their actions, content, and tools. In the context of these activities, the teachers successfully teach the children literacy and numeracy knowledge and abilities (see, for example, van Oers 2007, 2010).

Conclusion and Discussion

Starting out from Vygotsky's and Elkonin's notion of leading activity, it was argued here that role play is actually a format for the developmentally appropriate activities for children from four to eight years old. On the basis of a theoretical analysis of play, we listed a set of characteristics that defined play as a particularly formatted activity. The implementation of these characteristics in a curriculum for the early grades of primary school leads to an *institutionalization of play* in that school in the form of a play-based curriculum.

For an innovation to become sustainable, at least two important conditions have to be achieved. First, the innovation must produce stable, high learning outcomes, both for maintaining teacher motivation and for convincing external stake holders (like parents and policy makers). Several evaluation studies carried out by engaged researchers and independent researchers have confirmed the claim that pupils can achieve good learning results in a play-based curriculum, as intended in the context of developmental education. Secondly, the teachers involved must appropriate the theoretical ideas and tools of the innovation for independent and creative application in their everyday classroom practices. Careful guidance of the teachers in appropriating the abilities of working in a play-based curriculum is thus an essential precondition for the sustained institutionalization of play as a learning context in school.

The project reported here produced evidence that the interaction between teacher educator, teacher, and pupils indeed can yield meaningful and sustainable innovations in school and valuable learning outcomes. It was clear from our research that consistent teaching in the context of a play-based curriculum might change the relative weight of (traditional) indicators of development, but it is also plausible that the implementation of a play-based curriculum can produce learning outcomes in both pupils and teachers that eventually lead to a sustainable strategy for the promotion of development in pupils and teachers.

References

Daniels, H. 2001. *Vygotsky and Pedagogy.* London: RoutledgeFalmer.

Edelebos, P. 2003. *Realisatie en effecten van ontwikkelingsgericht onderwijs. Het stimuleren van probleemoplossende vaardigheden* [Realization and effects of developmental education. Promoting problem solving abilities]. Groningen: RION.

Elkonin, D.B. 1972. Toward the problem of stages in the mental development of the child. *Soviet Psychology*, vol. 10, 225–251.

Harskamp, E. and C. Suhre. 2000. *Praktijkbrochure ontwikkelingsgericht lezen* [Brochure for reading Practices in developmental education]. Groningen: RION.

Janssen-Vos, F. 1997. *Basisontwikkeling* [Basic development]. Assen: van Gorcum.

Karpov, Y.V. 2005. *The neo-Vygotskian approach to child development.* New York: Cambridge University Press.

van Oers, B. 1996. Are you sure? The promotion of mathematical thinking in the play activities of young children." *European Early Childhood Education Research Journal*, 1996, vol. 4, no. 1, 71–89.

———. 1997. The narrative nature of young children's iconic representations: Some evidence and implications. *International Journal of Early Years Education.* 1997, vol. 5, no. 3, 237–246.

————. 1998. The fallacy of decontextualization. *Mind, Culture, and Activity*, vol. 5, no. 2, 135–142.

————. 1999a. Quality of diagnostic teaching abilities in early education." *European Early Childhood Education Research Journal*, vol. 7, no. 2, 39–51.

————. 1999b. Teaching opportunities in play. In *Learning activity and development*, ed. M. Hedegaard and J. Lompscher, pp. 268–289. Aarhus: University Press.

————. 2002. Teachers' epistemology and the monitoring of mathematical thinking in early years classrooms. *European Early Childhood Education Research Journal,* vol. 10, no. 2, 19–30.

————. (ed.) 2003a. *Narratives of childhood. Theoretical and practical explorations for the innovation of early childhood education.* Amsterdam: VU press.

————. 2003b. Learning resources in the context of play. Promoting effective learning in early childhood." *European Early Childhood Education Journal*, vol. 11, no. 1, 7 –26.

————. 2007. Helping young children to become literate: The relevance of narrative competence for developmental education. *European Early Childhood Education Research Journal,* vol. 15, no. 3, 299–312.

————. 2009. Developmental education: Improving participation in cultural practices. In *Childhood studies and the impact of globalization: Policies and practices at global and local levels—World Yearbook of Education 2009,* ed. M. Fleer, M. Hedegaard, and J. Tudge, pp. 293–317. New York: Routledge.

————. 2010. Children's Enculturation Through Play. In *Challenging play: Post developmental perspectives on play and pedagogy,* ed. L. Brooker and S. Edwards. Maidenhead: McGraw Hill .

van Oers, B., F. Janssen-Vos, B. Pompert, and T. Schiferli. 2003. "Teaching as a joint activity. In *Narratives of childhood. Theoretical and practical explorations for the innovation of early childhood education,* ed. B. Van Oers, pp. 110–126. Amsterdam: VU press.

van Oers, B., W. Wardekker, E. Elbers, and R. van der Veer (eds.) 2008. *The transformation of learning. Advances in cultural-historical activity theory.* Cambridge: Cambridge University Press.

Poland, M. 2007a. Bergopwaarts in taalontwikkeling [Reaching higher in language development]. *De wereld van het jonge kind*, vol. 35, no. 3, 79–84.

————. 2007b. *The treasures of schematising. The effects of schematising in early childhood on the learning processes and outcomes in later mathematical understanding.* (Dissertation). Enschede: Ipskamp.

Rogoff, B. 1990. *Apprenticeship in thinking.* New York: Oxford University Press.

——. 2003. *The cultural nature of human development.* New York: Oxford University Press.

Smirnova, E.O. 1997. *Psichologija rebënka* [Child psychology]. Moscow, Russia: Škola Press.

Suhre, C. 2002. Functioneel lezen en schrijven in de groepen 3 en 4. [Functional reading and writing in grades 3 and 4]. Groningen: RION.

Vygotsky, L.S. 1978. *Mind in society.* Cambridge, Mass.: Harvard University Press.

——. 1982. *Myšlenie i reč* [Thinking and Speech]. Moscow: Pedagogika.

Part IV

Regional and Global Implications

CHAPTER ELEVEN

MAKE-BELIEVE PLAY VS. ACADEMIC SKILLS: A VYGOTSKIAN APPROACH TO TODAY'S DILEMMA OF EARLY CHILDHOOD EDUCATION

ELENA BODROVA

Today, educators in countries across the globe face the same pressure to start teaching academic skills at a progressively younger age, at the expense of traditional early childhood activities: in Russia, it leads to preschools being transformed into "miniature schools" (Kravtsova 2005) while in the United States, kindergartens as we know them seem to be disappearing, giving way to classrooms focused on test preparation and devoid of play (Miller and Almon 2009). This increased emphasis on teaching academic skills to the little ones is largely caused by concerns about children not being ready for school as well as concerns about children falling behind in their later academic learning (Zigler, et al. 2006). However, an examination of the effects of academically-oriented preschool programs reveals that they do not necessarily guarantee future academic success, especially in the long term, and that they may even exacerbate children's problems in social and emotional areas (Miller and Almon 2009). At the same time, the only alternative to academically-oriented classroom is often expressed as the idea of a classroom where the teacher's role is relegated to "following the child's lead." For too many children this alternative does not seem to be a viable one (Whitehurst 2001).

The Vygotskian approach provides a new answer to this dilemma: intentional instruction in preschool and kindergarten can and should foster the prerequisites for the academic skills but it should do it by promoting foundational competencies that are "uniquely preschool" and promoting them through play. Alexander Zaporozhets, one of the closest colleagues and students of Lev Vygotsky and a life-long advocate for high quality preschool programs describes this approach as "amplification of development" which focuses on the expansion and enrichment of the content of appropriate activities, thus presenting an alternative to the artificial "acceleration of development," which forces preschool children into inappropriate activities:

> Optimal educational opportunities for a young child to reach his or her potential and to develop in a harmonious fashion are not created by accelerated ultra-early instruction aimed at shortening the childhood period—that would prematurely turn a toddler into a preschooler and a preschooler into a first-grader. What is needed is just the opposite—expansion and enrichment of the content in the activities that are uniquely "preschool": from play to painting to interactions with peers and adults
>
> (Zaporozhets 1986, 88)

The Vygotskian approach has both the theoretical framework and practical strategies that may help resolve the dichotomy that seems to exist between the contemporary proponents of "adapting rearing to development" (Vygotsky 1997, 224) and those who believe that the primary mission of preschool should be to support early academic learning. One of the important contributions of the Vygotskian approach is a thorough study of "uniquely preschool" activities in general and make-believe play in particular along with the analysis of the effects of children's engagement in these activities on their learning and development.

Make-Believe Play: The Vygotskian Perspective

One of the major differences in Vygotsky's approach to play compared to the theories of his contemporaries is that in Vygotsky's view, play is more than a reflection of the child's current level of development: most importantly it is a mechanism propelling the child's development forward:

> In play the most important thing is not the satisfaction the child receives through playing, but the objective use and objective meaning of the play, of which, the child himself is unaware. This meaning, as is well known, involves the development and exercise of all the child's powers and latent strengths.
>
> (Vygotsky 2004, 65)

Another distinguishing characteristic of Vygotsky's approach to play is that he did not view play as a "naturalistic", i.e. as an outgrowth of children's instinctive tendencies. Instead, he believed play to be a cultural-historical phenomenon largely dependent on the degree and quality of adult mediation (Karpov 2005). Finally, Vygotsky's approach to play is characterized by its distinct focus on a specific kind of play—namely make-believe or dramatic play of preschoolers and children of primary school age. This narrow definition distinguishes Vygotsky from most educators as well as non-educators who use the term "play" to describe a broad range of activities that "are freely chosen and directed by children and arise from intrinsic motivation." (Miller and Almon 2009, 15)

The Structural Components of Make-Believe Play

Make-believe play, according to Vygotsky, is defined by its three main components, in which children:

- create an imaginary situation,
- take on and act out roles, and
- follow a set of rules determined by specific roles.

While imaginary situations and roles in make-believe play have been often mentioned by other researchers in their analysis of play, the idea that play is not totally spontaneous but is instead contingent on players abiding by a set of rules was first introduced by Vygotsky. At first, the notion of play being the most restrictive context for children's actions seems to contradict the long tradition of defining play by its spontaneity and open-endedness. However, Vygotsky argues that this rule-based nature is an essential characteristic of children's make-believe play:

> Whenever there is an imaginary situation in play, there are rules—not rules that are formulated in advance and change during the course of the game, but rules stemming from the imaginary situation. Therefore, to imagine that a child can behave in an imaginary situation without rules, i.e., as he behaves in a real situation, is simply impossible. If the child is playing the role of a mother, then she has rules of maternal behaviour. The role the child plays, and her relationship to the object if the object has changed its meaning, will always stem from the rules, i.e., the imaginary situation will always contain rules. In play the child is free. But this is an illusory freedom.
>
> (Vygotsky 1967, 10)

Make-Believe Play as a Source of Development

Vygotsky assigned play a special place in his theory listing it specifically as one of the social contexts responsible for creating young children's Zone of Proximal Development (ZPD):

> In play the child is always behaving beyond his age, above his usual everyday behaviour; in play he is, as it were, a head above himself. Play contains in a concentrated form, as in the focus of a magnifying glass, all developmental tendencies; it is as if the child tries to jump above his usual level. The relationship of play to development should be compared to the relationship between instruction and development... Play is a source of development and creates the zone of proximal development.
>
> (Vygotsky 1978, 74)

Vygotsky defined other sources and mechanisms involved in creating children's ZPD relatively vaguely in his other writings. His statement on play as a source of ZPD was specific enough to lead to a series of experimental studies, which proved that young children's performance in play context was indeed "a head above" their performance in non-play contexts. For example, Manuilenko (1975) found children exhibiting higher levels of self-regulation of their physical behaviours in play compared to non-play contexts. For example, when a boy was asked to be the lookout, he remained at his post and did not move for a longer period of time than he could when the experimenter asked him to stand still in a laboratory condition. In another study, Istomina (1977) compared the number of words children could deliberately remember during a dramatic play session involving a grocery store with the number of words they could remember in a typical laboratory experiment. Istomina found that preschoolers remembered more items in the dramatic play condition, functioning at the same level that older children could demonstrate in a non-play condition that was similar to a typical school task. These findings support Vygotsky's insight that new developmental accomplishments do become apparent in play far earlier that they do in other activities. Vygotsky maintained that for children of preschool and kindergarten age, their mastery of academic skills is not as good a predictor of their later scholastic abilities as the quality of their play.

Make-Believe Play as a Prerequisite for Academic Learning

Vygotsky considered play to be similar to instruction in its ability to foster child development, but emphasized that unlike instruction play impacts not isolated areas of development, but the entire course of development:

> The play-development relationship can be compared with the instruction-development relationship, but play provides a background for changes in needs and in consciousness of a much wider nature.
>
> (Vygotsky 1967, 16)

In regards to child development in general, Vygotsky viewed play as an important mechanism and source of development of Higher Mental Function—mediated, intentional and internalized mental processes. In its mature state, Higher Mental Functions are an outgrowth of specific cultural practices including formal schooling; however, children's successful functioning in the very context of formal schooling depends in turn on their existence even if in their nascent form. Play has an important role in formation of the higher mental functions in affecting the development of children's abstract and symbolic thinking, their ability to act internally or on an "internal mental plane," and their ability to engage in intentional and voluntary behaviours.

Developing internalized symbolic representations

Play promotes the development of internalized representations because in play children act in accordance with internal ideas rather than with external reality: The child sees one thing, but acts differently in relation to what he sees as when she uses a long block as a computer keyboard. In Vygotsky's words, *a situation is reached in which the child begins to act independently of what he sees.* (Vygotsky 1967, 11)

In regards to the development of internalized representations, play presents a transitional stage from children being limited by the images of their immediate environment to them being able to operate with most abstract constructs. Role-playing in an imaginary situation requires children to carry on two types of actions simultaneously—external and internal. In play, these internal actions, "operations on the meanings," are still dependent on the external operations on the objects. However, the very emergence of the internal actions signals the beginning of a child's transition from the

earlier forms of thought processes—sensory-motor and visual-representa-
tional—to more advanced abstract thought:

> A child learns to consciously recognize his own actions and becomes aware
> that every object has a meaning. From the point of view of development,
> the fact of creating an imaginary situation can be regarded as a means of
> developing abstract thought.
>
> (Vygotsky 1967, 17)

Another aspect of the development of Higher Mental Functions as
mediated and internalized processes is associated with children's ability to
use increasingly complex symbols such as mental models and language. In
play, children model real-life objects, actions, and relationships: since they
act out not the exact actions of a fire fighter or a doctor but rather synopses
of these actions, they, in fact, generate a model of reality. This modelling
requires children to isolate and abstract essential features of these objects,
actions, and relationships that lay the foundation for further development of
abstract thinking and imagination.

Children's discovery of the symbolic nature of language also emerges
in play as children use props, gestures, and later words to represent objects
and actions. Assigning new names to the play props as these are used in new
functions helps children master the symbolic nature of words as the child
first "unconsciously and spontaneously makes use of the fact that he can
separate meaning from an object" (Vygotsky 1967, 13). It leads to children's
eventual realization of the unique relationship that exists between words
and the objects they signify.

Developing Self-Regulation

Another way make-believe play contributes to children's development of
Higher Mental Functions and thus to their readiness for formal schooling
is by promoting their intentional behaviours. The relationship between
children's ability to act with intentionality (i.e., to self-regulate their social
and cognitive behaviours) and their success in academic learning has long
been observed by practitioners and now is documented in research (Blair
and Razza 2007, McClelland, et al. 2007). The Vygotsky's theory of how
play affects self-regulation is based on his idea of internalized (or "intra-
mental") higher mental functions evolving from shared ("inter-mental" in
Vygotsky's words) behaviours. Vygotsky called this transition from shared

to individual *the general law of cultural development,* emphasizing that in the course of development of higher mental functions, and *social relations, real relations of people, stand behind all the higher mental functions and their relations.* (Vygotsky 1997, 106)

Development of self-regulation in play becomes possible because of the inherent relationship that exists between roles children play and rules they need to follow when playing these roles. This relationship requires children to practice self-regulation both in its shared and its individual form. In play, the shared form of self-regulation exists as "other-regulation," as children monitor their play partners' "playing by the rules," while at the same time following directions issued by other players. By engaging in "other-regulation," preschoolers gain awareness of the rules of play that they will be later able to apply to their own behaviour.

In regards to self-regulation proper, for preschoolers, play becomes the first activity where children are driven not by the need for instant gratification, prevalent at this age, but instead by the need to suppress their immediate impulses. In play,

> at every step the child is faced with a conflict between the rule of the game and what he would do if he could suddenly act spontaneously. In the game he acts counter to what he wants...[achieving] the maximum display of willpower in the sense of renunciation of an immediate attraction in the game in the form of candy, which by the rules of the game the children are not allowed to eat because it represents something inedible. Ordinarily, a child experiences subordination to a rule in the renunciation of something he wants, but here subordination to a rule and renunciation of acting on immediate impulse are the means to maximum pleasure.
>
> (Vygotsky 1967, 10)

Make-believe play thus equips children with the beginnings of symbol-mediated, intentional, and internalized behaviours. Having developed these prerequisite competencies, a preschool child can make the necessary transition from learning that *follows the child's own agenda* to the learning that *follows the school agenda*: one of the basic ways that the social situation of development in school differs from that of preschool. (Vygotsky 1956, 426–427). In the words of post-Vygotskians, play is an activity within which new developmental accomplishments emerge than make possible the development of learning activity—the leading activity of school aged children.

Characteristics of Play as a Leading Activity

Speaking of play as "the leading source of development," Vygotsky (1967) used the term "leading activity" more as a metaphor than as a theoretical construct. The Vygotskian idea that a leading activity may be used as an indicator of a specific age was later extended and refined in the work of Alexei Leont'ev (1981) and Daniel Elkonin (1972) who described leading activities throughout childhood and identified their role in bringing about the main developmental accomplishments of each age period. In Elkonin's theory of periods in child development, play is placed on the continuum of leading activities following the adult-mediated, object-oriented activity of toddlers and followed by the learning activity of primary school aged children (Elkonin 1972). While some elements of play emerge in infancy and toddlerhood, there are other kinds of leading activities that drive child development in these periods (Elkonin 1972; Karpov 2005). Only mature make-believe play with all play elements fully developed becomes the leading activity of preschool- and kindergarten-aged children.

What is Mature Play?

The idea of mature play comes from the work of Daniel Elkonin (1978), who had studied the development of play from infancy through primary grades. He defined advanced play as a *unique form of children's activity, the subject of which is the adult—his work and the system of his relationships with others* (Elkonin 2005a, 19) thus distinguishing this form of play from other playful activities children engage in. Although Vygotsky himself never used the terms "mature" or "advanced," the play vignettes in his writings seem to describe play that is fairly advanced. Based on the work of Vygotsky and Elkonin as well as the work of their students it is possible to identify several components of mature play (Bodrova and Leong 2007a).

    First, mature play is characterized by the child's use of objects-substitutes that may bear very little if any resemblance to the objects they symbolize: they use a pipe cleaner as a stethoscope or a box as a boat. In a similar way, children use gestures to represent actions with real or imaginary objects. The second characteristic of mature play is the child's ability to take on and sustain a specific role by consistently engaging in pretend actions, speech, and interactions that fit this particular character. The more mature the play, the richer are the roles and the more complex are the relationships between them. Another sign of mature play is the child's ability to follow the rules associated with the pretend scenario in general (playing restaurant vs. playing school) and with a chosen character in particular (playing a chef vs. playing a teacher). Yet another characteristic of mature play is high quality of play scenarios that often integrate many themes and span the time of several days or even weeks. When reflecting on our own childhood many of us can remember playing in such a way.

Is Play of Today's Preschoolers a Mature One?

Unfortunately, play that exists in many of today's early childhood class-rooms and on the playgrounds does not fit the definition of mature play. Even 5- and 6-year-old children who according to Vygotsky and Elkonin should be at the peak of their play performance often display signs of immature play that is more typical for toddlers and younger preschoolers: they play only with realistic props, their play scenarios are stereotypical and primitive, and their repertoire of themes and roles is rather limited. With the main elements—imaginary situation, roles, and rules—underdeveloped, this "immature" play cannot serve as a source of child development or create the Zone of Proximal Development. This was demonstrated in a recent Russian study which replicated Manuilenko's experiment, which was described earlier. The original study compared preschoolers' and schoolchildren's ability to follow directions in play and non-play settings. The preschoolers of the 1940s followed directions better in play situations than in non-play settings, but in the 2000s that difference did not show up until the children were much older. Demonstrating superior self-regulation in play first and being able to transfer it to non-play contexts later had been in the past a characteristic of preschool children, but this no longer is the case (Smirnova and Gudareva 2004). In addition, the researchers found that the ability to follow directions at all ages and in all conditions had generally declined compared to that found in the 1940's study: 7-year-olds of today have self-regulation levels more like those of the preschool children of the 1940's. The authors attributed this phenomenon to the decline in both quantity and quality of play in preschool and kindergarten. Similar findings were obtained in another study in the United States, where a correlation between play and self-regulation was found in children playing at a high level but not in the ones playing at a low level (Berk, Mann, and Ogan 2006). Researchers from different countries agree that the make-believe play of today's children is not simply different from the play of the past, but that it has declined in both quality and quantity (Miller and Almon 2009, Karpov 2005).

The decline of make-believe play is associated in play literature with such factors as an increase in adult-directed forms of children's learning and recreation, proliferation of toys and games that limit children's imagination, and safety limits set by parents and teachers on where and how children are allowed to play (Chudacoff 2007). The most important factor, however, is the decrease in adult mediation of make-believe play (Karpov 2005) affecting not one but all if its components.

Viewing play as a cultural-historical phenomenon, as is consistent with the Vygotskian tradition (Elkonin 1978), one can conclude that today's social situation almost guarantees that children may not develop mature play unless adult mediation is restored. The idea that we need to teach young children how to play is not a new one. However, until recently it has been primarily discussed in the context of special education. While children with language delays or emotional disorders were thought to benefit from play interventions, typically developing children were expected to develop play skills on their own. This approach, while valid in the past, can no longer be adopted if we want all young children to develop mature play.

The changes in the social context of young children's development do not mean that make-believe play is destined to disappear for good. These changes also create new opportunities such as the availability of high quality preschool programs for scaffolding make-believe play, although the mechanisms for play scaffolding need to be designed to fit the new social context. For many children enrolled in centre-based ECE programs their classroom is the only place where they can learn how to play. However, learning how to play in today's early childhood classroom cannot simply emulate learning to play in an informal peer group of yesterday. First of all, in the past, most play existed in multi-aged groups where children had an opportunity to learn from older "play mentors," practice their play skills with the peers of the same age, and then pass their knowledge on to the "play novices." In today's classrooms, children are almost always grouped by age and have to interact with play partners that are as inexperienced as they are. As a result, many of the play skills that children were able to learn in the past by observing and imitating their older playmates now have to be modelled and taught directly by the teachers. In addition, unlike unstructured play of the past that often lasted for hours and days, play time in today's early childhood classroom is limited and rarely exceeds one or two hours. This means that to achieve rapid progress in the quality of play, play scaffolding in the classroom needs to be designed to strategically target its most critical components.

Tools of the Mind: Scaffolding Make-Believe Play in an Early Childhood Classroom

Tools of the Mind (Leong and Bodrova, in press) is a comprehensive early childhood curriculum for children in preschool and kindergarten that explicitly focuses on the role of self-regulation in learning and academic ability by using specific activities that promote self-regulation and by embedding self-regulation promoting activities in instruction designed to build foundational skills in literacy, mathematics and social-emotional competence. It is one of the first attempts in the United States to create a comprehensive Vygotskian-based curriculum that could be used in early childhood classroom. While several Vygotskian-based curricula have been designed in the West for older students, most of the previous attempts to use Vygotskian-based pedagogy with younger children were limited to individual instructional strategies (e.g., "Elkonin blocks") or focused on only one type of scaffolding (e.g., teacher-assisted learning in one-on-one setting).

Tools of the Mind includes systemic play intervention as a one of the principal strategies to promote the development of self-regulation. The intervention is based on Vygotsky and Elkonin's theories of make-believe play and uses specific strategies to scaffold such critical play components as using toys and props in a symbolic way; developing consistent and extended play scenarios; being able to take on and to stay in a pretend role for an extended play episode or a series of play episodes; and being able to consistently follow the rules determining what each pretend character can or cannot do. In *Tools of the Mind* classrooms, children spend a significant amount of their day—around 60 minutes—playing and play is scaffolded and organized in a particular way to ensure that children create an imaginary situation, act out well-defined roles, and follow the rules built in the pretend scenario.

Scaffolding the Use of Toys and Props in a Symbolic Way

Many of today's preschoolers grow up using extremely realistic toys and as a result have a hard time with the concept of "pretend." For these children, teachers model how to use props in a symbolic way, gradually expanding the repertoire of different uses for the same object. Over the period of several months, the teachers introduce more unstructured and multi-functional props at the same time removing some overly realistic ones such as plastic fried eggs. Older preschoolers and kindergartners can start making their own props while younger preschoolers should be shown how to make minimal changes in the existing props to change their purpose. An important part of adult scaffolding is monitoring children's language use making sure that changes in the prop use are accompanied by the changes in prop labelling.

Scaffolding the Development of Consistent and Extended Play Scenarios

Scaffolding play scenarios has several components. First, children often lack background knowledge to build their scenarios. Even to play "house" or "hospital" requires knowledge of the setting, roles, and actions associated with these roles. To build this knowledge, teachers use field trips, guest speakers, books, and videos. The choice of places to take children on a field trip as well as the choice of books and videos is guided by Elkonin's idea of role being the core unit of play. In other words, when field trips or books centre on objects or animals, very little of their content gets re-enacted in make-believe play. Discussing the use of books as a fodder for make-believe play, Elkonin (2005b) commented that *Only those works that clearly and understandably described people, their activities, and how they interacted caused the children to want to reproduce the content of the story in play* (p. 41). Positive impact of explicit modelling of play scenarios on children's engagement in play was found in several studies that involved demographically varied groups of children (Karpov 2005). It indicates that in today's context not only at-risk children, but all preschoolers benefit from in-classroom scaffolding of pretend scenarios.

Scaffolding the Development and Maintaining Play Roles and Rules

As Elkonin (1978) pointed out, the focus points of mature play are the social roles and relationship between people—something that children cannot learn by simply observing adult behaviours. Therefore, to promote mature play, teachers in the *Tools of the Mind* classrooms engage children in discussions of the purpose of adult behaviours, their sequence, and the cause and effect relationships between different behaviours, for example.

The rules that hold make-believe play together are not arbitrary but are based on the logic of real-life situations (Elkonin 1978). Not knowing how these life scripts unfold will keep children from practicing self-regulated behaviours by following these rules. This calls for greater involvement of early childhood teachers in children's play than most teachers are used to. However, for most children this involvement needs to last for a relatively short time: soon they would be able to use models provided by the teachers to build their own roles and rules thus require only occasional support of the adult.

Another way to scaffold roles and rules in make-believe play in *Tools of the Mind* classrooms is by teaching children to plan ahead. Elkonin identified planning as one of the features of highly developed play describing play of older children as consisting mostly of lengthy discussions of who is going to do what and how followed by brief periods of acting out (1978). As with other components of play, role planning can benefit from adult scaffolding. Teachers start with asking children what they want to play or what they want to be encouraging them to discuss the choice of the roles with their peers. Later in the year, the teachers ask children about more specific details of their future play scenarios including what props they might need or whether they need to assume a different role. By making planning a necessary step in play, the teacher directs children's attention to the specifics of their roles and to the existence of rules associated with them. The planning process can take place orally, but if children are encouraged to represent their plans in drawing or pretend writing this process produces even greater benefits (Bodrova and Leong 2005, Bodrova and Leong 2007b). First, as children engage in drawing they are able to focus on their future play for a longer period of time, thus thinking over more details of their pretend scenarios. Second, having a tangible reminder helps children to regulate their own and their partners' behaviours: if a child has a picture of princess with her name on it, it becomes is harder for another child to usurp this role. Finally, by using play plans in their play, children learn about communicative and instrumental purposes of written language—thus engaging in authentic literacy behaviours in the situation that in Vygotsky's (1997) words *satisfies their need for writing*.

How Does the Vygotskian Approach Resolve the Dilemma of Play vs. Academic Skills?

The results of the implementation of *Tools of the Mind* in over 600 preschool and kindergarten classrooms nationwide indicate that the current social context in play scaffolding in ECE classrooms can and should be provided in order to support mature play. When this scaffolding does address the most critical components of play, not only the quantity and quality of play improves, but so do many other competencies—language, cognitive, social, and emotional—for which mature play creates Zone of Proximal Development (Leong and Bodrova in press, Barnett, et al. 2008, Diamond, et al. 2007). In addition to promoting general foundations for learning academic skills in the formalized school environment, mature make believe play also has the potential to affect specific literacy skills, especially early writing (Bodrova and Leong 2005, Bodrova and Leong 2007b).

The implementation of the *Tools of the Mind* curriculum can itself be considered an example of the use of Vygotsky's (1997) experimental-genetic method to investigate the effects of adult mediation of play on the development of critical developmental accomplishments of early childhood. Consistent with Vygotsky's theory the results prove that by scaffolding make-believe play and making sure it does exist in its most mature form we can positively impact not only the development of play itself but also the development of early academic skills. Thus Vygotsky's ideas on play and the decades of post-Vygotskian research can provide an answer to today's dilemma of early childhood education.

References

Barnett, W.S., J. Kwanghee, D.J. Yarosz, J. Thomas, and A. Hornbeck 2008. Educational effects of the Tools of the Mind curriculum: A randomized trial." *Early Childhood Research Quarterly,* 23 (3): 299–313.

Berk, L.E., T.D. Mann, and A.T. Ogan. 2006. Make-believe play: wellspring for development of self-regulation." In *Play=Learning: how play motivates and enhances cognitive and social-emotional growth*, eds. D.G. Singer, R.M. Golinkoff and K. Hirsh-Pasek, 74–100. New York: Oxford University Press.

Blair, C., and R.P. Razza. 2007. Relating effortful control, executive function, and false belief understanding to emerging math and literacy ability in kindergarten." *Child Development,* 78 (2): 647–663.

Bodrova, E. and D.J. Leong. 2007b. Play and early literacy: A Vygotskian approach. In *Play and literacy in early childhood, Second edition*, eds. K.A. Roskos and J.F. Christie,185–200. Mahwah: Lawrence Erlbaum Associates.

———. 2007a. *Tools of the Mind: The Vygotskian approach to early childhood education, Second edition.* Columbus: Merrill/Prentice Hall.

————. 2005. "Vygotskian perspectives on teaching and learning early literacy." In *Handbook of early literacy research* (Vol. 2), eds. D. Dickinson and S. Neuman, 243–256. New York: Guilford Publications.

Chudacoff, H.P. 2007. *Children at play: An American history.* New York: New York University Press.

Diamond, A., W.S. Barnett, J. Tomas, and S. Munro. 2007. Preschool program improves cognitive control. *Science,* 318.

Elkonin, D. 1978. *Psychologija igry [The psychology of play].* Moscow: Pedagogika.

————. 2005b. The psychology of play: Chapter I. *Journal of Russian and East European Psychology,* 43 (1): 22–48.

————. 2005a. The psychology of play: Preface. *Journal of Russian and East European Psychology,* 43 (1): 11–21.

————. 1972. Toward the problem of stages in the mental development of the child. *Soviet psychology,* 10: 225–251.

Istomina, Z. 1977. The developmental of voluntary memory in preschool-age children. In *Soviet Developmental Psychology*, ed. M. Cole. New York: M. E. Sharpe.

Karpov, Y. 2005. *The neo-Vygotskian approach to child development.* New York: Cambridge University Press.

Kravtsova, E. 2005. Shkola dlya malen'kikh ili malen'kaya shkola? [A school for the little ones or a little school?]. *Psychology and Education,* 2.

Leong, D.J., and E. Bodrova. In Press. Tools of the Mind: A Vygotskian based early childhood curriculum. *Early Childhood Services: An Interdisciplinary Journal of Effectiveness.*

Leont'ev, A. 1981. *Problems of the development of the mind.* Moscow: Progress Publishers.

Manuilenko, Z. 1975. The development of voluntary behavior by preschool-age children. *Soviet Psychology,* 13: 65–116.

McClelland, M.M., C. McDonald Connor, A.M. Jewkes, C.E. Cameron, C.L. Farris, and F.J. Morrison. 2007. Links between behavioral regulation and preschoolers' literacy, vocabulary, and math skills. *Developmental Psychology,* 43: 947–960.

Miller, E., and J. Almon. 2009. *Crisis in the kindergarten: Why children need to play in school.* College Park: Aliance for Childhood.

Smirnova, E. and O. Gudareva. 2004. Igra i proizvol'nost u sovremennykh doshkol'nikov [Play and intentionality in modern preschoolers]. *Voprosy Psychologii,* 1: 91–103.

Vygotsky, L.S. 1956. "Obuchenije i razvitije v doshkol'nom vozraste [Learning and development in preschool children]." In *Izbrannye psychologicheskije trudy [Selected psychological studies]*, Lev Vygotsky, 426–437. Moscow: RSFSR Academy of Pedagogic Sciences.
———. 1967. "Play and its role in the mental development of the child." *Soviet Psychology*, 5 (3): 6–18.
———. 1978. *Mind in society: The development of higher mental processes*. Cambridge: Harvard University Press.
———. 1987. *Thinking and speech*. New York: Plenum Press.
———. 1997. *The history of the development of higher mental functions*. New York: Plenum Press.
———. 1998. *Child psychology* (Vol. 5). New York: Plenum Press.
———. 2004. Imagination and creativity in childhood. *Journal of Russian and East European Psychology,* 42 (1): 7–97.
Whitehurst, G.J. 2001. "Much too late." *Education Next,* 1 (2): 9, 16–20.
Zaporozhets, A. 1986. *Izbrannye psychologicheskie trudy [Selected works]*. Moscow: Pedagogika.
Zigler, D.G., R.M. Golinkoff, and K. Hirsh-Pasek, eds. 2006. "The cognitive child vs. the whole child: lessons from 40 years of head start." In *Play=Learning: How play motivates and enhances cognitive and social-emotional growth, eds.* R.M. Golinkoff, K.A. Hirsh-Pasek, and D.G. Singer, 15–35. New York: Oxford University Press.

CHAPTER TWELVE

ZONES OF PROFESSIONAL DEVELOPMENT: ARGUMENTS FOR RECLAIMING PRACTICE-BASED EVIDENCE IN EARLY CHILDHOOD PRACTICE AND RESEARCH

MATHIAS URBAN

Introduction

There are powerful concepts that influence and shape how we understand early childhood institutions and practices, both locally and globally. Majority and minority world countries have adopted ambitious policy goals to increase the quality and quantity of early childhood services—which are recognised as effective means of addressing issues of economic prosperity, gender equality, educational achievement and social inclusion and children's rights. Often, policies are linked to a debate on the early childhood workforce, its members, their qualifications, and how to best guide their practices.

Internationally, an emerging discourse on professionalism in early childhood emphasizes the importance of critical reflectiveness, professional autonomy, and habits over the mere acquirement of skills and techniques. At the same time, practitioners in many countries are facing a parallel and increasingly influential discourse on outcomes, quality, and effectiveness, etc., which leaves them with a fundamental dilemma: they are expected to achieve predetermined outcomes in a working context that is increasingly diverse, uncertain, and less predictable.

This chapter begins with looking at the prevailing conceptualization of the early childhood profession, which, I argue, is constructed out of a particular, hierarchical mode of producing and applying expert knowledge. I will argue that this notion of professional knowledge and practice is not appropriate for the complex field of working with children, families, and diverse communities.

In the light of the work of two thinkers who have been most influential in shaping our understandings of early childhood practices—Lev Vygotsky and Paolo Freire—the chapter then explores an alternative paradigm of a relational, systemic professionalism that embraces openness, diversity and uncertainty. This approach encourages the co-construction of professional knowledges, practices, and practice-based evidence. Professional practice, learning, and research, in this frame of thinking, are understood as dialogic activities of asking critical questions and creating understandings across differences.

Professionalism—A New Paradigm in Early Childhood?

In the past decade, early childhood has moved up policy agendas in an unprecedented way. Many countries have set ambitious policy goals to increase both quantity of services and quality of provision. As the OECD points out in the *Starting Strong* report (OECD 2006), the political agendas are quite often driven by common socio-economic concerns, e.g. the wish to increase women's labour market participation and to reconcile work and family responsibilities on a basis that is more equitable for women. Falling birth rates and aging populations present challenges for most OECD countries, and that, too, gives reason to look at early childhood institutions as a possible solution (OECD 2006). There is a strong belief that "economic prosperity depends on a high employment/population ratio," (OECD 2006) and therefore, policies to bring more women into the workforce have been put in place in most OECD countries. But besides being a condition for gender equality and economic prosperity, there are other rationales, too, that have moved early childhood onto political agendas and into the public debate. Early childhood is increasingly recognized as a critical period in human life. Young children's experiences, beginning with the very first day of their lives, form the basis for lifelong learning and development. But children's everyday experiences cannot be reduced to simply being the preparation for something that has yet to come. Their interactions with parents and caregivers in their families, and with practitioners in early childhood institutions, especially with other children, have a value of their own. Young children are not incomplete beings—future pupils and future adults—to be shaped through education in order to meet assumed needs of an adult society. While young children are particularly vulnerable and affected by social injustice and inequality, they are also fellow citizens with rights of their own which we must respect. But above all, early childhood is an opportunity, writes Martin Woodhead:

Each young child has a unique potential for development of human capacities, for communication and cooperation, for skill and feeling, for reason
and imagination, for practicality and spirituality, for determination and
compassion.

(Woodhead 1996)

The care and education of young children lies at the very heart of any
human society. And it is not just something that we as adults provide for, or
do to, children. It is a fundamental need of human society:

Through the care and education of young children, a society constructs
and reconstructs community and economy, ensures continuity of tradition
between generations, and makes innovation and transformation possible.

(ibid)

Along with an increasing division of labour, modern societies, over the
last two centuries, have tended to successively extend the responsibility for
the upbringing of young children from the family domain to public institutions. Care and early education, which once used to be common social
practice, have become specialised tasks—and occupations—for those who
are specifically identified as early years practitioners: childcare workers,
preschool teachers, preschool nurses, pedagogues, to name only a few.
Roles, work contexts, levels of qualification, and remuneration, etc., of
early years practitioners always varied widely in different institutions, in
different countries, and in different periods of time. In recent years, however,
a common thread appears to have emerged within the debate: most national
and international policy documents, as well as the increasingly globalised
scholarly discourse, are referring to the early years workforce and its
members as something that has to be *professionalized* in order to meet the
increasingly challenging requirements of the work.

Professionalism, it seems, has become the new buzzword in early
childhood and it links seamlessly with the similarly prominent discourse
on *quality*. There have been important European and national discussions
on what quality entails in early childhood institutions and services. They
include the publication, in 1996, of *Quality Targets in Services for Young
Children* by the European Commission Network on Childcare and other
Measures to reconcile Employment and Family Responsibilities (1996).
This is an important document as it offers a multi-dimensional framework
for quality, including, among others, targets for policy, investment, participation, and professionalism.

While there are good reasons, in many countries, to argue for better quality early childhood services, it is necessary to keep in mind that the concept of *quality* itself is highly problematic. It has been widely challenged for its implicit relatedness to notions of universality, technocratic manageability, and measurability (Pence and Moss 1994; Dahlberg, Moss, et al. 1999; Urban 2003; Urban 2005; Dahlberg, Moss, et al. 2007). Too often, the language of quality is employed to legitimise the proliferating maze of regulations in early childhood education, and to undermine instead of support professional autonomy. We should, therefore, be cautious not to lose the "shared unease" with the terminology and the implications of this concept, as Dahlberg, Moss, and Pence remind us (2007). *Quality* remains a questionable concept, a problem that needs to be explored rather than to be presented as the solution.

At first sight, the discourses on *quality* and *professionalism* seem to merge without major difficulty. It is generally recognized today that the workforce is central to achieving the ambitious policy goals of increasing both quantity and quality of provision. Recent research supports this notion (Siraj-Blatchford, Sylva, et al. 2002; Dalli 2003; Dalli 2005; Mac Naughton 2005; Oberhuemer 2005), and along with policies to increase *quality*, many countries have been introducing policies that aim at *professionalizing* the workforce. In England, for example, the extensive *Every Child Matters* policy (Department for Education and Skills 2004) links explicitly to *Children's Workforce Strategy* (Department for Education and Skills 2005) which aims at building a "world-class workforce for children and young people" (ibid). The message is clear: early childhood practitioners need to be *qualified*, *trained* and *skilled* in order to achieve the highly ambitious outcomes of the strategy. In addition to that, the strategy resulted in redefining the workforce on the whole. The new status of *Early Years Professional* (EYP) has been established, introducing to—or imposing on, as some authors write (Miller 2008)—the notion of professionalism to the early years workforce.

In work contexts that are challenging and changing, practitioners, as individuals, are increasingly expected to *act professionally* but quite often, it remains largely obscure what that means. In the following section I will argue that this focus on the individual creates a number of dilemmas (for the individual practitioner as well as for the early years profession) and is part of a powerful discourse that creates a particular—and highly questionable—notion of professional practice.

Talking the Talk—Who Defines What Counts as Professional?

What is a profession? How did professions come about in modern societies and what are their roles and functions? There is, of course, more than one way of approaching the answer to these questions (for a more detailed discussion see Urban 2008). For Talcott Parsons, for example, the American sociologist who looked at modern societies from a structural-functionalist perspective, professions are a particular way of *solving social problems* (Parsons 1968). Parsons' definition of a profession has been—and still is—highly influential. In order to fulfil their role in society, professions build social sub-systems that consist of a *central regulatory body* (in order to ensure the quality of the performance of the individual professional), a professional *code of conduct* and an effective means of *producing and managing the professional body of knowledge*. It is crucial for the professional system, according to this perspective, to have an effective control over entrance, too, because numbers, selection, and training of future professionals need to be controlled.

Marxist sociologists have taken a radically different angle. A profession, they suggest, is a highly effective means of an *intellectual class* of gaining influence and power, and of securing social status and economic advantage in an unequal society:

> Professionalization is thus an attempt to translate one order of scare resources—special knowledge and skills—into another—social and economic rewards. To maintain scarcity implies a tendency to monopoly: monopoly of expertise in the market, monopoly of status in a system of stratification.
>
> (Larson 1977)

Whatever way we look at it, *knowledge* is central to the professional system. Whatever the actual practice, *knowledge*, and the way it is produced, distributed and applied plays a central role, and is the key to power inequalities within the system. Who defines professionalism? What stands out in the debate (and in the influential policy documents) is the clear distinction between those who talk and those who are talked about. Early childhood, as a professional system, is highly stratified. There are, for instance, considerable gaps between the Education Committee of the OECD and the individual early childhood practitioner. Consultations at the national level, to introduce and discuss new policies, seldom involve the practitioners who are expected to realize them. And within the professional system, the stratification is clearly visible, too. Scholarly discussions about what it entails to be professional in early childhood often express expectations towards the individual practitioner; they seldom acknowledge the inequities of the knowledge producing and processing structures that are highly effective as tools of regulation and self-regulation. There is an *epistemological hierarchy* in our field that consists of distinct layers, where the professional body of knowledge is *produced* (academic research, scholarly debate), *transferred* (professional preparation, pre- and in-service training) and *applied* (practice). This top-down stream of knowledge and expectations constantly increases the pressure on practitioners. The hierarchical layout of the professional system also suggests there is a distinction between knowledge production and its application, between *theory* and *practice*. This theory/practice divide links well with the structural-functionalist framework, where a social *problem*, and the way it is defined, is distinct from its *solution*. In this frame of thinking, the role of the professional is clearly defined as contributing to the solution of a given social problem by applying specific knowledge and skills, which they have acquired through formalized training.

The notion of the early childhood professional as an expert, applying expert knowledge to achieve specific outcomes is part of a broader—and increasingly dominant—discourse that is concerned with guiding educational practice through scientifically provided evidence. Educational practices, not only in early childhood, have been accused of failing largely because they are not informed by educational *research knowledge*. Considerable efforts are being taken (and considerable amounts of money spent) to promote the idea of education as an *evidence-based practice* and of teaching as an evidence-based profession (Biesta 2007). The concept of evidence-based practice is supposed to close the gap between research, policy, and practice. It does so in a very specific way that weakens democratic control over research as well as practice, Gert Biesta argues:

> On the research side, evidence-based education seems to favour a technocratic model in which it is assumed that the only relevant research questions are questions about the effectiveness of educational means and techniques, forgetting, among other things, that what counts as 'effective' crucially depends on judgments about what is educationally desirable.
>
> (Biesta 2007)

When effectiveness is defined externally, and decisions about outcomes are already made, it is almost impossible for practitioners to make judgments about what is relevant or desirable for their work or to engage in meaningful dialogue with the children, families, and communities they are working with. An overemphasis on evidence—based practice can disqualify practitioners and prevent the asking of critical questions:

> The focus on 'what works' makes it difficult, if not impossible to ask the questions of what it should work for and who should have a say in determining the latter.
>
> (ibid)

The concept of educational practice, based on research evidence may appear neutral at first sight, but of course, it is not. Values and judgments (e.g. about what counts as evidence, what research questions are considered relevant, which methodological approaches are considered as being more valid than others etc.) lie at the very core of the concept. But the *processes* of valuing and judging are steered away from practitioners, thus systematically excluding them from the contextual meaning-making that should build the basis for professional practice. The result is a concept of professional practice as *intervention*, with the underlying assumption that professionals (as experts) act in particular ways to bring about certain effects (outcomes) that can be determined beforehand. But early childhood practice is highly complex; many things can happen, and will happen, in the day-to-day encounters with children's and families' complex and diverse life situations. It is not about pushing the right buttons and, therefore, the powerful conceptualization of the early childhood professional in a paradigm of clearly defined problems, predetermined outcomes, and evidence-based, hence "right" practice, implies failure. "Outcomes" of any interaction between early childhood practitioners and children are likely to be uncertain and surprising. My argument is that in order to capture those surprising and uncertain "outcomes," the professional knowledge system needs to acknowledge practitioners' experiences and systematically enable and encourage their contributions to building and interpreting the professional body of knowledge. Practitioners are key actors, not recipients, in the professional system—and so are researchers, managers, and trainers, etc. They all contribute to providing what I want to call *practice-based evidence*. The environment that encourages such processes of joint learning and meaning-making can best be described as *critical learning community*.

Learning from Vygotsky—Can We Create Zones of Professional Development?

Early childhood practitioners do not "solve" given problems by applying certain technologies. Instead, they find themselves involved in meaning-making activities that require value-based decisions and experience. In his classic book on reflective practice, Donald Schön writes:

> In real-world practice, problems do not present themselves to the practitioner as givens. They must be constructed from the material of problem situations which are puzzling, troubling, and uncertain. In order to convert a problematic situation to a problem, a practitioner must do a certain kind of work. *He must make sense of an uncertain situation that initially makes no sense.*
>
> (Schön 1983, emphasis added)

From this perspective, *practice* becomes inseparable from *making sense*, hence is an inseparable part of the sphere where professional is produced. The problem remains, however, that practitioners in early childhood are scarcely recognized as co-constructors of professional knowledge and providers of practice-based evidence.

Let us look, for a moment, at the invaluable contribution Lev Vygotsky made to our understanding of how children learn. In the process of establishing itself as an academic discipline in the nineteenth and early twentieth centuries, developmental psychology had successfully constructed its subject—the developing child. In line with the implicit logic of emerging scientific disciplines, this child had to be constructed as both *universal* and *distinct*, as Erica Burman (2008) argues in her book *deconstructing developmental psychology*. The idea of a largely *decontextualized child* whose development and learning could be explored and explained by applying *scientific* methods formed the basis for many theories of child development that are influential today. One example is the concept of developmental *stages* that follow a particular order from simple to more complex. Only if these stages are seen as universal (meaning they occur in every child, regardless of the social and material world the child grows up in) can they be employed to inform and legitimate *developmentally appropriate practices*. There are indeed many examples of early childhood programs and practices that are seen as *right* for children of a particular age group, regardless of their life situations. Not even within developmental psychology is this view uncontested. It is by no means the only way of understanding children's learning, as Helen Penn (2008) clearly demonstrates.

Lev Vygotsky argued that children—humans—are social beings from the beginning. Their learning takes place in social interactions which, in turn, are embedded in a complex reality determined by the social, cultural, and historical context. Both aspects of his theories—learning as interaction and the importance of the context of these interactions—are most important for early childhood practices. First, children's learning builds on their social experiences—which may vary widely, depending on the society a child is born into: "Being poor in Mali, or even in Britain, is a different life experience from being rich in America" (Penn 2008). Second, if children's learning takes place in interactions, then who they interact with, and in what way, is crucial. This points to the important role of teachers, or early childhood practitioners, in any learning process. Adult-child-interactions, Vygotsky argued, should be based on children's *meaningful activities*—but the teacher should always encourage children to take these activities one step further. He referred to this productive tension as opening up "Zones of Proximal Development" (ZPD) (Vygotsky and Cole 1978) which provide an intellectual space where the child is "engaged in a particular kind of meaningful activity, in which he or she wants to participate, but cannot yet carry out all actions independently" (van Oers 1995; van Oers 2003). Vygotsky is explicit about the adult's role in this interaction:

Education must be based on the student's own activity and should involve nothing more than guiding and monitoring this activity. In the interaction with children the teacher should open a zone of proximal development.

(Vygotsky and Cole 1978)

There is a widespread consensus on this social co-constructivist view on learning today. Children are not empty vessels, waiting to be filled by adults. On the contrary, they are active learners who *make sense* of the experiences and activities they are engaged in. In order to be able to open ZPDs, practitioners are urged to engage in a "pedagogy of listening" (Rinaldi 2005). Recent research emphasizes that children's exploring and meaning-making activities unfold to their full potential only when they are engaged in meaningful, child-led interactions between children and adults—in activities Siraj-Blatchford and Sylva (2004) refer to as *sustained shared thinking*.

It remains a challenge, however, for the early childhood professional system to encourage similar activities for adults—to systematically open *"zones of professional development."*

Crucial questions for professional learning could be derived from this perspective:

- How can practitioners and students, together with parents, managers, researchers, and other adult actors, become engaged in meaningful activities in order to explore, understand, and change practice?
- How can they be guided and monitored—in a process of reciprocal meaning-making?
- How can they be encouraged to move on to the next step—to create change?

The early childhood profession, conceptualized as *critical learning community*, would allow moving on from questioning individual practices of individual practitioners to questioning the system as a whole—including individual and collective practices in early childhood settings, training and professional preparation and learning, policy, administration, and research. All of these elements of the professional system are embedded in—and contributing to—the wider social, historical, economic and political context of society with its local, national, and increasingly global dimensions. They are part of a complex socio-ecological system. The challenge is to work toward a *critical ecology of the profession* (Urban and Dalli 2008) that is informed by the political and social realities that bring about knowledges and practices, "together with the use of this knowledge to *strategically transform* education in socially progressive directions" (Mac Naughton 2003, emphasis added).

Creating Understandings—Can We Bring Professionalism, Research and Joint Learning into One Frame of Thinking?

Critical learning communities provide spaces for asking critical questions. They challenge the hierarchy between theory and practice, between those who produce knowledge and those who apply and deliver. Critical authors in the human and social sciences have suggested an alternative model which is more suitable to making sense of the complex interactions between "self-interpreting, meaning-making human beings" (Taylor 1995). Their thinking is rooted in the work of German philosopher Hans-Georg Gadamer on *hermeneutics* (Gadamer 1960; 2004). From a hermeneutic perspective, research can be understood as a dialogic activity of *coming to an understanding*. Hermeneutic inquiry challenges traditional approaches to research (and their inherent power inequities) as its dialogic process is something "in which one participates, not an activity over which one exercises method-ological control" (Schwandt 2004). The mutual activity of coming to an understanding of a phenomenon or a situation resembles Donald Schön's description of practitioners' constant engagement in reflective conver-sations with the situation. However, it adds a new dimension, because it systematically involves all participants in the system that generates profes-sional knowledge. Such an approach comes with a number of ethical impli-cations. The most important questions, in a dialogic framework of thinking and acting, are not only about choosing appropriate methods for research with (as opposed to *on*) practice. They are about choices to make and about taking a stand: to be open to others and to respect their autonomy, presuming "they possess an independence and voice we must address and by which we ourselves are addressed" (Warnke 2002).

The—necessarily participatory—project of *creating understandings* through systematically organizing dialogues, in which all participants equally talk and listen, challenges the hegemony of expertise and dominant knowledge and bridges the gap between the *ways of being* and the *ways of knowing* in the professional system. It offers a way to overcome the inherent dilemma of the early childhood profession as it "embraces difference, diversity, and the messiness of human life rather than seeking, in the first instance, to resolve it" (Schwandt 2004).

Dialogue, as a key principle, has guided the educational and political work of Paolo Freire throughout his life. His early work is concerned with dialogue as a way to overcome the hierarchical relationships between teacher and student who, in the process, become teacher-students and student-teachers, "both responsible for a process in which all grow" (Freire 2000, first published in 1970). In his later writings he emphasises the radical nature of the dialogic project in education and society. Dialogue, he insists, is not a tool for teaching. Dialogue is a requirement of human nature and a sign of the educator's democratic stand—but also an "epistemological requirement" (Freire and Freire 1997) as it brings together *ways of being* and *ways of knowing* of the educational practitioner-researcher.

Policy Implications

What are the policy implications of such a reciprocal understanding of research and practice? First and foremost it will be necessary to recognise that *evidence*, i.e. the professional body of knowledge, is continuously produced by *all* actors in the professional system—which brings into the picture a new focus on practitioners' everyday experiences in working with young children and their families. These experiences, as Schön (1983) argues, are gathered in situations that are complex, open and necessarily *uncertain*. Early childhood practice is itself an on-going experiment, a continuous invention that is risky because its outcomes are not predictable. It is a practice that unfolds in situations that offer "untested feasibilities" (Freire 2004). The "effects" of early childhood practices are manifold and complex, as are the "outcomes" they produce. A system which overemphasizes top-down models, where "effective" practices are supposed to be guided by externally produced "evidence," is most likely to lose sight of the surprising, promising, and innovative effects and outcomes of early childhood practices. Policy can, alternatively, provide an alternative and secure framework (in terms of funding, resources, recognition) to gather, document, disseminate, and theorize these experiences. It is possible, as forward-looking examples in many countries show, to reconcile the notions of evidence-based-practice with *practice-based-evidence*.[1]

Successful examples differ in their contexts, aims, and approaches. However, a number of key messages can be drawn from all of them. First, they shift perspectives from the individual practitioner (who has to be professionalized in order to apply and deliver) to the interactions between the various actors in a complex *critical ecology* of the early years professional system. *Professionalism* is understood as an attribute of the entire system that is to be developed in its reciprocal relationships.

Secondly, successful examples point to a key feature of the professional system: its ability to encourage and systematically create spaces for asking critical questions at every layer of the system—and to value the multitude and diversity of possible answers as a key to creating new understandings. They create professional learning environments with an "ethos of inquiry" (Urban 2007) and they encourage critical explorations of the context and preconditions of early childhood practice—including the cultural, historical, economic, and political realities and inequalities that shape them. Paolo Freire has described this as a process of "*conscientization*."

Finally, they build on a notion of *hope*—which is an ontological need, as Freire (2004) argues. Educational practice is there for a purpose and it implies change. The *hoped-for* has to be debated—and this directs the attention from the simplistic question of *what works* to questions of meaning, value, and purpose.

---

[1]   E.g. the Centres of Innovation initiative in New Zealand, the éist project in Ireland, the bildung:elementar project in Germany (cf. Urban 2008)

References

Biesta, G. 2007. "Why 'what works' won't work: Evidence-based practice and the democratic deficit in educational research." *Educational Theory,* 57 (1): 1–22.

Burman, E. 2008. *Deconstructing developmental psychology.* London: Routledge.

Dahlberg, G., P. Moss, et al. 1999. *Beyond quality in early childhood education and care. Postmodern perspectives.* London: Falmer.

———. 2007. *Beyond quality in early childhood education and care: languages of evaluation.* New York: Routledge.

Dalli, C. 2003. "Early childhood policy in New Zealand: Stories of sector collaborative action in the 1990's." *Education International Working Papers* (10).

———. 2005. *The New Zealand story of EC professionalisation.* International conference on Change Agents in Early Childhood Education and Care, EC+P. Early Childhood and Profession. International Centre for Research, Studies and Development. Martin-Luther-University Halle-Wittenberg.

Department for Education and Skills. 2004. *Every child matters: Change for children.* London: DfES.

———. 2005. *Children's workforce strategy. A strategy to build a world-class workforce for children and young people.* London: DfES.

European Commission Network on Childcare and Other Measures to Reconcile Employment and Family. 1996. *Quality targets in services for young children : proposals for a ten year Action Programme.* European Commission.

Freire, P. 2000. *Pedagogy of the oppressed.* New York: Continuum.

———. 2004. *Pedagogy of hope. Reliving pedagogy of the opressed.* London: Continuum.

Freire, P. and A.M.A. Freire. 1997. *Pedagogy of the heart.* New York: Continuum.

Gadamer, H.G. 1960. *Wahrheit und methode: Grundzüge einer philosophischen hermeneutik.* Tübingen: Mohr.

Gadamer, H.G. and J. Weinsheimer, et al. 2004. *Truth and method.* London, New York: Continuum.

Larson, M.S. 1977. *The rise of professionalism: a sociological analysis.* Berkeley: University of California Press.

Mac Naughton, G. 2003. *Shaping early childhood. Learners, curriculum and contexts.* Berkshire: Open University Press.

————. 2005. *Doing Foucault in early childhood studies: applying post-structural ideas*. London: Routledge.

Miller, L. 2008. "Developing professionalism within a regulatory framework in England: challenges and possibilities." *European Early Childhood Education Research Journal* 16 (2): 225–268.

Oberhuemer, P. 2005. "Conceptualising the early childhood pedagogue: Policy approaches and issues of professionalism." *European Early Childhood Education Research Journal* 13 (1): 5–16.

OECD. 2006. *Starting Strong II. Early childhood education and care*. Paris: OECD.

van Oers, B. 1995. "How to define the zone of proximal development?" *Studi di Psichologia dell'Educatione* 14 (1, 2, 3): 157–165.

————. *Marking out pupils' learning trajectories: Developmental narratives as a tool for teachers*. European Early Childhood Education Research Association (13th Annual Conference), University of Strathclyde, Glasgow.

Parsons, T. 1968. Professions. *International encyclopedia of the social sciences,* eds. D.L. Sills and R.K. Merton. 12: 536–547. New York: Macmillan.

Pence, A.R. and P. Moss, eds. 1994. *Valuing quality in early childhood services : new approaches to defining quality*. London: P. Chapman.

Penn, H. 2008. *Understanding early childhood: issues and controversies*. Maidenhead: McGraw-Hill/Open University Press.

Rinaldi, C. 2005. *In dialogue with Reggio Emilia: listening, researching, and learning*. London, New York: Routledge.

Schön, D.A. 1983. *The reflective practitioner. How professionals think in action*. New York: Basic Books.

Schwandt, T.A. 2004. Hermeneutics: a poetics of inquiry versus a methodology for research. *Educational research: difference and diversity,* eds. H. Piper and I. Stronach, 31–44. Aldershot: Ashgate.

Siraj-Blatchford, I. and K. Sylva. 2004. "Researching pedagogy in English pre-schools." *British Educational Research Journal,* 30 (5): 713–739.

Siraj-Blatchford, I., K. Sylva, et al. 2002. *Researching effective pedagogy in the early years*. London: Department for Education and Skills.

Taylor, C. 1995. *Philosophical arguments*. Cambridge: Harvard University Press.

Urban, M. 2003. *From standardized quality towards 'good enough' practice: a dialogic approach to evaluation and quality development in early childhood settings*. European Early Childhood Education Research Association (13th Annual Conference), University of Strathclyde, Glasgow.

———. Quality, autonomy and the profession. In *Questions of Quality*, eds. H. Schonfeld, S. O'Brien and T. Walsh. Dublin: Centre for Early Childhood Development and Education.

———. 2007. Strategies for change: Reflections from a systemic, comparative research project. *A decade of reflection. Early childhood care and education in Ireland: 1996–2006*, eds. N. Hayes and S. Bradley, 44–64. Dublin: Centre for Social and Educational Research.

———. 2008. "Dealing with uncertainty. Challenges and possibilities for the early childhood profession." *European Early Childhood Education Research Journal*, 16 (2): 135–152.

Urban, M. and C. Dalli, eds. 2008. "Professionalism in early childhood education and care." *Special Edition. European Early Childhood Education Research Journal* (EECERJ).

Vygotsky, L.S. and M. Cole. 1978. *Mind in society: the development of higher psychological processes*. Cambridge, London: Harvard University Press.

Warnke, G. 2002. Hermeneutics, ethics, and politics. In *The Cambridge companion to Gadamer,* ed. R.J. Dostal, 79–101. Cambridge: Cambridge University Press.

Woodhead, M. 1996. *In search of the rainbow. Pathways to quality in large-scale programmes for young disadvantaged children*. The Hague: Bernhard van Leer Foundation.

Part V

Conclusion

CHAPTER THIRTEEN

BUILDING BRIDGES, BUILDING FUTURES:
ISSA AND CHANGES IN EARLY CHILDHOOD
DEVELOPMENT AND EDUCATION IN THE
POST-COMMUNIST REGION

AIJA TUNA

"...every step toward truth in our science belongs to us. After all, we did not choose one of the two roads because we liked it, but because we consider it to be true."

Lev Vygotsky, from *The Historical Meaning of The Crisis in Psychology*

Recent decades have been a very rich and crucial time for those working in the field of early childhood development and education (ECDE). Increasingly, research from a wide range of countries and diverse cultures is coming to similar conclusions, demonstrating that important benefits for children, and, therefore, for all societies, are produced by high quality early childhood experiences. This brings attention to the quality of programs and professionals providing services for young children.

With the growing impact and speed of globalization, information and communication technologies, as well as changing political, economic, and environmental realities, the 21st century presents significant challenges and opportunities for new generations. The ability of education systems and society to support each child's development and learning within this changing world is becoming an important criterion in judging the quality and success of educational policies and practices.

This phenomenon is taking place in all parts of the world. However, for countries where major political and social-economic changes have taken place, it has been an exceptionally challenging task to incorporate into their policies and practice the most recent innovations and findings in early education. Whether in academic discussions about professionalism in ECDE or conversations of practitioners on improving the quality of home learning environments and community support for children's early stimulation and development, the need to understand the best mechanisms for reaching a child remains crucial.

Meanwhile, neuroscience research continues to illuminate the correlation between positive interactions with significant adults and long-term developmental outcomes for children. Such research, coupled with the on-going experience of practitioners across cultures, suggests that a loving, secure, and stimulating relationship with parents, family members, and caregivers/preschool teachers has a highly beneficial impact on every aspect of a child's development, from birth through the preschool and early primary years. Children (and, indeed, adults) gain strength when they are surrounded by people who believe in their potential. Such positive support helps them to grow, develop, reach new horizons, and contribute back to the community and the whole society.

It is interesting to realize, however, that many of the ideas essential for today's approach to quality ECDE were already introduced and practiced many decades ago in different regions of the world. One such unique example has been the theories of developmental psychologist Lev Semionovich Vygotsky (1896–1934).

Vygotsky was born and raised in Belarus, which was then part of the Russian Empire. He studied law at Moscow University and worked as a teacher in various institutions. Vygotsky then became a researcher at the Moscow Institute of Experimental Psychology, where he founded the discipline of cultural historical psychology. His work contributed significantly to the fields of psychology, education, and child development. In his short 36 years of life, Vygotsky completed important research on many diverse topics, including the origins and psychology of art, development of higher mental functions, philosophy of science and methodology of psychological research, the relationship between learning and human development, concept formation, the interrelationship between language and thought, play, and the study of learning disabilities, among others. He is most well-known for his innovative work on the key concepts of *Zone of Proximal Development, psychological tools, cultural mediation, scaffolding,* and *internalization,* among others. Vygotsky left behind a large body of research that continues to have a profound influence on a range of psychological and educational theories and the work of numerous scholars.

From many examples in many corners of the education world, there is a growing consensus that diversity creates the most perfect wholeness, and exposure to many different seemingly non-related ideas, opinions, and even cultures provides fresh ideas and perspectives for solving complex problems. Linking together ideas and knowledge from different fields allows us to see problems or challenges from new angles and opens new horizons.

The life and work of Vygotsky has been a perfect example of drawing on ideas from a broad spectrum of disciplines to come up with fresh, new ideas. His open mind, eclectic interests, and knowledge of languages enabled him to explore the vast intellectual realms of education, psychology, history, culture, and art and to create a legacy which is still of the greatest interest to researchers and practitioners around the world. Vygotsky's international influence is astonishing, considering his short life span and the time in which he lived. His theories moved from the east to the west and then back, often being understood, interpreted, and applied differently in different contexts, countries, and cultures. Today, Vygotsky's concepts, insights, and formulations are very much alive and continue to inspire and influence a new generation of researchers.

The authors and editors, hope that this publication will serve as a meeting place for professionals from different parts of the world and will further delve into the richness of Vygotsky's ideas and the multitude of ways they can be understood, used, and further developed in today's context.

Coming Together to Rediscover Vygotsky

Vygotsky's contribution to the world has been very diverse. His cultural-historical approach has not only greatly influenced developmental psychology and education, but has also been successfully applied in clinical psychology, neuropsychology, and other fields. It has become well known on both sides of the Atlantic and on both sides of the now-defunct Iron Curtain. The approach has served as the basis for many educational programs, both for preschool age children and for schools, and continues to gain recognition and respect.

Building on the phenomenon of the growing interest in Vygotsky's theories and ideas, in 2007, the European Early Childhood Education Research Association (EECERA), a prominent European professional organization in the field of ECDE, devoted its 17th Annual Conference to Vygotsky under the title *Exploring Vygotsky's Ideas: Crossing Borders*.

The conference was organized in cooperation with International Step by Step Association (ISSA), a network of early childhood professionals from the region in which Vygotsky was raised and completed his work and research. In spite of Vygotsky's origins, for several decades his work

was virtually unavailable to ECDE professionals in Central and Eastern
Europe, due to the political situation within the Soviet Union at the time of
his works' publication. When his work finally became widely available, the
traditions of early childhood education practice had developed throughout
the region in ways which made the application of Vygotsky's ideas significantly challenging for practitioners and schools.

The Vygotsky conference was a unique event, bringing together professionals interested in the field of early childhood care and education from
different parts of the world, including the former communist countries of
Eastern and Central Europe and the former Soviet Union where interest
in and actual application of Vygotsky's ideas has been growing in recent
years. The conference was able to gather a variety of rich experiences from
different academic schools and regions, from researchers and program
implementers, to discuss, share, and disseminate ideas and lessons learned.[1]

A special highlight of the conference was the keynote speech by
Professor Elena Kravtsova, PhD, granddaughter of Vygotsky, Professor and
Director of the Vygotsky Institute of Psychology at the Russian University
for the Humanities, as well as a brief video-presentation by Vygotsky's
daughter, Gita Vygotskaya, who shared her memories of her father and
his ideas, both from the perspective of a child and that of a professional.
Vygotskaya's comments were especially illuminating on the reasons that
Vygostsky's ideas were long silenced in his own country, and, therefore,
the entire former Soviet Union. In her presentation, Vygotskaya expressed
her sincere gratitude for the conference participants' interest in the life and
creative work of her father, saying:

"Now, this name is well known in the world. Several times I have attended
conferences where representatives from all five continents were present.
His works have been published in scores of countries, and books have been
written about him in many countries. However, I remember well those times,
just a few dozen years ago, when it was not advisable even to mention his
name, let alone make references to Vygotsky. It was still impossible to read
his works after the official ban on his name was lifted, because in those
years, when his name was banned, a great many of his books were simply

---

[1]   Abstracts of the presentations and keynotes of the 2007 EECERA Conference
       are available at http://www.easyprague.cz/eecera2007/download/files/abstract-
       book_web.pdf.

destroyed. A new generation of psychologists arrived who didn't know anything about him. My contemporaries and I had more luck. We were fortunate to have a chance to listen to lectures by his pupils, who, notwithstanding all of the bans, would tell us about him and his work. Those few books that I had at home I would surreptitiously bring to my fellow students to read—I did it in secret as if they were illegal. Now—thank heavens!— everything has changed."

(Vygotskaya 2007)

Reconsidering ECDE in the Post-communist Region

While preschool services were well established in the former Soviet Union, and they were accessible to an impressively large percentage of children, early childhood education under the Communist system had an authoritarian, hierarchal structure, strongly influenced by a behaviourist approach towards child development and learning, as well as a transmission paradigm of teaching. The teacher's (воспитатель) job was to implement whole group activities from approved programmes, plans, and textbooks, with all children doing and learning the same things at the same time, as it was believed that such upbringing (воспитание) was the best for all children. Very few alternatives were officially recognized, even if they existed in practice, as these alternatives were mainly initiated by the teacher's personal experience and personality, rather than the system or requirements from the administration and other authorities. Of course, there were dedicated, reflective, teachers who were sensitive to children's needs and feelings and tried to incorporate good practice within the existing rigid system. However, these teachers had to fight a daily, upstream battle against a system or to implement their approach "unofficially"—outside officially recognized practice.

There were also some differences in sub-regions of communist countries, influenced by the previous history of schooling and the political system in each sub-region. For example, in most parts of the former Soviet Union preschool services were wide-spread, as it was expected that both parents would work outside the home. However, these provisions lacked flexibility and choice for both teachers and children. Children were involved in full-day provisions with strictly assigned times for group activities, eating, sleep, going outside, 'free time' in the afternoons, etc. All children were expected to accomplish the same tasks and achieve same results in order to be considered successful. The concept of children having the opportunity to select and play with toys and different materials according to their own ideas was not valued as a learning experience; in most of the communist bloc countries, *serious learning* and *free play* were treated as completely separate activities.

The social aspects of development were much less emphasised than cognitive and physical skills. Children were encouraged to act as a group through collective actions. The goals, actions, and outcomes for the group were always established and communicated from the outside, by the teacher/program. The use of language was often restricted. Teachers led (dominated) conversation or discussion. In some cases, there could be guided exchange on a particular topic, but exchanges among children—children engaging with each other—was not viewed as valuable pedagogical activity.

A hierarchical atmosphere was also present in relationships between schools, teachers, and families. What took place in the preschool or school was considered to be the responsibility of the professionals, and parents' intervention was not welcome or needed. Parents/family members had almost no access to the premises of the preschool classes, other than during special events (performances by children), to which parents were invited as observers.

In spite of the fact that teacher preparation contained a substantial emphasis on theoretical knowledge, there was very little linking to practical applications of these theories. As for Vygotsky, while some educators in the region may have been familiar with his theories, there was no evidence that their practical implications were implemented.

After the fall of the Iron Curtain and the breakup of the Soviet Union, it was clear that a fresh approach to education was necessary in order to provide new generations with the skills needed to thrive in newly democratic societies and rapidly changing economies. Thus, increased attention to the engagement of students in their own learning, applying interactive teaching methodologies, making citizenship education alive and participatory, and involving parents and communities in decision-making about education have been features of the range of projects and programs introduced in Central and Eastern Europe and the former Soviet Union during the last 10–15 years.

Introducing Change—Step by Step

One of the programs targeted specifically at preschool and primary school has been the Step by Step (SbS) Program, brought to life by the visionary approach and support of the philanthropist George Soros and implemented in the former communist bloc region by the Open Society Institute (OSI).[2] Being a broad network project with considerable know-how, funding, and technical assistance capacity for educators and educational managers in the countries, the SbS program introduced a child-centred approach into preschool and primary education, promoted respect for family as the child's first and most important teacher, and encouraged educators, parents, and communities to see the earliest years of each child's life as the foundation for learning to think critically and becoming productive, active members of democratic societies. The program began in 1994 in a limited number of classrooms in 15 countries in the former Communist Bloc. Today, the program operates in 29 countries, and has had a major impact on policies and practices in ECDE in the region. The Step by Step approach should not be considered to be alternative pedagogy or complete and fully developed

---

[2] Investor and philanthropist George Soros created the Open Society Institute (OSI) in 1993 as a private operating and grant-making foundation to support his foundations in Central and Eastern Europe and the former Soviet Union. Those foundations were established, starting in 1984, to help countries make the transition from communism. OSI has expanded the activities of the Soros foundations network to encompass the United States and more than 60 countries in Europe, Asia, Africa, and Latin America. Each Soros foundation relies on the expertise of boards composed of eminent citizens who determine individual agendas based on local priorities.

The Open Society Institute works to build vibrant and tolerant democracies whose governments are accountable to their citizens. To achieve its mission, OSI seeks to shape public policies that assure greater fairness in political, legal, and economic systems and safeguard fundamental rights. On a local level, OSI implements a range of initiatives to advance justice, education, public health, and independent media. At the same time, OSI builds alliances across borders and continents on issues such as corruption and freedom of information. OSI places a high priority on protecting and improving the lives of people in marginalized communities.

To read more about OSI, visit www.soros.org.

curricula. Rather, it is a philosophy and framework for methodology that is open to the situations and needs of children, teachers, and families. The implementers of the SbS program, at both the national and international levels, have taken great care to respect and preserve the educational traditions in each country and the SbS methodology has been adapted to meet the national educational requirements of participating countries. The combination of best practices and theory in this program has successfully blended with the efforts of other international agencies and donors actively contributing to the region in the 1990s, such as UNICEF, the World Bank, the Nordic Council of Ministers, the British Council, and many others.[3]

The Step by Step Program has very special links with Vygotsky and his theories. In the theoretical underpinnings of the program, Vygotsky's work holds a prominent place. His theories have informed a new approach to teacher professional development and have emphasised the importance of interactions with children in the classroom and relationships with families and communities. As noted by Vladimir Zinchenko in his book *Pedagogical Psychology*, in 1926 Vygotsky had already proposed discussion on such issues as the relationships between teaching and development, teaching and upbringing, and personal, learning-related activities of pupils, writing that "the child will act himself, whereas to the teacher is left only the task of guiding and directing the child's activity" (Zinchenko 2007).

The Step by Step Program was built and implemented around the main principles that are directly related to Vygotsky's idea of the prominent role of the child in his/her own development. Teaching based on individualization, activity centres with freely accessible materials and tasks in the classrooms, developmentally appropriate practices, planning guided by and based on children's knowledge and interest, family participation, and on-going professional development of teachers and staff are the main cornerstones that were introduced in the region (Burke-Walsh and Kaufman 1998) by the SbS program. These principles have provided significant influence on developing national policies, curricula, and guiding documents, especially in the area of preschool education.

---

[3] Please visit www.issa.nl for a complete list of partners.

Rediscovering Profession, Providing Support to Professionals

The Step by Step Program was and continues to be implemented by many thousands of classroom practitioners under the leadership of program administrators and managers who have become recognized experts in the field of ECDE in their countries themselves. Successes and lessons learned have been shared through the annual conferences of ISSA over the past 10 years, as well as in articles published in the professional journal of the International Step by Step Association. The journal was intended for teachers and faculty who instruct preschool and/or primary school teachers, as well as other educational professionals interested in child-centred teaching methods. With articles based on the experiences of countries in transition, the journal emphasized change and educational transformation. It solicited articles on the challenges, confronting all democracies, of providing educational experiences necessary to the continuation of open and free societies. The first issue of *Educating Children for Democracy* was published in 2000 and was continued semi-annually in English (in print and on-line) and Russian (on-line only) until Winter/Spring 2006. Articles were reprinted in other professional journals in countries throughout the network.

Another resource that documents changes in the region is ISSA's Case Study Project, which commenced in 2004. Case Studies were produced to illustrate efforts to improve early childhood care, development, and education in the region. The Case Studies covered the following topics: promoting high-quality, child-centred teaching, ISSA standards and certification, creating child-centred environments and learning opportunities, reforming and decentralizing teacher training, social inclusion, quality education for Roma children, inclusion, children with disabilities, reaching children outside of preschools, and family and community environment.[4] This initiative served two main objectives—to improve research capacity in the ISSA region, especially in applying qualitative methods, and to document change that had been taking place as a result of interventions of the SbS program. The results present interesting resources for an international audience, providing materials from a region that has had limited international representation so far.

Many research findings and articles about implementation of the SbS program and its impact on the change in ECDE have been published in

---

[4]   The complete Case Studies are available for download and review at www.issa.nl.

the national languages of participating countries in professional journals, books, and other media. As shared by Tatjana Vonta, a SbS veteran and highly respected ECD professor in Slovenia (2007) "incorporating Vygotsky's ideas into early childhood education has the potential to change our societies, to value and improve social interactions and to promote individuals' participation in civil society."

Reflection of Vygotsky's Ideas in New ECDE Paradigms

There are many ways that researches across the world classify the ideas and theories of Vygotsky. However, there are some key points that facilitate translating his ideas into practice. Elena Kravtsova (2007) offers three ideas central to Vygotsky's thinking that are very useful to illustrate changes brought about in the region by the Step by Step Program.

Relationship between Education and Development

One of Vygotsky's central ideas about the close connection and relationship between education and development is, as mentioned by Kravtsova (2007), that "only an education leading to development is a good one."

Interestingly enough, this statement can and has been interpreted in quite different ways. According to one interpretation, most common in former Soviet states and satellite countries, the teachers' main task is teaching, based on what they themselves know and the system-imposed curriculum requirements. In this view, children's interests or characteristics are of minor concern. Others, including the authors represented in this book, take this same idea to make the case that children's learning should be active and driven by the child's interests, strengths, and needs.

Recent research indicates that when children are in settings in which free choice activities predominate, where there are fewer whole group activities, and where there are an increased number and variety of materials, children's later language and cognitive performance improve significantly (Montie, Xiang, and Schweinhart 2006). Other research indicates that where children are in settings that encourage them to engage in sustained shared thinking with teachers and peers, academic performance increases (Siraj-Blatchford, Sylva, Muttock, Gilden, and Bell 2002).

These findings are consistent with and support Vygotsky's thesis that in order to help a child enter their Zone of Proximal Development (ZPD), it is crucial for teachers to create learning environments in which children have choices, are able to develop from their actual developmental stage, and engage in interactions with others who can subtly direct activities in ways to ensure the maximum development of each child.

Building on Vygotsky's notion that learning occurs in interactive processes, the Step by Step approach helps children develop and learn by providing situations where children are able to choose groups, learning topics, and projects, thus allowing them a variety of opportunities to listen and speak with others and share experiences. Educators combine whole group and small group activities during the day, provide opportunities for children to make choices in their work activities, create mixed-age groups (if possible), and provide opportunities for the inclusion of children with additional support needs and from diverse backgrounds.

Introducing the Step by Step Program included rearranging the physical environment of existing classrooms in order to allow more space for individual and small group work when children are engaged in performing different tasks according to their interests, level of mastery, social relationships, etc. Such arrangements required a new approach to planning, as the teacher had to provide multiple tasks and materials in different parts of the classroom, and also guide children to acquire more self-regulatory behaviour, to become better problem solvers, to negotiate and agree, and to develop and apply self-assessment skills. Instead of all children doing the same activity at the same time (and being allowed to spend an equal amount of time in spite of different needs and abilities), children learn something new by practicing it on their own at their own pace with an adult/teacher or peers available to provide guidance or support, if needed.

The Step by Step Program's support to families and the high value placed on the role of parents as the first educators of children also echoes Vygotsky's beliefs about the strong link between education and development. Involving parents in their children's formal education was a rather challenging task at the start of program implementation, due to the cultural taboo against parents' involvement in schools. But parents inherently want to be involved in their children's education and development, and their active participation has grown into a very strong aspect of the program, resulting in the establishment of parent associations in several countries. Encouraging and supporting parents to engage in meaningful developmental activities with their children, and to use everyday situations as learning opportunities and teachable moments, has always been part of the child-centred approach promoted by ISSA (Landers 2005, Tuna and Tankersley 2007).

Conception of Personality

Another of Vygotsky's key ideas is the *conception of personality*. Each child behaves with a distinct, personal character when she perceives herself as a source of her own behaviour and activity. "...Education helps personal development only if children perceive themselves to be both the source and the subject of education, in other words, as active participants" (Kravtsova 2007).

This idea of valuing child-initiated education and development is very different from the traditional system of the former Soviet region, in which the child's main task is to simply follow adult direction, imitate examples and be as similar to peers in learning ability and performance as possible. Traditionally, uniformity, conformity, and consistency were strongly emphasized. Students were expected to master the same material and produce the same product, whether it was a drawing of a certain image, memorizing a poem, or following a proscribed method to solve a math problem. Individuality and creativity were not at all valued in this system. Children learned that the "right" answers were valued; the teacher was supposed to know all answers her/himself and children were to strive to learn what the teacher knew. Children were taught to fit in, not to stand out (Cincilei, David, and Grob 2000, 10).

Obviously, to change this mind-set the Step by Step Program needed to provide intensive training to teachers, school administrators, and education authorities to challenge existing paradigms and offer new ways of thinking about a child. Initial trainings had two main emphases: to introduce the concept individualization and its practical implementation and providing children with choices. During training and mentoring, teachers were encouraged to observe children more carefully and to exchange information with families in order to better support each child's development and learning. The perception of play was revisited, as play offers endless opportunities for learning, both individually and through interactions with peers and teachers, who can give subtle direction.

Vygotsky's idea of the Zone of Proximal Development (ZPD) is also closely related with the personality of a child and is at the core of individualisation. Each child's developmental needs, interests, learning styles, knowledge, skills, and experiences are taken into consideration. The educator builds a bridge between official curriculum demands and her observations and knowledge of each individual child, as well as her judgment about how best to support their learning. Scaffolding involves taking risks, testing hypotheses, and learning from mistakes, which can provide successful learning experiences only in environments where children feel psychologically and physically safe. To create this kind of environment, a strong feeling of community must be constructed through interactions among children, families, educators, administrators, and community members.

After initial trainings and on-going support to change their practice, teachers in Step by Step classrooms were happy to notice, value, and support the individuality of their students, as well as to respect their differences and nurture their creativity. As described by Cincilei et al, "When a small group of third graders had completed a painting to depict the emotion "sad," two children from the group, rather than just one, stood up to present their work in front of the class. Why? Because they said their ideas differed—one painted red dots, the other black dots. The teacher accepted their different approaches and wisely asked them to explain their thinking, and they did" (Cincilei, David, and Grob 2000, 10). Such an episode which can seem very simple for established child-centred environments was almost a radical change of attitude in that part of the world.

Difference between Spontaneous and Reactive Education

A third key area central to education and development, deals with the types of education. According to Vygotsky, there is a particular *difference between spontaneous and reactive education*: if in spontaneous types of education, children create their own program, in reactive they have to study according to someone else's. In his own era, Vygotsky emphasized what is being promoted now as the most crucial characteristics for life in the 21st century: the ability to identify and solve problems, flexibility, curiosity, ability to learn, etc. Skills and habits developed during experiences of spontaneous education become crucial for the success of individuals and communities. At the same time, a child left alone without any support cannot create the ideal environment for spontaneous education; the teacher must be skilful in observation and building on children's interests and teachable moments. In other words, a teacher must have much higher level of internalized knowledge and understanding about children's development and developmental goals that should be achieved. As Sizer (1999) argues, the only way to individualize instruction is to know each student well.

The Step by Step program has capitalized on Vygotsky's reflections on spontaneous education by introducing strategies on how to collect and use children's interests and previous knowledge and develop them into powerful motivating tools for future learning. As mentioned by one teacher implementing the Step by Step methodologies in Moldova, "I know my children much better because they have the possibility of expressing themselves at any point during the day. The room arrangement and the classroom management make the children be themselves … I feel much closer to the children. I have the possibility to observe them in greater detail," (Cincilei, David, and Grob 2000, 11).

One of the most successful strategies introduced by the Step by Step program was the "KWL" strategy, in which the teacher encourages children to communicate what they k*now,* what they *would like* to know, and what they have *learned* at the end of the new topic/thematic area. This strategy was a discovery for most of the preschool and primary teachers in the region as it opened a completely new way of communication with children and made teachers reconsider their plans once they learned what children already knew and where their interests were. Now this strategy has become an integral part of teaching in many classrooms across the region. It allows children to contribute their knowledge, to set learning goals, to learn how to find information from multiple, diverse sources, and to assess achieved results at the end. By deeply listening to children and observing their knowledge through the KWL strategy, teachers can more easily find each child's Zone of Proximal Development.

Using this strategy has also contributed significantly to building cooperation skills, mutual support, and community spirit—concepts embedded in Vygotsky's theories and applications. Such strategies have been also helpful for teachers in giving ideas and advice to parents on how they can engage in meaningful conversations with their children and build links between in-formal and non-formal learning, preschool, and school.

Dialogue and Cooperation for the Benefit of Children: Work in Progress

More than 150 years ago, the Danish philosopher Kierkegaard argued that "it is not enough for us to know what our student understands, we must also know the way he understands it." In the 21st century, learning *how* to learn has been recognized as one of the most essential competences for success throughout the life. It has also been noted that knowing how to learn and having the capability to explore the ways in which you learn directly affect your sense of well-being.

In mid-90s, the Step by Step Program helped to the region to rediscover Vygotsky and to make a significant shift to more meaningful, successful, and pleasant learning environments and practices for young children. Thousands of educators changed their practice, developed examples of good pedagogy, and were eager to engage in discussion with professionals from all over the world. ISSA's conferences have become prominent professional events where east and west, north and south come together to discuss better ways to support children's development and learning.

In early 2010, ISSA launched *Competent Educators of the 21st Century: ISSA's Principles of Quality Pedagogy*. ISSA's *Principles* are an excellent example of the blending of Vygotsky's ideas with the most recent findings on quality pedagogy, international trends and international rights documents. ISSA's intention in publishing the *Principles* is to offer grounds for further reflection, dialogue, and cooperation, because increased participation, equity, and quality in education for all children—especially in the early years—are still tasks for education systems, professionals, and communities throughout the world.

On behalf of ISSA and the editors of this volume, we hope that the research and observations shared in this book will inspire lively exchange among those involved in ECDE, in spite of the different cultural and historical backgrounds from which they originate. We also hope that the research and discussions in this text will be for future teachers and a rich resource for continuous professional development programs for practicing caregivers and teachers. Representatives of civil society, non-governmental organizations, and groups of activists involved in piloting and implementing high quality early childhood programs, as well as decision makers at the national and international levels who seek the latest research and theory as a basis for supporting best-practices in education programs and systems may also use this book as a tool to further dialogue and ensure that children in their countries are receiving the highest quality early education and developmental support.

Vygotsky's early education ideas are directly applicable to creating high quality education programs and environments for young children today, and the Step by Step program has played a very special part in bridging theories, practices, and regions, as well as setting an example of implementing significant systemic change in education in the new democracies. Incorporating Vygotsky's ideas into early childhood education has proven to have great potential to change our societies, to value and improve social interactions, and to promote individuals' participation in civil society. Vygotsky's ideas have brought important changes to the region of new democracies in Central and Eastern Europe and the countries of the Commonwealth of Independent States. ISSA and all of the authors of this book are pleased to enhance the discussion of Vygotsky's theories, contributing significantly to the dialogue as the world reflects on and implements development of new types of preschools and schools, new types of teacher practices, and, most importantly, significant changes in lives of children supporting development and becoming active, responsible, and caring citizens of their countries and the world.

References

Burke Walsh, Kate and Roxane Kaufman. 2000. *Creating Child-Centered Classrooms—3–5*. New York: Open Society Institute.

Cincilei, C., J. David, and B. Grob. 2000. Changing to Child-centered Approach: Teachers Reflect on the Moldovan Experience. *Education Children for Democracy. Journal of the International Step by Step Association*. 1: 9–13.

ISSA. 2002. *Step by Step Program and Teacher Standards for Preschool and Primary Grades*. Budapest: International Step by Step Association.

———. 2005. *ISSA Pedagogical Standards for Preschool and Primary Grades*. Budapest: International Step by Step Association.

———. 2006. *Educating for Diversity: Education for Social Justice Activities for Classrooms: Teachers' Guide*. Budapest: International Step by Step Association.

———. 2006. *Effective Teaching and Learning for Minority-Language Children—Compendium of Learning Materials*. Budapest: International Step by Step Association.

———. 2006. *Speaking for Diversity: Promoting Multilingualism in Early Childhood Education—A Teachers' Guide for the Effective Teaching and Learning for Minority Language Children Program*. Budapest: International Step by Step Association.

———. 2010. *Competent Teachers of the 21st Century: ISSA's Principles of Quality Pedagogy*. Budapest: International Step by Step Association.

Kolpakova, V. 2000. Encouraging Children's Exploration in Activity Centers: Stories from Latvia. *Educating Children for Democracy. Journal of the International Step by Step Association*. 1: 25–26.

Kravtsova, E. 2007. Vygotsky's Approach to education. *Children in Europe*. Vygotsky Issue: 8–9.

Montie, J.E., Z. Xiang, and L.J. Schweinhart. 2006. Preschool Experiences in 10 Countries: Cognitive and Language Performance at Age 7. *Early Childhood Research Quarterly*. 21: 313–331.

O'Toole, L. 2008. Understanding Individual patterns of Learning: implications for the well-being of students. *European Journal of Education.* 43: 71–86.

Siraj-Blatchford, I., K. Sylva, S. Muttock, R. Gilden, and D. Bell. 2002. Researching Effective Pedagogy in the Early Years: Research Report RR 356. London: Department for Education and Skills (DfES).

Sizer, T.R. 1999. No Two are Quite Alike. *Educational Leadership* 56: 8.

Tuna, A., and D. Tankersley. 2007. *Opening Magic Doors. Reading and Learning Together with Children. Activities with 6–8 year old children using ISSA Reading Corner books.* Budapest: International Step by Step Association.

Vonta, T. 2007. Vygotsky's ideas in the new democracies. *Children in Europe.* Vygotsky Issue: 21–23.

Vygotskaya, G. 2007. Recorded Comments presented at the opening of the 17th Annual EECERA Conference, August 29–September 1, 2007 in Prague, Czech Republic. http://www.easyprague.cz/eecera2007/download/files/Gita%20Vygotskaya_Eng%20final.pdf.

Zinchenko, V. 2007. Lev Vygotsky: From "silver age" to "red terror". *Children in Europe.* Vygotsky Issue: 5–7.

Appendices

APPENDIX A

The Children Follow-up Instrument (CFI)[1]

CFI Phase 2
*Analysis and Conclusions Concerning the General Evaluation
of the Group and Context*

Group Evaluation		
Emotional well-being	What pleases me:	
	What worries me:	
Involvement:	What pleases me:	
	What worries me:	
Context Evaluation		
Consider the contextual aspects: educational offerings, group climate, room for initiative, organization, and adult style:		
Consider the characteristics and resources of the community and families, and the school's curriculum project:		
Children's opinions about kindergarten	Positive aspects:	
	Negative aspects:	
	Interests referred:	

[1] CFI is inspired in Laevers, F., Vandenbussche, E., Kog, M. & Depondt, L. (1997). A process-oriented child monitoring system for young children (POMS). Experiential Education Series, nº2, Leuven: Centre for Experiential Education. Its development/contextualization for Portuguese early childhood settings is still being worked out within a project funded by the Portuguese Foundation for Science and Technology (PTDC/CED/67633/2006) and will be completed in October 2010 (contact information gabriela.portugal@ua.pt).

CFI Phase 3

Intervention: Objectives and Initiatives towards the Group

Considering the analysis and conclusions of 2g (directed to the group and context), what changes/intervention do we want?

Possible aspects to be considered in change or intervention	1. Specific objectives of change:	2. Initiatives or actions to develop:
Educational offerings		
Group climate		
Room for initiative		
Organization		
Adult Style		

Ideas for the development of the curricular project of the group:

CFI Phase 2

Characterization and Individual Analysis of Children

1. Global levels of emotional well-being and involvement (1, 2, 3, 4, 5)	
Emotional well-being	Involvement

2. Overall impression

3. Family details

4. Relationships
(Consider the child's relationship with the teacher, with other children, with the school world, and with members of the family and close friends.)

5. Involvement
(Consider the activities available in the kindergarten and its organization: working or playing in groups, individually, as a compulsory or optional activity, guided by the adult, or not guided by the adult.)
The child is highly involved in activities such as: Developmental areas implicit in these activities:
The child is not highly involved in activities such as: Developmental areas implicit in these activities

6. Child's opinion about kindergarten
(Consider the child's relationship with the teacher, with other children, with the school world, and with members of the family and close friends.)

What I like most to do is... because...   **What I like least to do is... because**

7. Development and Learning (attitudes, group behaviour, and basic acquisitions)	
Attitudes **Well-being and self-esteem, self-organization, and initiative** **Curiosity, willingness to learn, creativity, and relationship with the world**	
Group behaviour (social competence)	
Basic acquisitions: fine and gross motor skills; art; language, logical, conceptual, and mathematical thinking; understanding of the physical and social world	

APPENDIX B

Curriculum Guidelines for Preschool Education

Translation retrieved from: Ministério da Educação (Vasconcelos, T.) (1998). Early Childhood Education in Portugal. Lisboa: Ministério da Educação, Departamento de Educação Básica, Gabinete para a Expansão e Desenvolvimento da Educação Pré-Escolar (ISBN 972-742-094-X).

Introduction

Curriculum Guidelines are a common reference for all preschool teachers working within the national preschool education network and are intended to provide organization for the syllabus component. They do not constitute a curriculum in themselves, since they are intended as guidelines rather than a prescriptive list of learning targets to be achieved by the children. They may also be differentiated from the curriculum notion since they are more general and wide-ranging, i.e., they include the possibility of using various types of learning/teaching options and, therefore, various types of curriculum.

- Curriculum Guidelines are based on the following foundations:
- Development and learning are indissociable from each other;
- The child is the subject of the education process—which means an educator should start with what the child already knows and value his/her knowledge as the basis for new learning. This learning fundamentally envisages the development of curiosity, a critical approach and the ability to learn how to learn;
- Articulated building of knowledge—which implies that the different areas should not be seen as closed compartments, but approached in a global and integrated way;
- All children should be responded to—which presupposes differentiated teaching methods centred on children's cooperation, in which the child benefits from the educational process developed within the group.

Based on these foundations, curriculum development will take into account:

- Organization of the educational environment—the environment should be structured to support the curriculum and the fulfilment of its intentions. The educational environment includes different interaction levels: organization of the group, classroom space, and time; school organization and management; and relationships with parents and other partners in the educational process.

- Learning areas—these are the general areas to consider in planning and assessing learning situations and opportunities. There are three learning areas:
  - Personal and social development
  - Creativity and communication, covering three domains
    a) Different forms of art—kinetic, dramatic, plastic, and musical expression;
    b) Language, literacy, and an initial approach to writing;
    c) Mathematics
  - Knowledge of the world

- Educational continuity—as a process which starts from what children already know, and creates conditions for success in later learning.

- Educational intent—which results from a process of reflecting on observation, planning, action and assessment carried out by the teacher, with the aim of matching classroom practice to the children's needs.

1. General Principle and Pedagogic Aims Listed in the Preschool Education Framework Law

The Preschool Education Law establishes as a general principle that:

- *Preschool education is the first step in basic education and is seen as part of lifelong learning, and complements the education provided by the family, with which it should establish close cooperation, fostering the training and balanced development of the child, with a view to his/her full integration in society as an autonomous, free, and cooperative individual.*

This principle provides the grounds for the rest of the dispositions of this law, and for the general pedagogic aims defined for preschool education:

a) *To promote the child's personal and social development based on experiences of democratic life within a perspective of education for citizenship;*

b) *To foster the child's integration in different social groups, teaching respect for different cultures and encouraging a growing awareness of his/her role as a member of society;*

c) *To contribute to equality of opportunity in access to education and foster successful learning;*

d) *To stimulate each child's overall development, with respect for his/her individual characteristics, inculcating patterns of behaviour favourable to significant and diversified learning;*

e) *To develop creativity and communication through different forms as a means of relating, informing, and raising aesthetic awareness and understanding of the world;*

f) *To arouse curiosity and critical thought;*

g) *To ensure each child's welfare and safety, especially in terms of individual and collective health;*

h) *To correct precocious, deficient or socially unacceptable behaviour, promoting the best guidance for the child;*

i) *To encourage family participation in the educational process and establish real cooperation with the community.*

2. Foundation and Organization of Curriculum Guidelines

Considering preschool education as the *first step in basic education seen as part of lifelong learning*, implies that it is at this stage that the conditions are created to enable children to continue learning, i.e., it is important that during their preschool years children should learn how to learn.

This statement is also the starting point for the general aim "*to contribute to equality of opportunity in access to education and foster successful learning.*" The intention is not that preschool education should be organized in such a way as to prepare children for primary education, but rather it should prepare children for lifelong learning. However, it should prepare children to deal successfully with the next stage of education.

To enable preschool education providers to contribute to greater equality of opportunities, these curriculum guidelines stress the importance of a structured teaching approach, which implies intentional and systematic organization of the learning process and requires that the teacher plan his/ her work and then assess the process and its effects on the children's development an learning.

Adopting an organized and structured pedagogical approach does not mean bringing into preschool education certain "traditional" practices which make no sense to children, nor does it mean undermining the importance of the "play" side of many learning activities, since the pleasure of learning and mastering certain skills requires real effort, concentration, and personal investment.

Preschool education creates the conditions for successful learning in all children, insofar as it promotes self-esteem and develops skills which enable each child to recognize his/her own potential and progress.

The different contexts for preschool education are thus spaces where children build their own learning processes, in such a way as to *foster the training and balanced development of the child.*

This aim of stimulating *each child's overall development, with respect for his/her individual characteristics, inculcating patterns of behaviour favourable to significant and diversified learning* points towards the interlinking of development and learning, defended by a series of different modern strands of psychology and sociology, which consider that the human being develops through a process of social interaction. Within this perspective, the child plays an active role in his/her interaction with the environment which, in turn, should provide favourable conditions for development and learning. Admitting that the child plays an active part in the construction of his/her own development and learning means that s/he should be seen as the subject and not the object in the educational process. In this sense, it is important to stress that preschool education should start from what the child already knows, their own culture and individual knowledge.

Respecting and valuing the individual characteristics of each child—the fact that each child is different—is the basis for new learning. The opportunity to take advantage of a diversified range of educational experiences in a context which facilitates broad social interaction with other children and adults allows each child to contribute to the development and learning of others as s/he builds his/her own development and learning.

Respect for differences in others includes children who do not follow normal patterns, and preschool education should respond to any and every child. Within this perspective of the inclusive school, preschool education should adopt the practice of a differentiated teaching approach, centred on cooperation, including all children, accepting all differences, supporting learning and responding to individual needs.

The inclusive school concept assumes that the planning process should take the group into account. This plan is adapted and differentiated in line with children's individual characteristics, so as to offer each child stimulating conditions for his/her development and learning. By its reference to the group, it goes further than the view of integration that posited the need for individual and specific plans for "different" children. Thus even children diagnosed as having special educational needs are included in the group and benefit from the educational opportunities made available to all.

The conditions considered necessary for an inclusive school, such as the efficient working of the educational establishment; the involvement of all interested parties including staff, children, parents, and community; and team planning, are all aspects to be taken into account in the educational process to be developed in preschool education.

The response which preschool education should provide for all children is organized with a *view to his/her full integration in society as an autonomous, free, and cooperative individual.* This last statement of the general principle guiding preschool education is directly related with the following aims:

- *To promote the child's personal and social development based on experiences of democratic life within a perspective of education for citizenship.*

- *To foster the child's integration in different social groups, teaching respect for different cultures and encouraging a growing awareness of his/her role as a member of society.*

In its search to provide education for citizenship, the Curriculum Guidelines attribute particular importance to the organization of the educational environment as a context for democratic life in which all children participate, where they come into contact with and learn to respect different cultures. It is this experience that provides the foundation for the area of personal and social education, which is considered to be an area integrating the whole process of preschool education.

It is also an aim of preschool education *to ensure each child's welfare and safety, especially in terms of individual and collective health.* Welfare and safety also depend on the educational environment, in which the child feels welcomed, listened to, and valued, all of which contributes to his/her self-esteem and willingness to learn. A preschool should be an environment in which s/he feels comfortable because his/her physical and psychological needs are satisfied. To improve welfare related to individual and collective health, a preschool also has a chance to provide health education, which is part of anyone's education as a citizen.

But the child's education, aimed at the children's full integration in society as an independent, free and cooperative being, also implies other ways of developing and learning, as referred to in the aim of developing *creativity and communication through different forms as a means of relating, informing, raising aesthetic awareness and understanding the world.*

This aim is dealt in the areas of *expression and communication* and *knowledge of the world.* There is a link between these two areas, but the first includes different types of expression divided into three main domains:

- Different forms of art—kinetic, dramatic, plastic, and musical expression;

- Language and literacy, which includes other languages such as informatics and audio-visual technology, as well as a possible introduction to a foreign language;

- Mathematics, considered as a language, which is also part of the area of expression and communication.

Although mastery of these forms of expression is important in itself, they are also a means of relating, raising aesthetic awareness, and obtaining information. Thus the areas of *expression and communication* form a basic area which contributes simultaneously to personal and social training and to the child's knowledge of the world. In its turn, the *knowledge of the world* area makes it possible to articulate the other two, since it is through relationships with others that personal identity is constructed and one's posture in the social and physical *world* takes shape. Making sense of this *world* depends on the use of symbolic and cultural systems.

Since these areas are not to be considered sealed compartments, it is important to interlink the different content areas and contextualize them in a given educational environment. Thus the organization of the educational environment in its relation with the general environment is a support for curriculum development. Only this articulated process makes it possible to achieve another aim which should run through all preschool education *to arouse curiosity and critical thought.*

This objective is made concrete in the different content areas which are articulated in a global education, and it is this early training which will be the grounds for lifelong learning.

Another statement contained in the general principle of the Law considers preschool education as complementing *the education provided by the family, with which it should establish close cooperation.* This statement which stresses the importance of relationships with the family can be seen in the objective of encouraging *family participation in the educational process and establish real cooperation with the community.*

Parents or guardians are legally responsible for the child as their first and main educators. Since the prevailing fashion has now swung away from the idea of education compensating for what parents cannot provide, it is thought that the effects of preschool education are closely related with the degree of articulation with families. The intention is not to compensate for the family background but rather to use it as a starting point and take into account the culture/s from which the children come. This is to ensure that preschool education is then able to mediate between the children's culture of origin and the culture they will have to appropriate to learn successfully.

Since preschool education is to be seen as complementary to the upbringing provided by the family, there must be articulation between the educational establishment and families, aimed at finding within a certain social context the solutions best suited to children and families. It is thus the parents' right and duty to participate in the drafting of the educational plan of the school in question.

However, not only the family but also the social environment in which the child lives influences his/her education, and the school benefits from the united effort and the resources any community will make available for the education of its children and young people. Parents and other members of the community may therefore work together to develop the school's educational plan.

This process of collaboration with parents and the community has effects on children's education and consequences for the development and learning of adults involved in their education.

3. Overall Guidelines for Preschool Teachers

Basic Tenets

Observing

Observing each child in the group to learn their abilities, interests, and diffi-culties, and to gather information on family context and the environment in which the children live, is necessary to understand the children's charac-teristics and to mold the educational process to respond to their needs. Knowledge of the child and his/her development are the basis for the different teaching approach which begins with what the child knows and is able to do, then broadens his/her interests and develop his/her potential. This knowledge is the result of continuous observation and presupposes the need for references such as what the children produce and different types of registers and records. This is fundamentally a question of having infor-mation which may be analysed periodically so as to be able to understand the process and its effects on each child's learning. Observation is thus the basis of planning and assessment, and serves as a support to the underlying intention of the educational process.

Planning

Planning the educational process in line with what the educator knows about the group and each child, his/her family and social background is an essential condition to ensure that preschool education provides a stimu-lating environment for development and promotes significant and differen-tiated learning experiences contributing to greater equality of opportunity.

Planning implies that the educator reflects on underlying intentions and the ways of adapting these to the group, anticipating learning situations and experiences and organizing the material and human resources necessary to ensure that they take place. Planning the learning environment allows children to explore and use the spaces, materials, and instruments placed at their disposal, providing them with a range of diversified interaction with the whole group, in small groups and in pairs, and the possibility of interacting with other adults. This planning takes into account the different content areas and their articulation, as well as foreseeing the various possibilities which arise or change in accordance with situations and the children's proposals.

It is therefore the teacher's job to plan learning situations which are sufficiently challenging to interest and stimulate each child, providing support to enable the child to reach levels which s/he could not reach alone, but avoiding the danger of being overly demanding, which might discourage the child and lead to low self-esteem.

Planning carried out with the participation of the children allows the group to benefit from the diversity, ability, and skills of each child, in a sharing process which facilitates learning and development for each and every one.

Acting

Putting educational intentions into action, adapting them to the children's proposals, and taking advantage of unforeseen situations and opportunities is important. The participation of other adults—auxiliary staff, parents, and other members of the community—in bringing to fruition the educational opportunities planned by the early childhood teacher is a way of broadening children's interactions and enriching the educational process.

Assessing

Assessing the process and its effects implies being aware of action in order to mould the educational process to the needs of the children and the group and their development. Assessment done with the children is an educational experience, and it also serves as a basis for assessment of the teacher. Reflection based on observed effects makes it possible to establish a progression in the learning experiences to be developed with each child. In this sense, assessment is a support for planning.

Communicating

The knowledge the preschool teacher acquires of the child and how s/he develops is enriched by sharing with other adults who also have responsibility for the child's education, especially fellow teachers, auxiliary staff, and parents. While teamwork by professionals is a means of self-training which benefits the child's education, exchanging opinions with the parents provides greater knowledge of the child and other contexts influencing his/ her education: family and community.

Articulating

It is the teacher's duty to promote educational continuity in a process which begins with entry into preschool education and ends with the move to primary school. The relationship established with parents before the child attends nursery school facilitates communication between the teacher and parents, thus encouraging the child's adaptation. It is also the early childhood teacher's job to provide conditions for the child to be a successful learner in the next phase, and to work with both the parents and primary school staff to make the child's move to primary school as easy as possible.

LIST OF CONTRIBUTORS

Lynn ANG

Dr. Lynn Ang is Senior Lecturer of Early Childhood Studies in the Cass School of Education, University of East London. She has worked in the field of early childhood internationally in a variety of early years settings and institutions in Singapore, Scotland, and England. Her research specialisms include early years curriculum, issues of diversity, and early childhood across cultures. She was awarded a British Academy research grant in 2007 to conduct an empirical study on the kindergarten curriculum in Singapore. She was also granted a collaborative research bid from the Economic and Social Research Council to hold a series of seminars on 'Critical Issues for Preschool Education: towards a research agenda'. Dr. Ang works with both undergraduate and postgraduate students, is Programme Leader for the MA in Early Childhood Studies, and supervises PhD students. She is also convenor of the Early Childhood Studies Research Group in Cass School of Education.

Elena BODROVA

Dr. Elena Bodrova is a Principal Researcher at Mid-continent Research for Education and Learning (McREL) and a Research Fellow at the National Institute for Early Education Research (NIEER). Prior to joining McREL, she was a visiting professor of educational psychology at the Metropolitan State College of Denver. Her work on applying Lev Vygotsky's theory to education started in Russia, where she worked at the Institute for Preschool Education. Dr. Bodrova is the author of multiple articles and book chapters on the subjects on early literacy, self-regulation, play, and assessment. She is a co-author of *Tools of the Mind: The Vygotskian Approach to Early Childhood Education*; *Basics of Assessment: A Primer for Early Childhood Educators*; and *For the Love of Words: Vocabulary Instruction that Works*.

Stig BROSTRÖM

Stig Broström is Associate Professor of Early Childhood Education at the School of Education, Aarhus University. His main areas of research are based in cultural historical theory related to preschool, transition to school, the first years in school, curriculum theory, children's play, social competence, and friendship. His Ph.D. thesis, an ethnographic and comparative study, deals with transition issues exposed through children's social competence and learning motivation in a Danish and American classroom.

Jacqueline HAYDEN

Jacqueline Hayden BA, MEd, PhD is Professor of Early Childhood and Social Inclusion at Macquarie University, Australia. She has worked or researched in the field of ECD in diverse contexts and regions, including Africa, North America, Europe, and Australasia. Jacqueline has published or presented over 150 papers. Her most notable publications include the edited book *Landscapes in Early Childhood Education: Cross National Perspectives on Empowerment*, and the co-authored *From Conflict to Peace Building: The Power of Early Childhood Initiatives- Lessons from around the World*.

Yulia KARIMOVA

Yulia Karimova is the Quality Education and Innovative Teaching Programs Manager at the Center for Innovations in Education. She holds an MA from Baku State University in Russian Literature and Language. She joined CIE in 2004 as an associate coordinator for Open Society Institute Higher Education Academic Fellowship Program. She spent 2006 at Kent State University in Ohio, US on an Edmund S. Muskie Fellowship. She graduated from Kent State University with an MA in Curriculum and Teaching Studies in 2007. She works closely with the national Ministry of Education and is a member of the expert group on early childhood methodology development.

Linda E. LEE

Linda E. Lee is a partner in Proactive Information Services Inc., a Canadian social research and evaluation company. She has worked in research and evaluation since the late 1970s. She has conducted training in program evaluation, research methods, data use, student assessment, school improvement, and education for social justice. Her projects have taken her across Canada, to South America, and to Europe, where she has worked extensively on issues concerning Roma communities. She is passionate about using evidence to improve programs, giving young people a voice, and engaging school communities in improving educational equity and access, all with the intention of creating a more socially just world.

Susanna MANTOVANI

Susanna Mantovani is Professor of Education at the University of Milano-Bicocca and, at present, Dean of the Faculty of Educational Sciences. Her work in the past thirty years has dealt with early childhood and ECDE policies, making her one of the leading figures in ECDE in Italy. She has been involved in the OECD ECDE projects since the 70s, was a co-founder with Loris Malaguzzi in 1978 of the Gruppo Nazionale Nidi-Infanzia, the largest Italian network of researchers, administrators, and educators in early childhood, has served in the National Committees for the Guidelines for Nursery Schools, and in 1986 started the project *Tempo per le famiglie* funded by the Bernard van Leer Foundation, which has now developed into a network of infant/toddler centres across Italy.

Ulviya MIKAILOVA

Ulviya Mikailova is the Executive Director of the Center for Innovations in Education, Baku, Azerbaijan. She has a teaching degree from Baku State University and a Ph.D. in biology from Tbilisi State University, Georgia. In 1998 she became Step by Step Program Director at the Open Society Institute—Azerbaijan National Foundation. She has extensive experience in teaching, including courses on gender and politics and education policy at the university level. In 2006, she was awarded a Fulbright Scholarship Award and spent three months doing research at the International and Comparative Education Department at the Columbia University, New York. She is a member of Azerbaijani National Society of Psychologists, and Acting Chief of the Child Protection Network in Azerbaijan. She has served on the ISSA Board.

Bert van OERS

Bert van Oers is Professor of Cultural-Historical Theory of Education at the Department of Theory and Research in Education (Faculty Psychology and Education) of the VU University Amsterdam. His research interests are the elaboration and implementation of Developmental Education, the potentials of play as a context for learning of young children, and the promotion of literacy, mathematics, and art in young children. He received an honorary doctor's degree at the University of Jyväskylä in Finland. A few of his recent publications are Narratives of childhood (Amsterdam: VU University Press 2003) and the co-edited book The transformation of learning (Cambridge University Press 2008).

Gabriela PORTUGAL

Gabriela Portugal is a senior teacher of Early Childhood Education at the Department of Educational Sciences at the University of Aveiro (Portugal), where she is responsible for early years training and development at pre-service and in-service levels for early years professionals. She coordinates the development of the project "Evaluation in Early Childhood Education—children follow-up instrument," leading a research team that includes Paula Santos, Aida Figueiredo, Ofélia Libório, Natália Abrantes, Carlos Silva, and Sónia Góis (research assistant). Among this group there is extensive experience of working with young children and of providing training and courses for teachers and other professionals in the areas of psychology and pedagogy. As current interests, members of the group can highlight the following: Experiential Education, Quality-Inclusion, Early Intervention, Special Education, Education, and Teacher Training.

Aija TUNA

After serving as ISSA's Program Director from 2006–2009, Aija Tuna currently serves as a Program Specialist for ISSA, as well as an independent consultant through her company "Knowledge Creation Lab." For decades, Tuna has been actively involved in promoting systemic and purposeful change in education at the classroom, school, national, and international levels in the post-communist region through different national and international projects. Tuna has provided consultancy and technical assistance in many countries, including Azerbaijan, Belarus, Bulgaria, Kosovo, Latvia, Lithuania, Moldova, Pakistan, and Russia, working in close partnership with colleagues in the UK, US, Nordic countries, and elsewhere.

Mathias URBAN

Dr. Mathias Urban, Reader in Education, works for the Cass School of Education, University of East London, where he is Director of the International Centre for Research on Professionalism in Early Childhood. He is Visiting Fellow at the Thomas Coram Research Unit, Institute of Education, University of London. His research interests unfold around questions of diversity and (e)quality, evaluation, and professionalism in working with young children, families, and communities in diverse contexts. He is a founding member of a consortium of European Universities to develop and deliver the first European Joint

Masters programme in Early Childhood Education and Care. His recent work includes international case based comparisons on change processes in early childhood systems (Strategies for Change, Urban, 2007) and on professional epistemologies and habitus (A Day in the Life of an Early Years Practitioner, Dalli, Miller, Urban, forthcoming).

Piotr Olaf ZYLICZ

Piotr Olaf Zylicz is a senior lecturer at the Warsaw School of Social Psychology, Warsaw, Poland. His major academic research involves moral psychology and child development. He has been involved in two international research projects: "Growing up in cities" and "Parenting for the 21st century". Piotr Olaf Zylicz wrote among others: 1. Oliner, S., Zylicz, P.O. 2008. *Altruism, Intergroup Apology, Forgiveness, and Reconciliation*. St. Paul: Paragon House. 2. Zylicz, P.O. 2002. Adapting during time of great change. In *Growing up in an urbanizing world*, Ed. Louise Chawla. London: UNESCO Publishing/Earthscan Publications.

Elena YUDINA

Elena Yudina, Ph.D. is a department head at the University of Psychology and Education, Moscow. She is a researcher and professor of Early Childhood Development and Education. An expert in cultural-historical psychology, especially concerning preschool education, currently Dr. Yudina serves as an expert for the World Bank (WB) and UNESCO and leads several WB projects in preschool education. Dr. Yudina is interested in the intellectual and social-emotional development of preschool children, teacher-child interaction, teacher training, and the ethical problems of developmental psychology. She is the author of more than 60 books and papers, some of them used in elaboration of standards and guidelines for preschool education in Russia.

INDEX